M000120453

FIGHTER PILOT:
FROM COLD WAR JETS
TO SPITFIRES

THE EXTRAORDINARY MEMOIRS OF
A BATTLE OF BRITAIN MEMORIAL
FLIGHT PILOT

FIGHTER PILOT:
FROM COLD WAR JETS
TO SPITFIRES

THE EXTRAORDINARY MEMOIRS OF
A BATTLE OF BRITAIN MEMORIAL
FLIGHT PILOT

CHRISTOPHER COVILLE

AIR WORLD

AIR WORLD

FIGHTER PILOT: FROM COLD WAR JETS TO SPITFIRES
The Extraordinary Memoirs of a Battle of Britain Memorial Flight Pilot

First published in Great Britain in 2021 by
Air World
An imprint of
Pen & Sword Books Ltd
Yorkshire – Philadelphia

Copyright © Christopher Coville, 2021

ISBN 978 1 39901 557 8

The right of Christopher Coville to be identified as Author of this work has been asserted by him in accordance with the Copyright, Designs and Patents Act 1988.

A CIP catalogue record for this book is available from the British Library.

All rights reserved. No part of this book may be reproduced or transmitted in any form or by any means, electronic or mechanical including photocopying, recording or by any information storage and retrieval system, without permission from the Publisher in writing.

Typeset by SJmagic DESIGN SERVICES, India.

Printed and bound in the UK by CPI Group (UK) Ltd, Croydon, CR0 4YY

Pen & Sword Books Limited incorporates the imprints of Atlas, Archaeology, Aviation, Discovery, Family History, Fiction, History, Maritime, Military, Military Classics, Politics, Select, Transport, True Crime, Air World, Frontline Publishing, Leo Cooper, Remember When, Seaforth Publishing, The Praetorian Press, Wharncliffe Local History, Wharncliffe Transport, Wharncliffe True Crime and White Owl.

For a complete list of Pen & Sword titles please contact

PEN & SWORD BOOKS LIMITED
47 Church Street, Barnsley, South Yorkshire, S70 2AS, England
E-mail: enquiries@pen-and-sword.co.uk
Website: www.pen-and-sword.co.uk

Or
PEN AND SWORD BOOKS
1950 Lawrence Rd, Havertown, PA 19083, USA
E-mail: Uspen-and-sword@casematepublishers.com
Website: www.penandswordbooks.com

Contents

A Glossary of Terms – Essential Pre-Reading

Aircraft/Aeroplane – Never plane!

The Boss – Squadron commander (Sqn Cdr); normally of wing commander (Wg Cdr) rank, but occasionally squadron leader (Sqn Ldr) of training units.

Station Commander (Stn Cdr); usually a group captain (Gp Capt). Less courteous titles are occasionally used. Commands the entire station, with Wg Cdrs immediate subordinates.

CO – Commanding officer; an officer of any rank who is designated as a unit commander.

Break – A run in and break is a manoeuvre used by tactical crews to get an aircraft rapidly on the ground. The airfield is approached at high speed, typically 400 knots; over the top of the runway, the aircraft is turned with 3–4 G, with airbrakes out and throttle closed, culminating in arriving at the downwind leg to land with gear and flaps going down. A real fighter pilot does this with sufficient panache to remain unsure of a safe outcome until he flares the aircraft to land.

Weenies – Anyone other than fighter aircrew.

Bomber Pukes – Bomber aircrew; also known as Mud Movers.

Truckie – Transport aircraft aircrew.

Stall – Encountered when speed is too low to sustain lift, resulting in loss of control. Can be recovered in less advanced aircraft by easing stick forward and increasing power.

Spin – A stall in which one wing produces more lift than the other, resulting in a rotation towards the 'more stalled' wing. Usually bad news in swept wing aircraft.

Met Man – Meteorological Forecaster; synonymous with/related to Sorcerer, Alchemist and Fortune Teller. Has all necessary modern equipment: Radar, Laser, Satellites, Computers, Seaweed and Pine Cones. A coin usually kept handy in case an immediate decision needed.

QFE/QNH/QTE etc – Aircrew set a pressure value on their altimeters according to their stage of flight. When taking off or landing, a pressure setting is used which gives zero on the altimeter – QFE; once airborne, the height above sea-level is more important, especially when operating in high ground; QNH is then set. When flying at high level, especially in airways or under radar control, all aircraft need to be on a standard pressure setting; this is QTE, and by convention is 1013 millibars or equivalent. Not to be confused with:

QFI/QWI – Qualified Flying Instructor (QFI), who is responsible for 'pure' flying skills, such as handling, turning, circuits and landings, stalling and spinning etc. Usually a person who smokes a pipe and wears carpet slippers at home. A Qualified Weapons Instructor (QWI) teaches applied flying, i.e. how to turn an aeroplane into a weapon for war: air gunnery, air combat, bombing etc., c.f. Top Gun, Tom Cruise, Ray Ban Sunglasses and, historically, Brylcreem.

IRE – Instrument Rating Examiner; responsible as the name suggests for maintaining high skills in instrument flying, including instrument approaches. Conducts the annual IRT (Instrument Rating Test) on all squadron pilots, including the Boss. Can be used by some to guarantee a few free beers annually. Boss rarely failed.

G-Force – The force to which aircrew are subjected in manoeuvre. We normally live at 1-G. Go over a hill rapidly in your car and you get a bit of negative G-Force. On a fairground machine, you might experience 2-G. Fighter aircrew operate up to 9-G, which can be alleviated by bearing down and grunting (requiring understanding spouse when the underwear arrives in the laundry basket), special suits and physiological training, all to avoid 'blacking out' as G exceeds 5.

Control Column – Also called 'joystick' or just 'stick'.

Gear – Aircraft undercarriage, which on advanced aircraft is selectable up or down. This should be in the order 'Up' after take off, and 'Down' before landing. But just occasionally ...

Flaps – High lift surfaces towards the back of the wing, deployed at lower speeds to reduce stalling speed, especially for take off and landing. Similar devices at the front of the wing are called leading edge flaps or slats.

FNG – F***ing New Guy. Used especially by the Red Arrows Aerobatic Team; has American origins.

Knots – Measure of speed used in aviation and sailing; means (air) nautical miles per hour. This is slightly higher than statute miles per hour. Lots of knots = good; no knots = bad.

Beat Up/Wire/Beat the Sh*t Out Of – To fly extremely low, normally resulting in a Bollocking.

Bollocking – A severe telling off, normally in Number One Uniform and hat on; coffee is rarely offered by the senior officer delivering the bollocking. Punishments range from 'Now get out of here', to doing additional Orderly Officer duties, and occasionally posting off the squadron.

Happy Hour – A tradition of the Service, at which at precisely 1700 on Friday, drinks are served at half price; the end time is less precise. Very popular with Scottish and Yorkshire aircrew.

Ranks in the RAF:
- OR: Other Ranks; all who are below WO/SNCO rank.
- SNCO: Senior Non-Commissioned Officer: sergeants (Sgt), chief technician (Ch Tech), flight sergeant (Flt Sgt).
- WO: Warrant officer; promoted ex-SNCOs who run the RAF; normally in their late 40s/50s and have 'seen it all before, Sir'. Can be very frightening, especially to junior officers.
- Commissioned Officers: Everything from pilot officer (PO) to air chief marshal (ACM). Ranks normally abbreviated, so:
  - Fg Off – flying officer
  - Flt Lt – flight lieutenant
  - Sqn Ldr – squadron leader
  - Wg Cdr (not Wingco!) – wing commander
  - Gp Capt – group captain
  - Air Cdre – air commodore
  - AVM – air vice-marshal
  - AM – air marshal

Squadron Engineering Officer (SEngO) – Overworked officer, normally the fall guy when flying task not achieved.

JEngO – see above. Junior Engineering officer, to whom blame for not achieving flying task is delegated.

Afterburner/Burner/Reheat – The afterburner, which is a long extension at the back of the engine, combines much of the remaining oxygen from the compressor with jet fuel, squirted into the high-speed exhaust stream from the engine's turbine, and ignites the mixture. The resulting 'blowtorch' shoots through a nozzle at the back of the engine, providing a hard kick of extra thrust, but at the expense of a lot of fuel.

Gash Shag – Junior Officer aircrew with no supervisory responsibilities.

Limo, or wheels – A car, or something resembling one. Not to be confused with:

Wheel/Exec – Squadron executive.

Minimum height/minimum separation distance – The height at which pilots say they never went below.

Bullshit – Hyperbole, exaggeration, lies; extremely common in fighter aircrew.

Some other abbreviations:

- No 43(F) Sqn; Number 43 (Fighter) Squadron;
- AOC – Air officer commanding, normally of a Group (Gp), for example 11(F) Gp. Usually an AVM.
- CinC – Commander-in-Chief, of a Command, comprising several Gps. Normally an AM or ACM.
- 'Stars' – Air Rank Officers, and RN/Army equivalents, are designated as 1–4 Star.
  - 1-star Air Cdre.
  - 2-star AVM
  - 3-star AM
  - 4-star ACM

THE EARLY YEARS

We all have dreams. But in order to make dreams come into reality, it takes an awful lot of determination, dedication, self-discipline, and effort.

Jesse Owens

Prologue

'Does Chris like Scouse?' Irene's mother enquired, in a manner which I later came to recognise as shyness, but which at the time suggested I could not be trusted to speak for myself.

'Yes he does', Irene replied, continuing to ignore me and finish her make-up. Around me the Johnson family, a couple of passing friends and those who aspired to friendship, munched on Margaret Johnson's lashings of lamb stew, which with the addition of a few secret ingredients, was transformed into Scouse; indeed, by repute, the best Scouse in the Walton area of Liverpool. The origins of Scouse go back many years to Lobscaus, a Nordic sailors' dish made from fish and vegetables, which was transmogrified over the centuries by Liverpool seamen into something more akin to Irish Stew. I sat somewhat self-consciously on the edge of the sofa, plate perched on lap, totally inept in the art of eating from a plate balanced so precariously, anxiously looking for a flat surface to avoid what I saw as an inevitable and humiliating catastrophe.

Sensing my plight, Mrs Johnson made room on the tiny parlour table, and furnishing me with a knife to supplement my fork, I was squeezed into a place that became mine for the next few years. I had arrived and, it seemed, been accepted by the main authority in the household, and despite the obvious suspicion and mistrust by some, I was there to stay. In consequence, Scouse, the dish that gives Liverpudlians their name, had become part of my staple diet, at least when I was visiting Irene in 29 Appleton Road, Walton, Liverpool; one of many terraced houses in a congested, working-class area of the city, but conveniently close to Everton football ground. How my life was to change!

Chapter 1

I had wanted to fly for a living for many years. Having flown in a Chipmunk at RAF Woodvale near Southport as a 16-year-old air cadet, I was totally smitten, and following a week-long selection test at RAF Hornchurch in Essex and at the RAF College at Cranwell, I was selected for a Scholarship leading to a permanent commission. I confess I nearly blew it at the medical. For some reason, the Coville family had been blighted with poor hearing (selective, my mother would have argued), and I was no exception. When the rather crusty ENT consultant whispered at impossible range the words 'Pit' and 'Bun', I replied with 'Tit' and 'Bum', no doubt inspired by the clear connection between the two words. I was obviously passed on the basis of sense of humour rather than aural acuity.

I returned to De La Salle Grammar School £500 a year better off, with the only requirement on me being to work hard enough in the Sixth Form to get two pretty average A-Levels. Life seemed very comfortable: I had gained a Private Pilots Licence (PPL) through a flying scholarship with the Air Training Corps; I had been selected to represent my Air Cadet Wing on the International Air Cadet Exchange, and spent an amazing four weeks in the USA, and I was gliding with my friend Aldon Ferguson every possible weekend. Then everything changed.

One day in late 1961, I was walking around the school yard during the afternoon break, when I saw my younger brother, Terry, and my mother's brother, Uncle John, standing near the school gate. As I approached them, I could see at once from my uncle's face that something was badly wrong.

'I'm afraid your mum's been taken ill; looks like pneumonia', he said. By the time we got home, it was clear that Mum had suffered a stroke. She died that evening, age 47. Mike, my elder brother, Terry and I were suddenly left without the loving mother we had all taken for granted. It was a terrible blow, and I still grieve for her today, partially through a sense of guilt that I was not the comfort she so needed. After the funeral, my father asked the Parish Priest, Father O'Brien, if there were any widows looking for domestic work, who could help us get through the next few months. My beloved Aunt Emily and her husband Arthur were a great source of support, but they couldn't be with us every day. Shortly after returning to school, I came home to find a stout lady peeling potatoes and preparing the evening meal. To my shame, I was less than welcoming to Mrs Kilfoyle, seeing her initially as an intruder. But she was such a kindly soul that after a while we became good friends. She was indeed a widow, mother of eleven children. But she was especially proud of one, her son Peter, who alone had passed the eleven-plus exam, and was at St Edwards Grammar School, where he was fly-half for the First XV, and expected to move on to university in due course. The next time I was at St Edwards, I looked him up, and after a few beers we agreed to meet regularly, which we did for the next couple of years. He did well at A-Levels, decided to do a gap-year in Australia, and disappeared off my radar screen forever – or so I thought … park this for a while, please.

But let's get back to my school, with me now in the Sixth Form, but with no great inclination to academic work. My old headmaster, Brother John, had written earlier of me: 'If Coville could put as much effort into his academics as he does into athletics and flying, he would be an extremely successful student.' These words turned out to be prophetic, as a combination of hormonal development, flying and a growing taste for beer resulted in my falling short of the required standards in the final exams, and I had to eat humble pie with the long-suffering Brother John and beg to be given another chance. Against his better judgement, and no doubt despite advice and threats of resignation from the school staff, he eventually gave in, and thanks to the similar patience of the RAF, I went back to school to face another twelve months of tedium. Still, fate is a strange thing, as it was during this period that I met Irene, who was not only destined (some might say sentenced) to be my wife, but also my lifelong companion and soundest adviser. Irene was one of five sisters, and like Peter Kilfoyle was the only one to pass her eleven-plus and go on to a Grammar School. Unlike me, she was hard-working and academic, and clearly one of the brightest girls in her school. She was also blond, vivacious and very pretty.

I managed to scrape through the remaining A-Levels the following year with barely average marks, but just enough to get into the RAF. Irene, who did much better at her A-Levels than I did and had secured a place at Manchester University studying English and American Literature, agreed to join me at Butlin's Holiday Camp in Skegness for ten weeks. Working as bar staff, our wages and tips enabled us to save up enough money to hitch-hike down to the South of France. We got engaged on the beach at Nice at three o'clock in the morning, having been dropped off there by a lovely French family in an ancient van. I always was an old romantic.

So it came to pass that on 4 October 1964, leaving a tearful Irene as she started life as a student in Manchester, I arrived at the famous portals of the RAF College at Cranwell in Lincolnshire, a lonely place selected by the fathers of the RAF to ensure temptations of the flesh could be contained.

It was not a successful transition to military life. Cranwell in those days was an exclusive establishment, constructed to produce the core of high-quality senior officers for the future RAF. It was predominantly supplied from the Public School sector, with the majority of boys (no girls in those days) from well-heeled families in the Home Counties. My Liverpool accent (mild by Toxteth standards, but enough to outrage the Cranwell hierarchy), my Beatle hairstyle and my Marks and Spencer suit set me apart from all but a few other flight cadets.

'Now, gentlemen', grunted our drill sergeant, Noddy Slater, as he surveyed his latest challenges, 'You all need an 'aircut, and especially you, Sir', pointing his pace stick at me.

'But Sergeant', I protested, 'I only had one yesterday.'

'Don't you fret, Sir; you pay a pound a month 'ere and you can 'ave as many 'aircuts as you like!'

The following day, I had my arrival interview with our flight commander, Flt Lt Viv Warrington; a real gentleman, who had flown Vulcan bombers in his previous tours. After the usual arrival question and answer session, he cleared his throat, and with a little embarrassment asked about my suit. I naïvely believed he was about to praise my sartorial good taste, but it soon became apparent that my wool and mohair 'Director's Suit', despite its grand title, was perceived as more appropriate to a night club bouncer than a future RAF Officer. Viv especially commented on the width of my trousers, which was sixteen inches, and by contemporary Liverpool standards quite baggy; but as gently as he could put it, Viv suggested I get down to the Gieves shop on base and get myself a 'proper' suit. I duly did, and was leapt upon by the branch manager, one Mr Young, who immediately signed me up for a 'ledger account' with Gieves Tailors, so laying the foundations of what was to become a long impecunious period of discarded invoices and rather rude letters from creditors.

Having, as a grammar-school boy, basked in relative freedom, and having enjoyed senior status in my last years in the sixth form, I found the Public School antics by the more senior cadets, or 'Crowing' as it was called, difficult to abide. Today it would rightly be called bullying, but it did at least serve the purpose of uniting the 'new Entry', as we were called, against those more senior. It also had its funny side: one Cadet awoke in his bed after a night on the local beer to discover that he and his entire room's furniture had been uprooted and reassembled on the main Parade Square!

Cranwell was an odd mix of academics, General Service Training (GST) and Flying, and there was an uneasy tension between the three. The lecturers, who were Education Branch officers, thought we should devote all our spare time to Maths, Aerodynamics and Thermodynamics. The GST staff thought that their time was totally inadequate to turn this motley lot into real officers, and the poor old Qualified Flying Instructors (QFIs) had the difficult job of putting flying where it should have been in the priority list. The first year was demanding, and again I nearly flunked it by moaning and bucking the system. In no time at all I had a reputation for being 'Bolshie', and it was made clear to me that I had to pull my socks up or I would be back on the streets of Liverpool. Fortunately, my aforementioned flight commander, Flt Lt Viv Warrington, after giving me a lot of carrot, one day came down on me like a ton of bricks. I made a half-hearted attempt to sort myself out, but it was only when the squadron commander, Sqn Ldr Gary Bach, formally put me on review for lack of officer qualities that I realised that the dream of flying fighters I had held for so long was going to be thwarted; and it was entirely my own fault.

Fortunately, about this time we started flying, in a great little aircraft called the Jet Provost, or JP, which was fully aerobatic, capable of over 300 knots and could climb to 30,000ft. Initially, I had considerable trouble adapting to the more disciplined and methodical flying required by the RAF. My first flying instructor, Al Thomas, very quickly saw this weakness, and considered alongside my cockiness, bolshiness and laziness, he decided I was a very poor prospect indeed. Rather than ditch me at once, the flying flight commander, John Gibbon, decided I merited another chance and allocated me to a new instructor, Bill Howard, who was young, was a relatively new instructor, and had the sort of patience associated with one who had droned for hours around the UK's territorial waters in the ancient Shackleton Maritime Patrol Aircraft. We got on well, and I ended up with a fairly respectable mid-table position at the end of my first flying phase. It was just enough to get me off review, but nowhere near good enough to get me on to fighters, which was what I passionately wanted.

For some reason that has never been adequately explained, we were then taken off flying and put on a twelve-month intensive academics phase. Some thought that this was a ruse to weed out weak aircrew early; others saw it as a way to make the point that Cranwell was about officer development rather than flying excellence. The outcome was that it disrupted the continuity of our flying training, which as any skills instructor knows full well, is idiotic. My bolshiness returned in full measure, as we embarked on one of the most tedious years of my life, exacerbated because we had tasted the joy of flying, and because anyway the majority of us were, to put it mildly, not the academic types. How we got through that year is a testimonial more to the patience of our academic instructors than to our steadfastness. There were consolations: we were no longer the Junior Entry, so were allowed out on Wednesday and Saturday nights to Sleaford. Anyone who knows this charming Lincolnshire market town will know how ill-equipped it is to meet the requirements of energetic young A-Types. But in its favour, it did have fourteen excellent pubs, which made an interesting challenge at one pint per pub. With a good friend, Mike Smith, I tried three times, but seemed to lose my way on the first attempt, was denied entry to the tenth pub on the second attempt, and on the third we got into a minor altercation with a couple of the local mafia, and had to hightail it back to Cranwell before we had our posh suits ruffled up. I also managed to see a lot more of Irene, who had settled well into university life, and now had a flat she shared with a couple of great girls.

It was during this period that I met the officer who was to be my next flying instructor, Flt Lt David Morris. Unfortunately, the circumstances were less than auspicious. My Entry, Number 91, had put a lot of effort into preparing the backdrop to the graduating Entry's Ball; indeed the centrepiece was a rather splendid mock-up of a vintage bi-plane, precariously suspended from the roof of the Rotunda in the College entrance hall. The younger instructors, David Morris included, decided that this rather dodgy piece of aerodynamics required air testing, and proceeded to mount the flimsy craft and swing in it wildly around the circular Rotunda. Outraged by the sight of my masterpiece being so badly treated, and no doubt fired up by several pints of beer, I took it on myself to protect what remained of the disintegrating airframe with an armoury of water buckets and fire extinguishers, accurately deposited on, and aimed at, the QFIs below. Perhaps feeling bolder than his soaking counterparts, the majority of whom were more than content to leave retribution to the following week, David Morris decided to demonstrate leadership qualities and confront this impertinent wretch who had dared to take on his senior officers. He would no doubt agree today that this was not one of his better decisions, as I had just found a new fire extinguisher, and any part of him that had been spared a soaking during my first attack, received it in full measure on the second. Glaring at me through carbon dioxide foam, he proclaimed: 'I know who you are, Coville, and I'm going to get you next week.'

The following Wednesday, 91 Entry duly pitched up to restart flying training. Six instructors were waiting in the crewroom to greet us, and they all looked familiar.

David Morris spoke first, looking at me with glee: 'We took lots for you, Coville, and I won!'

Thankfully, David's professionalism surpassed his need for revenge, and there started a friendship that remains to this day.

All of a sudden Cranwell and its style started to make sense, and while I was glad to see graduation day approaching, I made friends and gained values which endured for life. However, it was never an easy ride, especially as I always appeared to be broke; indeed, Irene used to send me cash every time she received her student grant. I'm not sure whether everyone was in the same boat financially. Certainly, some cadets received a monthly allowance from home. I do recall that my financial situation was chaotic, and that most people seemed to be aware of it. One way to get out of trouble was through Uncle Frank. Uncle Frank was, in fact, Mr Frank Ullyatt, a very sincere insurance salesman, who sold personal kit cover at knock-down prices, no doubt as an inducement to buy Life Assurance policies later. I often wondered how the poor man survived, as many a cadet had to fend off the bailiffs by securing cash for 'lost' kit from Uncle Frank.

One especially bad period in my financial history prompted a letter from Mr Hogg, the section manager at Lloyds, Cox's and Kings' Branch, who had the misfortune to oversee my current account. In essence, Mr Hogg reminded me that the purpose of personal banking was that I was supposed to keep money with the bank, rather than the other way round. Feeling somewhat aggrieved at this affront to my personal management skills, I consulted with my financial advisers in the bar that evening. After several pints and a good raft of sound advice, I wrote a letter to Mr Hogg, which in essence said: 'Dear Mr Hogg, At the beginning of this month, I note that you had £24-3-4d of my money. I did not write to you to point this out. Kindly do not do the same when I have £23-5-5d of yours. You have the honour to be Sir, my obedient servant etc.' Chaired by my wildly supportive confidants, I posted the letter to Mr Hogg and returned to the bar to discuss more important matters.

The morning after has an unfortunate habit of reducing bravado, and it was with considerable remorse and apprehension that the following day

CHAPTER 1

I phoned Lloyds in Pall Mall. My worst fears were realised when the very acidic secretary announced that Mr Hogg had my letter, and was planning to contact me that very day.

'Hogg', came the humourless voice. I could picture him in a frock coat, Aladdin heater in the corner of the office, Hansom cabs driving past the window behind him in the swirling London fog.

'Mr Hogg, good morning, it's Flight Cadet Coville', I said cheerily.

'Ah, yes, Flight Cadet, I've got your letter in front of me.' Oh, God, take me now!

'Yes, I must apologise for that, Mr Hogg, you see … er … I'm afraid I got mixed up with the wrong crowd the night before last night, and … er … well, I did have a little too much to drink.'

'Hmm, I see', he replied dryly. 'You were drinking, and I see that you are now overdrawn to the tune of twenty-eight pounds three shillings and tuppence!'

In the end, he turned out to be a good sort, and after a strong lecture on living within my means (a ridiculous proposition), he agreed to let me have a loan of £50 to get my affairs in order.

With the wisdom and acumen of youth, now out of the red, I immediately dashed around to see a friend, Dick Shuster, who had let it be known that he had a splendid car for sale for £30. Now that I was a man of substance, albeit courtesy of Mr Hogg, I decided it was time to join the band of cadets with 'wheels'. In the event, it turned out to be Dick's father who was selling the car, a lovely old black Ford Anglia, VHX 970. Accompanied by a fellow cadet and good friend from Liverpool, Les Quigley, we duly turned up at Mr Shuster's residence in Skegness, money changed hands, and I proudly drove off in my new limo, 'L' plates front and back, Les in a supervisory role. Dick had proclaimed that the car went 'Like a Dingbat'. I've never been sure what a Dingbat is or was, but the expression was obviously meant to convey a feeling of speed, which was not readily apparent, even on the flat Lincolnshire roads. However, it seemed to go well enough, at least for the first twenty-five miles. Somewhere around a small village called Leadenham, with about five miles to go to the College, there was a sudden loss of power, followed by an ominous graunching noise, and a pronounced lurch to the left. Any doubts I might have harboured that this was a trivial issue were dashed when a wheel, attached to half a half-shaft, came rolling by on the left-hand side, mounted the kerb and rolled with a splash into the dyke alongside the road, causing the sky to fill with outraged ducks. This was the start of a long and troubled relationship between cars and myself, which nearly saw the AA go bankrupt.

Sport was a vital part of life at Cranwell. I remember the words of advice given to us at De La Salle by the much-loved Form Master, Brother Joseph: 'If ever you feel tempted by the sins of the flesh, take some vigorous exercise and then have a cold shower.'

Cranwell obviously thought likewise, as every afternoon and evening, randy young men appeared to be suppressing their hormonal urges with squash, judo, athletics and other similar pursuits. I loved squash and judo, but my closest friend at Cranwell, the aforementioned drinking partner Mike Smith, had introduced me to the joys of mountaineering, and Mike being a Glossop lad, we frequently found ourselves climbing at Stanage Edge in Derbyshire. I confess that we both had ulterior motives for the location: Irene was nearby at Manchester, and was occasionally able to join us, and Mike's girlfriend lived not too far away in Burton. It was a very satisfactory arrangement, until a tragedy struck.

From time to time, Mike and I would head off in the summer on Wednesday afternoon from Cranwell to Stanage. With the longer days we could expect to arrive there at about three o'clock, and get in a good four hours climbing before dropping in to the local pub for supper. More often than not, we would travel alone in Mike's van. This particular Wednesday, we were just about to set off when another Northern lad, John Capes, asked if he and Jeff Mathews could join us. Unfortunately the back of the van was loaded up with tents and climbing paraphernalia which we were pre-positioning for the weekend, so we agreed to meet John and Jeff at the Edge. They were both reasonable climbers, but needed Mike's local expertise to get them going, so we agreed to join them after they got there under their own steam. A few hours later, we were climbing together, and once they were happy with the unusual features of Stanage Edge, we split up and agreed to meet for a pint later. When they failed to turn up at the pub that evening, we were not unduly alarmed, as it was still light and we assumed they had stayed on for a little more climbing. As we pulled in to the College at about eleven o'clock, it was obvious that something was amiss. There were several staff cars in front of the main entrance, and the lights in the upper-floor offices were all blazing. On Mike's door there was a cryptic note: 'Urgent, report to the Commandant's Office at once.'

Ten minutes later Mike burst into my bedroom; his face was white.

'Capes and Mathews are dead,' he said, struggling to get his words out. 'They were found roped together at the bottom of a climb.'

CHAPTER 1

Mike left and I collapsed back on my bed. Just a few hours earlier, we had waved them on their way; and now two young lives were lost. It was never clear how the accident had happened, but it seems that John Capes, who was much the lighter but a more capable climber, had been leading, and after tying up at the top of the climb, was pulled off when Jeff fell. It was only a 25ft drop, but with rocks littering the floor below the chances of survival would have been slim. In fact, they were found by a group of nurses just after they had fallen, and both seemed to be breathing, but neither survived the journey to hospital and were pronounced dead on arrival.

While all this was going on, Irene was going through her own hell. The evening before, I had phoned to see if she could join us. Unfortunately she couldn't, but wished us good climbing. I mentioned that there would just be the two of us, as I believed at the time. So when the BBC News announced that night that two Cranwell Cadets had been killed climbing at Stanage Edge, Irene was convinced Mike and I were the casualties. Of course, the news release had every parent phoning the College, and she couldn't get through to establish the names. In desperation, she went to the BBC studios in Manchester, and forced her way in to the newsroom. The astonished broadcaster at first refused to give her any details, but when she burst into tears they asked for my personal details, and were able to reassure the poor girl that neither fatality was from Liverpool. Typically insensitive, I didn't think to phone her and got a well-deserved drubbing when I eventually got round to contacting her the next day. I suppose if nothing else, it helped prepare her for the inevitable tragedies that were all too common on fast-jet squadrons.

When I think back on my three years at Cranwell, I do so with mixed emotions. There was a lot of silliness, and I never really embraced the Public School ethos. But the College was a remarkable vehicle for generating friendships, and perhaps most importantly for inculcating values and standards that would stand us in good stead in the future. There were some moments when I could easily have thrown in the towel, but most of my colleagues had similar bouts of depression, and we always helped to pull each other through. Those that didn't make it rarely had any bitterness towards the College or its regime; indeed, those who ploughed their furrow elsewhere invariably acknowledged Cranwell as having defined their future characters. In my case, I believe it gave me far more self-discipline and self-confidence, but I still felt uneasy as I marched up the steps of College Hall on my graduation that I was made of the Right Stuff. Time would tell.

Chapter 2

Irene and I were married shortly after I left Cranwell and she had graduated from University. Perhaps with some misgivings, Cranwell had sent me off to be a fighter pilot, the first stage of which was the Gnat Course at RAF Valley in Anglesey, North Wales. The Gnat was a major leap forward over the Jet Provost: supersonic, very agile and with modern avionics. It had a bit of a reputation as a killer, and most courses lost a student or two, either permanently through a fatal crash, or following ejection injuries. I actually loved the aeroplane, and thanks to expert guidance from my instructor, Ching Fuller, took to it like a duck to water. Irene was less enamoured of Valley. With our baby son, Peter, now in the family and with a small cottage that was like a fridge in the Anglesey winter, Irene reckoned she was getting the raw end of the deal, as indeed she was. That said, we made lots of good friends in the service and civilian communities, and despite the constant 50-knot winds, came to love the island and its people. All too soon it was over, and I was given the wonderful news that I had been selected to fly the Lightning, the RAF's newest fighter. Second to the Spitfire, which of course I could never fly (!), this was my dream choice.

The next step, however, was to fly a short course on the ageing Hunter aircraft, to get a feel for operating an aircraft as a weapons system, rather than just an airborne vehicle. Unfortunately, the RAF was going through one of its many force reductions, and the consequent inability of the front line to accept new pilots meant that I had to 'hold' at a location I had never heard of. When I was first told, I thought I was going to Houston, probably on the embryonic space programme; however, the rather rude admin officer who had conveyed the posting pointed out that I was in fact going to Ouston in Northumberland, where I would be flying the Chipmunk basic trainer on an Air Experience Flight for six months, charged with giving basic instruction to school boys and girls in the Air Cadets. This was quite a drop down after the Gnat and seemed a very poor lead in to the Lightning!

CHAPTER 2

After consulting the map book, and identifying Ouston as being on Hadrian's Wall to the west of Newcastle, we set off in a ridiculously overloaded Mini, with baby Peter in a carry-cot on the back seat, and everything else we owned strapped above or behind the tiny vehicle. With some help from the local police force (both of them!) we eventually arrived at the gates of RAF Ouston, in its heyday an important unit, but now looking tired and unwanted. Still, we got a nice house on base, with rudimentary heating, which was an improvement on our little icebox in Anglesey.

After unpacking, which took about five minutes in those days, we went for a look around, and to our delight found a group of young people in the Officers' Mess bar. They were student officers with the Northumbrian Universities Air Squadron, and turned out to be a lively and friendly bunch, with whom we would share many merry hours over the next few months.

The flying turned out to be not too bad either. The flight commander was a veteran pilot, who had flown Mosquitoes towards the end of the Second World War, and who had at some time in his career been awarded the Air Force Cross. A self-effacing man, Flt Lt Frank Jones would only ever answer 'NAAFI Coupons' when asked how he had earned the decoration. The poor man had the unenviable job of monitoring a group of similarly frustrated young pilots, all waiting to go onto operational aircraft, but stymied by the constipation in the training system. Perhaps inevitably, we turned to mischief in the air and on the ground, to fend off the boredom of routine Chipmunk flying. Dogfighting was forbidden, but practised anyway by us all, and the climbout lane at Ouston became known as 'Mig Alley'. One day, I was engaged in a ferocious dogfight with a friend and colleague, Godfrey Cornish-Underwood, at a well-known meeting point, Stagshaw Mast. Unfortunately, one of the University QFIs, the then Flt Lt Sandy Hunter, was setting off on his annual holidays when he saw the re-enactment of the Battle of Britain over the Northumbrian skies. Outraged, but in the pre-mobile phone days unable to communicate with base, he decided to report it when he got back. Luckily for us, when he did some three weeks later, he got the date wrong, and two poor old part-time volunteer reserve aviators on the Flight got hauled over the coals by Frank Jones, and Godfrey and I got away scot-free. It suited us, as we had our full careers in front of us, and the Old Timers seemed to be quietly pleased that they had been caught doing something naughty; it certainly did their reputations no harm.

Inevitably the Devil found abundant opportunity to recruit when we were idle and bored, and on one such day Godfrey and I thought it would be a good wheeze to stir the station up with a bit of excitement. After a packet of cigarettes had changed hands, we persuaded the ground radio engineer to go for a walk while we used his radio equipment. Dialling the Ouston Air Traffic Control (ATC) Frequency, I transmitted over the ether:

'Ouston, Ouston, this is Whisky Mike Charlie One One, important message, over.'

Ouston ATC, somewhat mystified: 'Whisky Mike Charlie One One, loud and clear, go ahead.'

'Roger, Ouston from Whisky Mike Charlie One One, VIP aircraft en route Ouston, please confirm arrangements made to receive twenty-four VIPs, including for lunch?'

Ouston ATC – after long pause:

'Er, Whisky Mike Charlie One One, confirm destination Ouston?' Not an unreasonable question, as nobody ever visited Ouston, least of all VIPs!

'Whisky Mike Charlie One One, affirmative, as reported new estimated time of arrival at Ouston 1200 hours local.' It was now 1130.

While I was causing havoc with ATC, Godfrey was busy sending a signal to Ouston operations (consisting of one corporal), asking for confirmation that the earlier signal concerning the VIP visit had been received and sent to the Station Commander. Oblivious to the other goings on, the corporal phoned the Station Commander's PA just seconds after the poor woman had had to tell her boss that he was about to receive a VIP flight literally out of the blue. So any doubts that this was an unfortunate misunderstanding were dashed, and the Station Commander scrambled back to his residence to find his best uniform, leaving his hapless PA to coordinate lunch and motor transport. There were already several nervous-breakdowns building up!

Not wishing to let things go too far, Godfrey and I were nevertheless distracted from calling it off in a timely fashion by the scenes of mayhem around the airfield, as ancient fire engines spluttered into action and were positioned around the perimeter tracks, Land Rovers raced around straightening up airfield information and warning boards that had remained where storms of many years before had deposited them, and the Station Commander arrived in a cloud of dust, desperately trying to button up his jacket over a large paunch as he leapt from his car. Out of sight, the Officers' Mess chef was wondering how he could turn Bangers and Mash or Cod and Chips into a culinary delight, and the Motor Transport (MT) Officer was screaming at several of his men who were trying in vain to start the Station's only thirty-eight seater coach.

The Senior Air Traffic officer (SATCO), Flt Lt Derek Exley, had just arrived on the scene, and started to smell a rat when I called 'Finals to

14

Land' and there was not an aircraft in sight. Within minutes the door of the Ground Radio section was wrenched open, and before Godfrey and I could make good our escape, we were clapped in irons and wheeled in front of a ferocious Station Commander. Fortunately, once his blood pressure was approaching normal levels, and following Frank Jones' pleas for clemency ('they're very young, Sir'), it was agreed that we should be fined a barrel of beer and do a weekend's Orderly Officer each.

Being a sleepy hollow, weekend Orderly Officer duties at Ouston seemed to consist of keeping the bar open as long as possible, and then formally closing it when it became impossible to bribe or cajole the barman into keeping it open any longer. Somewhere in the midst of all of this was the Ensign raising and lowering ceremony, which I confess was more often than not accomplished with less than the appropriate amount of decorum. Thus, while serving my penance the following weekend, it did not seem like an unreasonable suggestion when Godfrey and a few of the worst Northumbrian university students invited me to accompany them late on Saturday evening to one of Newcastle's favourite night clubs, the Cavendish. With the minor modification of a borrowed sports jacket, and in consequence resembling a policeman on a shopping expedition, the Station Commander's representative at RAF Ouston duly found himself in the front row of a cabaret, which as luck would have it turned out to be a hypnotist. Owing to my unfortunate seating position, and no doubt because of my obvious enthusiasm for his work, the artiste unwisely included me in his shortlist for hypnosis. In no time at all I was down to the last five performers, tasked with reproducing the antics of Elvis Presley, to the delight of the audience, not least my Ouston partners in crime. Fortunately for me, no one seemed to notice the uniform beneath the thin disguise, and I didn't feature in the Sunday edition of the Tyne *Chronicle*!

After the appointed six months at Ouston had passed, Irene and I packed baby Peter and other meagre possessions into our Mini, and headed off to RAF Chivenor, with a planned stop to visit family in Liverpool on the way. We were given a pleasant send-off, although I detected a sense of relief from the senior executive, including the new Station Commander, that at least one member of the 'Dynamic Duo' had departed to allow Ouston to sink back into its customary tranquil state!

After the usual low-stress journey associated with babies in nappies and unreliable cars, we arrived at my father's house in Liverpool and proceeded to disgorge vomit and detritus into his home. A short visit to the Queens

Arms satisfied the need to re-familiarise with real beer, and we started to prepare for the seven-hour journey to North Devon the next day.

'I think I'll touch base with Tony Bagnall and see if he knows anything about the flying programme,' I mused. Tony was a Manchester friend, who had not entirely involuntarily ended up in the Ministry of Defence for his holding posting. The phone was answered by his father, who, after establishing that I was not a spy intent on compromising his son, advised me that our course had been delayed a further six months! I decided to leave it until I had confirmed the facts the next day before telling Irene.

The following morning, the very sarcastic personnel officer at Chivenor confirmed that our course had indeed been delayed a further six months, and gave me a roasting for not knowing. I asked whether he had advised Ouston, to which he replied: 'Ouston, that's in Texas, isn't it?'

An hour or two later, a telegram arrived from the Station Commander at Ouston to say that I was absent without leave and would be court martialled if I didn't get back to the unit within twelve hours. Leaving a bewildered Irene and baby with an even more bewildered father, I hightailed it back to Ouston, making it just in time to avoid a night in the Guardroom. The next morning I was given a severe bollocking from the CO for being so naïve as to believe that a posting instruction written six months earlier could still be trusted, and warning me that any recurrence of such behaviour would most certainly result in formal action. With some trepidation, I phoned Irene that evening and told her in as cheery a voice as I could that I would be back that weekend to drag her and Peter all the way back to Northumberland; she was not at all consoled at my reminding her that we had left some coke in the coal shed, and now at least it wouldn't be wasted!

Irene's wrath and disbelief was nearly matched by that of poor old Frank Jones, who now saw Godfrey and I reunited. To his credit, he tried desperately to keep us sufficiently occupied to minimise mischief, but he largely failed. One wheeze he thought up was to form an aerobatic team, The Red Sparrows. Unfortunately, on our debut, and as it turned out our swan song, Frank got lost in cloud overhead Edinburgh, and we came out of the murk a few hundred feet over Princes Street, firmly in the Edinburgh Airport Control Zone. Several scheduled airline flights were disrupted, and The Red Sparrows never flew again. Not to be defeated, Frank gave us the tedious job of ferrying aircraft to Little Rissington in Gloucestershire for major servicing. The little Chipmunk couldn't make the journey in one hop, so we needed to refuel at Woodvale, which readers will recall was near Liverpool. On our first (and as it turned out, last) such trip, Godfrey and

16

CHAPTER 2

I decided that Woodvale needed a reminder of the significance of Ouston, and proceeded to 'wire' the airfield; a practice requiring less than well-disciplined low passes across the resident squadron's accommodation. Unfortunately, our antics took us across a home for the elderly, several long-standing noise-complainants, and a private hospital. I understand that there were no fatalities, but the subsequent outrage from locals was enough to ensure that we never went to Woodvale again.

In sheer desperation, Frank decided to put us back on flying air cadets, where at least he felt he could keep an eye on us. Over the summer months, the flying rate was anyway hectic, with Cadets resident on their summer camps, and there were not enough Volunteer Reserve pilots to meet the task. Most of the cadets seemed to prefer flying with Godfrey and myself, although we had to swear them to secrecy following more 'advanced' aerobatics. In addition to the Chipmunks, a Varsity aircraft, a large and lumbering twin-engine trainer, which could take some twelve cadets in the back, occasionally joined the Flight. On one Varsity detachment, we were surprised to see the aeroplane piloted by a sergeant, a rare breed in an essentially commissioned aircrew service. Nicknamed 'Noddy', he had been a Second World War Fighter Bomber pilot, and was almost as full of evil as Godfrey and myself. After some crewroom banter, he vowed to show us a thing or two if we ever met in the air. As luck would have it, I was returning to base the following day when this monstrous aeroplane suddenly appeared in my rear mirror, shortly followed by the triumphant cry of 'Tacka tacka tacka!' from an exultant Noddy. I managed after a few aggressive turns to shake him off, but the sight of twelve cadets clutching sick-bags as they trooped out of the back of the Varsity was enough to alert Frank Jones to the misbehaviour. Noddy told Frank to 'bugger off' when he tried to reprove him, but with a career ahead of me I had to take it on the chin. As usual, Frank found it difficult to be beastly, and I got off too lightly, agreeing to buy him a gin and tonic that evening and promising to behave better in the future.

Irene and I loved Ouston, especially the people and the Northumbrian countryside. But I was itching to move on, and when we eventually set off in our long-suffering mini, I was excited that I was getting a little bit closer to my dream of flying the Lightning.

Chapter 3

My bad relationship with cars hit an all-time low when I bought an Austin 1100 in Liverpool before setting off to Chivenor. It looked alright: British Racing Green, with more room than the mini and just a bit of extra power. Moreover, the salesman, Mr Allan of AA Car Sales (a shed in the Toxteth area of the city), seemed a nice enough chap. He gave me a disappointing part-exchange deal on the Mini: 'Been 'ammered a bit, Sir,' he unkindly observed, as his quick look under the bonnet revealed overflowing oil and coolant fluid. Nevertheless, after clucking his way round my pride and joy, touching parts of it with the look of a man probing the lesions on a leper, we fixed a deal. I proudly drove off to explain to an outraged Irene why, despite being totally broke, I had 'invested' in a new set of wheels. Not for the first, or last time, she was eventually won over; although my suggestion that we might need a bigger car if she got pregnant again nearly resulted in my castration.

The car seemed fine at first, and certainly coped better with the ever-growing load. Unfortunately it was jinxed, having probably been assembled in Cowley late on a Friday afternoon by a team anxiously watching the weekend approaching. The first mishap occurred as we set off for Chivenor. Passing through Chester, I became aware of a noticeable tendency for the vehicle to understeer on sharp bends. Progressively, the symptoms worsened, until eventually the car was virtually uncontrollable. Not being blessed with an especially analytical mind, I put this down to the characteristics of this particular marque, until a graunching sound pierced the calm of the cabin.

'You've got a puncture!' Irene exclaimed.

'Nonsense', I snorted, 'you don't get punctures in cars this young' (i.e. seven years).

But she was right, and after emptying the car and boot, I pulled the jack out of its oily bag.

'Is that it?' Irene asked in amazement.

'Just a bit rusty', I responded. 'Shouldn't be a problem.'

But it was, and it soon became clear that this piece of machinery's turning days were over. Fortunately, my father had, some years before, anticipated that the combination of my uselessness with machines and being poverty stricken could best be addressed with a long membership of the AA. In no time at all, a nice man on a motorbike and sidecar pitched up, raised his eyes when he saw the jack, and pulled a newer model from his massive toolbox. 'Have you on your way in no time at all, Sir', he promised. He was wrong. No sooner had he started to turn the jack handle when it became obvious that the jack was moving up but the car was not. The accompanying splintering sound gave a clue: the chassis was solid rust, painted over to give a semblance of solidity, but far too flimsy to bear any load. That nice Mr Allan had obviously been an accomplished con artist, and I had been suckered into taking on a write off with a false bottom! The AA man eventually found a long plank to spread the load, and after topping up a bald and totally flat spare tyre, we were on our way. 'Get that tyre changed as soon as you can, Sir', our Samaritan demanded. I promised him we would, but couldn't imagine when. We got on our way, hoping that the patches of red inner tube showing through the canvas of the spare tyre would hold out.

I had arranged, in the absence of available married quarters, for us to stay in an old fisherman's cottage in the pretty fishing village of Appledore, just across the Bideford Bay from RAF Chivenor. I was getting used to Irene being disappointed in me, but the sight of this minute dwelling in a narrow street on a wet October evening was probably the low point in terms of my reputation; at least up until then. After getting the fire lit and starting the process of drying out musty blankets, we eventually got Peter into his cot and I found some sherry left behind by earlier tenants. I have many times in my career called upon the healing qualities of alcohol to survive until better times; this was certainly one such occasion. Somewhat tiddly, we stumbled into the tiny, cold double bed and promptly fell into an exhausted sleep.

The alarm, which miraculously I had remembered to set, woke me up at six o'clock. I had to be at work by eight, and despite being only two miles across the bay, Chivenor was a good forty-five minutes by car. I grabbed a piece of toast, took Irene a cup of tea, and set off with a few minutes to spare. Perhaps inevitably, as the Gods favour the just, the car wouldn't start. After flattening the already feeble battery, and failing to find a crank handle in the bag of tools (*everything you want in that bag, Sir*), I had no choice but to coerce Irene out of bed to give me a push. I know this seems unchivalrous, but Irene had yet to learn to drive, and her one attempt to bump start from the driver's seat had ended up with me exhausted on the road and she and the car in a hedge.

After seeing her falling on her knees, I realised I wasn't going to get any faster and let out the clutch. I thanked my lucky stars as the engine reluctantly fired and I sped off down Irsha Street, leaving clouds of oily smoke, annoyed neighbours and Irene waving me goodbye, with her fists clenched.

It was very obvious that Chivenor was different. At Cranwell, and to some extent at Valley, all the instructors saw themselves as role models for future officers. At Chivenor, they considered their instructional tour as an irksome diversion from front-line flying. Students were by definition untrained and unworthy, and although several instructors were younger than us and had only completed one short tour on the Hunter in the desert, they assumed an air of elder statesmen to servile subjects. Instead of gleaming flying boots, most wore desert boots to prove their vast experience. The objective was unwritten if quite clear: if you didn't measure up you would be chopped and sent down to some less worthy role. I was at once considered slightly odd: married, and therefore unable to buy them beer every evening until the bar closed or they ran out of stories about 'Wadi-bashing' in mystical-sounding Arab locations. I could see that I had my work cut out!

To be fair to Chivenor and its staff, they saw themselves as guardians of the true fighter spirit, and while not all had the experience or professional skills to be so, they did act as a filter for those who could fly well but lacked the fighting edge: the 'Right Stuff', in modern parlance. The trouble was that the classical image of a fighter pilot was at odds with anyone who didn't cut the mustard in the air or in the bar, and for the first time in my flying career I struggled at both. Although I loved flying the Hunter, I hit a major block navigating at high speed at low level, a key qualification for any aspiring tactical pilot. I had been perfectly happy to follow a line on the map at 180 knots in the Jet Provost, or even 360 knots in the Gnat. But 420 knots required a totally different approach. In simple terms, it is possible at the lower speeds to fly along referring to railways, bridges and roads, but at higher speeds these just become a blur. I rapidly ended up leading my instructors on what became known as 'Coville's Mystery Tours'. My only defence was that at least we always ended up back at Chivenor, unlike my good friend Peter Bedwin who, similarly handicapped, finished one sortie landing at a civilian airport in Wales! Later, when flying a Lightning, he ended up landing at Norwich Airport when he ran short of fuel, and acquired the nickname 'Bedwin the wandering pilot.'

Funny aspects of this aside, it soon became apparent that if I didn't improve, I was not going to be a fighter pilot, and the prospect of hauling freight or passengers around the skies inspired me to step up a gear. Fortunately, there were a few older instructors around who identified my problem. One, Wally Willman, put it quite succinctly: 'Get your nose out of the bloody map and start looking for the big features.' He was right. I was looking for road junctions when my target lay on the other side of the biggest hill for twenty miles!

Things came to a head (no naval pun intended) when I was having a pre-flight nervous pee and the American exchange officer came to the urinal alongside me. In a hushed whisper, he muttered: 'Fly good, Chris; fly good.' Putting aside the poor grammar, the message was clear, if delivered in a somewhat unconventional manner: I was drinking in the Last Chance Saloon. Mercifully, the flight went well, and I moved on to the next stage: Air to Air Gunnery, referred to as the 'Sport of Kings'. And so it was, but in the ageing Hunter a massively demanding task. Owing to the several moving parameters in air combat, merely placing a fixed cross on the cockpit of the opponent wouldn't work; unless of course he chose to stay wings level in a straight line. As few opponents could be relied upon to be so obliging, all targets were assumed to be evading ones, which meant that bullets fired from the esteemed Aden Cannon would hit the empty airspace occupied by the target a split second before. To cope with this tricky equation, gunsights incorporated radar ranging and gyroscopic prediction systems. Sounds great, and it works if you can keep the 'pipper' on the target, but the expression 'trying to stuff a piece of soggy spaghetti up a wild cat's arse', was an absolutely accurate description of the challenge presented to the pilot! The major fault we all made initially was chasing the gunsight, giving insufficient time for the gyros to settle down. With practice we started to get the hang of things, and moved on to live firing on the air range out to sea. The target, a 24ft by 6ft banner, was towed behind a venerable (aka old) Meteor, a post-World War Two fighter. The Meteors were flown by an interesting group of pilots, most whose career prospects were zero, or who had been caught with their trousers down in circumstances deemed in those days inappropriate for an officer. There was even a Non-Commissioned pilot on the flight; the only NCO fighter aviator I ever met still serving, although there were many of course during the war. Apparently, he was an excellent pilot in training, but showed no officer qualities whatsoever, so some enlightened (if rare) staff officer arranged for him to graduate with wings but without the Queen's Commission. He no doubt remained hidden from senior scrutiny until he had acquired enough hours to move into a lucrative appointment in the airlines.

One thing linked all those who flew the Meteor: their totally reasonable fear of being shot down by a student pilot. For obvious reasons, the live firing could only commence when the Meteor was turning, so giving some separation between the target flag and the towing aircraft. Unfortunately, this was by no means a guarantee of safety, as pilots have traditionally found ways to exploit both Murphy's Law, and its corollary, Sod's Law. Murphy states that if anything CAN happen it WILL! Sod adds the rider: 'And at the worst possible time.' Thus, bullets did occasionally strike the Meteors, although more often than not it was 'Press-On-itis' rather than poor technique that caused such incidents. I shall return to these eternal constants in aviation from time to time, but any pilot who flouted them was highly likely to end up in a smoking heap.

After my previous shaky performance, especially at low-level navigation, I was relieved to find that I could perform well in air gunnery, and after a few low scores, I turned in an excellent result and ended up as the air-to-air ace of the course. Perhaps I would get through Chivenor after all!

But then something happened which could well have brought my time as a fighter pilot and my whole career to an abrupt halt.

A few months earlier, the breathalyser had been introduced to curb the ever increasing toll of death and injury on the British roads. The RAF had made its position clear: if you proved positive after breathalysing you were out of the service immediately. For this reason, I had started booking into the Mess following any event involving alcohol; the main ones being Friday evening Happy Hour and the monthly Formal Dinner Nights. It was after one of the latter when, the worse for sherry, wine and port, I stumbled back to my room in the Mess, only to find it already inhabited by another who, to put it bluntly, had allowed his beer intake to exceed the capacity of his stomach, with predictable consequences. Even had I been able to boot him out of bed, I didn't relish the prospect of sleeping in his vomit. So it was back to Mess Reception, only to be told that no other rooms were available. I tried for a few hours to bed down on a couch in the Ante-Room, but by five o'clock I had had enough and decided I would make a cautious dash for our home in Appledore. After all, I had been temperate for over six hours, and the chances of the police being around at this hour were surely remote.

CHAPTER 3

All went well until I was leaving Bideford when, in a layby on the left, I could clearly make out a large white car with a blue bobble on the top. I froze, especially when as I started to disappear around the next bend I could see the car pulling out after me. In a panic, I accelerated, looking for an escape route. In the near dark, I vaguely made out a gap in the hedge, and in a four-wheel drift scampered into a farmer's field. Mercifully, the gate was open. I put out my lights and waited, my heart beating furiously. The car drove past, accelerating when they realised I was out of sight on the bendy road. I dashed over and closed the gate, and with lights still out moved across the bumpy field until I felt I was well enough concealed in a group of high bushes. The car came back, this time with blue light flashing, but it turned down a side lane and shot off into the distance. I started to relax, when suddenly another blue light flashed its way into sight from the direction of Barnstaple. They were calling for reinforcements! Should I abandon the car and make a run for it across country? This didn't seem too sensible, dressed as I was in Mess Kit and bow tie, and I couldn't see the RAF accepting my explanation that I was merely doing some free-time escape and evasion practice. I decided to sit it out.

For what seemed an eternity, one or both cars cruised by, and on one occasion they stopped by the gate and I could hear their soft West Country accents discussing how I could have apparently vanished into thin air. After what seemed an eternity they got back in their cars and headed back towards Bideford. I dozed fitfully, the Austin getting increasingly like an ice box, until the sun gradually rose above the horizon, clearly revealing my tyre marks across the field. I would have to get away; but were they waiting for me, ready to pounce as soon as I emerged from my bolthole? Well, I would have to take my chance, and hope that the passage of time had reduced my alcohol level down to legal levels. I bumped across the field and poked the car's stub nose out of the gate. All seemed clear. Tentatively, I drove out onto the main road and headed for safety. I had only travelled a couple of miles when I saw coming towards me a large white car. My heart started to race again; to my relief it was not the police, but just another early riser. I wearily opened the front door of our little cottage in Irsha Street, to be confronted by a quizzical Irene, looking at my dishevelled appearance. 'Good God!' She exclaimed. 'You look as though you slept in those clothes!' Lesson learned!

23

We all knew we were in a risky business, where just a small mistake could cost you your life. But I suppose we didn't give it too much thought. Like most young people, we thought we were immortal. This belief took a bit of a jolt one day when, between sorties, a group of us were watching a Sea Vixen Naval fighter practising circuits on the easterly runway. Owing to the need for tight circuits around aircraft carriers, this young pilot and his observer were impressing us with the extreme bank angles he was using around the final turn.

Unfortunately, there was a strong, tightening crosswind dragging him through the runway centreline, and he really should have thrown it away and gone round for another approach. But he didn't, and foolishly tried to save face and persisted, with the inevitable outcome that he lost control of the struggling Sea Vixen. In slow motion, but in reality a split second, the aircraft flicked over on its back and plunged into the undershoot. We all gasped; slowly at first, but rapidly gaining strength, a lick of flame and then a mighty cloud of dense smoke marked the point in Devon where, in front of us, two young men had just lost their lives. I confess that I was shaken; perhaps more than I would have expected. We watched dumbstruck as fire engines and ambulances raced to the scene. An hour later, the fatalities having been confirmed, I was driving out of the station. An ambulance was just backing into the Station Medical Centre. Two white faced young medics were opening the back of the vehicle. Together with some assistance from the other medical staff, they lifted two stretchers out and hurriedly carried them inside and out of sight. But I had seen enough to understand that what was left of those two poor chaps was bundled into large plastic bags. It was a salutary reminder that even in peacetime, fast-jet flying was a risky business. It was not to be the last time I would be reminded so starkly of the realities of flying close to the edge of human and aircraft limits.

Tony Bagnall seemed frequently to be the first to pick up bad news. I was coming in one afternoon after a flight when he pulled me to one side. 'The bastards have chopped Glyn', he whispered secretively. Glyn Davies was a punchy little Welshman who had impressed the instructors at Valley with his sociability and aggressive flying. He had been rewarded with a streaming to the Hunter, and he and his new wife Margaret were among the minority of young marrieds going through flying training. Glyn was sitting in the crewroom, close to tears. I patted him on the shoulder, knowing what it meant to get so far and fail at this stage. Whatever the consolation prize offered, nothing was going to replace flying single-seat fighters. 'I don't know what I'm going to tell Margaret', he said. That night in the Mess, there was a little social gathering for the course, girlfriends and wives. Bravely, Glyn and Margaret turned up, although on one occasion I caught her alone with a handkerchief, brushing away the tears. I had already seen this happen several times before, and was to see it again, and in many different circumstances. The end result was always the same: a broken-hearted young man, who was going to have to pick up the pieces and start all over again down a different road in life.

The next day we came in to work to see Glyn gathering his things before departing, when to our surprise the squadron commander called him into his office. Glyn emerged with a grin all over his face: there had been some reconsideration, and he was to be given more time to get over a sticky patch. To his credit, he came good, and went on to enjoy a very successful career as a professional pilot in a fascinating range of roles.

With a bit of a struggle, I got through my final low-level navigation test, achieving average results for most disciplines, but above average for air-to-air gunnery and air combat. This augured well for my future as an interceptor pilot, but I was reminded that the bar was constantly being raised in front of me, and if I was to succeed in my chosen career path, I was going to have to work ever harder to achieve the necessary standards, in the air and on the ground.

Chapter 4

After a week of leave, those of us heading for the Lightning had to spend a few days at the Aero Medical Training Centre at RAF North Luffenham, in Rutland. The purpose of the course was to prepare us for the rigours of high-speed flight at high altitude, where the human body is operating at the edges of its capabilities. We were also to be issued with the special flying equipment needed to cope with these extremes: G-suits, special helmets and jerkins designed to cope with loss of cabin pressurisation. There were two highlights of the course: the decompression chamber and pressure breathing practice.

At sea-level, man breathes easily, having adapted to the oxygen levels available. However, as altitude increases, oxygen levels reduce, until at about 20,000ft humans cannot survive without long periods of preparation or supplementary oxygen. Above about 35,000ft, even 100 per cent pure oxygen is inadequate to maintain life, and the gas must be forced into the lungs under pressure to maintain the right oxygen levels in the blood. There are two consequences to this. The first is that loss of pressurisation or oxygen can lead to progressive unconsciousness, and where the cockpit pressurisation is above 35,000ft, pilots can only continue to fly if they are provided with oxygen under pressure, which requires practice to avoid gagging. The decompression chamber allows this to be practised in a realistic, if somewhat uncomfortable manner.

After some training in the insidious symptoms of hypoxia (oxygen starvation) and pressure breathing, we were scheduled to be tested in the chamber the following morning. Because of other consequences of decompression, especially evacuation from the gut of rapidly expanding gases, we were advised to eat sensibly the previous evening and refrain from drinking beer. True to form, we judged this advice to be exaggerated, and headed off for a curry washed down with several pints of the local Ruddles ale – well known for producing flatulence even under normal conditions.

CHAPTER 4

The results the following morning were both excruciating and nauseating, especially for the unfortunate AMTC technicians who, for safety reasons, were required to accompany us on our journey into near space. As we farted our way past 20,000ft, I noticed the technicians getting progressively greener, and switching to pure oxygen. At 36,000ft, the cabin was rapidly decompressed, and a sound rather similar to an exploding airship rent through the chamber. I swear the air turned a dark shade of vindaloo, if such a colour exists; certainly it turned blue with the expletives emerging from contorted faces, as trapped wind fought its way through tortured bowels until it could be mercifully released. The gradual return to earth was for most uncomfortable, for some painful, and for a minority who had turned air into matter embarrassing.

Another lesson learned, but plenty more to come!

The Lightning Operational Conversion Unit (OCU) took fully trained pilots, honed by their experiences on the Hunter, and turned them into fledgling operational pilots on the RAF's first supersonic fighter. The Lightning was a massive step forward over the aeroplanes it replaced, and presented aircrew, young and old, with a real challenge. Indeed, a lot of the very experienced Hunter and Javelin pilots who arrived at the OCU failed to complete the course. Most failures could in the end be attributed to two things: the first the RAF refers to as 'capacity', or lack of it; the second resulted from a not entirely unjustified fear of the beast! The Lightning had killed a lot of pilots in its early years, either through aircrew error in a high workload situation, or through technical malfunction. The aircraft had an unfortunate tendency to catch fire, and it was soon realised that with such ferocity that the titanium control rods to the tailplane would burn through in seconds, resulting in a fatal pitch up and spin into the ground. The ejection seat saved many, but at low level there was little chance of survival.

To most of us, none of this mattered. The Lightning was the best aircraft in the world, and we couldn't wait to get our hands on it. Like most RAF Stations, Coltishall was in the sticks; in this case North of Norwich near the Norfolk Broads. Irene was getting used to being parked with Peter in my father's home in Liverpool while I got accommodation organised. Being broke, the opportunities were limited, and in the end we had to settle for a summer holiday home in Mundesley, a seaside resort which was probably pleasant in summer, but with winter coming on it looked as bleak as the dark side of the Moon. I have often wondered how a house can be colder inside than it is outside, but this environmental phenomenon was common in the early Coville residences.

With a look of 'Oh my God, what have you set me up for this time?' on her face, Irene with Peter on her hip set about converting the chilly house into another home. I got ready for my first day on the Lightning.

After some brief arrival procedures, the group of us assembled in the briefing room for the progression of senior officers, from the flight commander through the squadron commander to the station commander, all of whom exhorted us to work hard, listen to our instructors, and not wreck the Officers' Mess. As well as some Cranwell colleagues, including Tony Bagnall and Nigel Holder, we had a few new faces. One was a wing commander, Erik Bennett, who had flown Hunters for years, set up several Arab Air Forces, and been an Aide-de-Camp (ADC) to King Hussein of Jordan. He was already a living legend in the air, but was on his way to be Officer Commanding Operations (OC Ops) Wing at Tengah, in Singapore, and so had to convert to the Lightning alongside a bunch of new kids. Erik was a tremendous friend and mentor to us during the difficult days at Coltishall, and he was to feature later in my life as a friend in retirement.

After the senior officers' finger wagging was over, we got changed for our first flight. Normally, this would take place after ground school and several trips in the simulator, but the staff at Colt (nickname) had sensibly calculated that with so much bad press around, they needed to reassure us that we were going to enjoy flying the aircraft. And so, almost five years after I had stepped across the portals of Cranwell, I climbed for the first time into the aircraft of my dreams.

It looked and felt big, after the tiny Gnat and pert Hunter; the difference between the MG Midget and an E-Type Jaguar. My instructor, Jerry Brown, started up the aircraft, and talked me through the complex instrumentation. 'Don't worry about the radar for this trip', he advised. I was relieved; there was going to be enough just taking in the basic cockpit. We lined up for take-off, Jerry selected full power on the mighty Rolls Royce Avon engines, and as I felt myself pushed back in the ejection seat he engaged reheat. Reheat, for those who lack a degree in thermodynamics, is like an extra engine in the back of the jet pipe. Extra fuel is poured into the jet efflux from the main engine, ignited, and then ... oh my goodness! The effect was phenomenal.

CHAPTER 4

The skin was pulled back across my face as, accelerating 100 mph every five seconds, the Lightning hurtled down the long tarmac runway before, with a gentle pull back on the control column, Jerry lifted her off the ground and pointed up almost vertically to the sky. It was electrifying, terrifying and absolutely wonderful. In seconds we were passing 5,000ft, the altimeter frantically winding round trying to keep up with the stunning rate of climb. After what seemed like just a couple of minutes we levelled off at 36,000ft, and accelerated to Mach 1.3.

'Try a steep turn, Chris', Jerry said, releasing the controls to me with the time-honoured expression: 'You have control.'

'I have control.' Came my response. It was sweet to fly, even at that speed.

'Do a roll', he suggested. I gulped; surely not at this speed? But she rolled beautifully around the horizon. 'OK, pull the stick back and climb at sixty degrees nose up', Jerry demanded. We zoomed up to 50,000ft, where the earth is visibly round and the sky becomes darker. I was in a different world; one visited by only a few people. All my previous training, in the air and on the ground, was really about this moment: flying an operational fighter.

I rolled the aircraft inverted and pulled the nose down to descend to low level. My ears felt as though they would burst as, with throttles back and airbrakes out, we hurtled down from over eight miles high to the dark North Sea below.

'Level at 250ft', Jerry instructed. 'Put the airbrakes in and select reheat.' The Lightning bucked like the thoroughbred she was and rapidly accelerated to 600 knots. 'OK, stick back again, Chris.' This time, now light on fuel, the aircraft climbed at an astonishing rate, and with some encouragement I levelled off at 25,000ft. 'Time to go home.' Surely not! We had only been airborne some twenty-five minutes; but in reheat the Lightning was a thirsty beast, and we had used most of the 900 gallons of fuel. Jerry turned us back towards the Norfolk Coast, showed me a quick loop on the way back, and a few minutes later put her back down on Colt's runway at nearly 170 mph.

That evening in the bar, we were all buzzing. It didn't matter that we had three weeks of hard graft ahead in the classroom and in the simulator. We had flown the Lightning, and despite a trace of apprehension which we all felt, but would never mention, we were heading for the RAF's front line in the best fighter in the world. But not all of us would survive the experience.

We were always broke in the early tours, and as a consequence were always looking for ways of saving money. Home brewing was common, and most of our flying underwear reeked of Cabernet Sauvignon as demi-johns plopped merrily in airing cupboards; frequently the only locations managing to stay warm enough to sustain fermentation. We were also constantly on the watch for cheap food. Sacks of spuds and onions at knock-down prices could often be found at roadside locations in Norfolk. Getting cheaper protein was a bit more of a challenge. One of the chaps on the course, Pete Hood, a pleasant Zambian ex-pat, persuaded me that we should buy a piglet at Swaffham Market, fatten it up over a few months, and then gorge ourselves on crispy suckling pig. Accordingly, one Saturday morning, Pete and his lovely wife Christine, picked us up and we set off to make the purchase. After a few emboldening ales in a Swaffham pub, we made our way to the marketplace, and eventually discovered a corralled area which appeared to be selling livestock. After watching proceedings for long enough to absorb the secret signals and processes, we started to make our bid for a cute little chap, who looked as though he would be ideal for our purposes. After several nods at the auctioneer, frowns from the gathered farmers, and threatening gestures from the other man intent on devouring the piglet, we outbid the rest at 'one hundred and five shillings', and went around the back of the fencing to pick him up. To our horror we found him back among the other twenty-five in the sale, with the auctioneer holding out his hand for more money than our cars were worth. Feeling appropriately embarrassed, we beat a hasty retreat back to the pub, where we lamented the lack of clear instruction in the pig selling process. But all was not lost. Pete came up with a great wheeze to fill our stomachs. He had read that Homo Sapiens has a far greater endurance than most animals, and given our levels of fitness we should be capable of driving to exhaustion any of God's creatures, including the plentiful and delicious Norfolk pheasant. Back in the car, with Christine driving, we set off in search of likely prey on the top road back to Norwich. After about twenty minutes two hapless birds ran across just in front of the car, Christine came to a screeching halt, and Pete and I dashed out in hot pursuit of supper. Unfortunately, Pete's source of information had failed to take account of rough terrain, or indeed for the propensity of wild creatures to fight dirty to survive; in this case by flying a few hundred yards just as we were making ground on them. After tearing our clothes, muddying our shoes and reaching a state of total exhaustion, Pete and I conceded defeat, and miserably returned to give the bad news to the ladies. It was turning into a totally forgettable day.

Happily, redemption was at hand, and after a few miles we came across an injured cock pheasant, flapping in distress at the side of the road. In no time his distress was terminated, and he was slung unceremoniously into the boot. That evening, putting aside the need to hang a game bird for at least a week, we dined royally at the Hoods' on pheasant casserole Zambian-style, and Chateau Coville red wine.

The progression from the Hunter to the Lightning was dramatic. The old Hunter was a delight to fly: relatively simple, with benign handling characteristics. The Lightning was a bit of a beast, and needed a degree of respect accordingly. I suppose it was like going from a spirited sports car to Formula One. The added complexity of the Lightning was in the weapons system; radar and missiles complementing eyeball and guns. Of course, many of the principles remained the same. Fighter pilots need to fly well, but aggressively. They need to hate losing, and tend to show disdain for all other forms of aviation. But the Lightning was definitely a step further, and the training was designed to ensure that the usual fighter spirit was tempered with a more technology-driven and methodical approach to finding and defeating the enemy.

The weapons system comprised the Ferranti AI 23 radar and the Firestreak Infra-red homing missiles; heat seekers, which would pick up engine exhaust and destroy with a lethal proximity fuse and blast fragmentation warhead. Normally, we could pick up a target on the radar at about twenty-five miles, but much lower at sea-level, where surface returns interfered with radar performance. The job of the ground-based radar system was to get the Lightning within radar contact, and then leave the pilot to do the necessary geometry to get into the rear hemisphere of the target, where the missile could 'see' the jet efflux. All this was happening, of course, at closing speeds of twenty miles a minute, so time for mental arithmetic was short. Perhaps more than for any other reason, this is where the older Hunter pilots found the transition to the Lightning challenging, and why so many failed to complete the conversion. The aeroplane had to be flown manually, accurately, while operating the radar and weapons. Although my old Maths teacher would have been astonished, I took to the Lightning not only in the pure handling, but also in the mental arithmetic needed to convert raw radar information into useful information on target speed, height and heading.

After it was decided that I would be going onto the latest, longer range version, the Mark 6 Lightning, a few of us split from those remaining on the older T4/FI versions, and moved a hundred metres to the sister squadron, where we would be introduced to a different radar and missile system, comprising the AI23B and the Red Top missile; more capable and with a better lethality envelope. In essence, this required no more than a mental technology upgrade, as the handling of the aeroplane was almost identical to earlier versions. But because the Red Top missile had a much bigger kill envelope than the older Firestreak, it did require some effort to learn how to get the best out of the radar and weapons. Again, the simulator was a great bonus, allowing precious time in the air to be spent to maximum value. I had the good fortune to fly with Flt Lt Henry Ploszek during this phase. Henry the Pole, as he was affectionately known, was an old-fashioned fighter pilot, who saw at once that I was being too robotic in my flying, and had become a slave to technology at the expense of flying in the spirited and aggressive way needed of a Knight of the Air. After flying a few sorties with me, Henry announced in his customary blunt fashion: 'Chris, you're a good pilot, but you're not going to be a good fighter pilot unless you pull your finger out and stop flying like an airline tart!' This 'something', 'right stuff' or 'spirit' was at the heart of fighter flying, and somewhere along the line I had lost it. I was left in no doubt that I had to rediscover the fighting edge, or risk being chopped onto another aircraft more suited to my precise form of flying.

I suppose in retrospect, I had been seduced by the different attitudes between Chivenor and Coltishall. At Chivenor there had been a total focus on tactics and skills very similar to those needed during the Battle of Britain. At Colt, we spent more time in the simulator and on academic subjects. Fortunately, Henry had reminded me of a fundamental truth of air combat: all the technology in the world will fail you unless you fight more aggressively than your opponent. There are no silver medals, and only contempt for those content to be in second place. After some rethinking of my priorities, I started again to consider every engagement as a personal not technical challenge, every other pilot to be someone I had to beat, and each opportunity to fly as a chance to prove my worthiness to fight and fly, to myself and to others. I made progress, started to really enjoy my flying again, and graduated at the top of the course. And so, at long last, I was on my way to an operational RAF Fighter Unit: No. 5(F) Sqn, at Binbrook, in Lincolnshire. After spending a few minutes finding the station on a road map, I gave the squadron a call, to be told that I was not to even think about arriving at the squadron for a couple of months, as they were fully engaged in an important Air Defence competition, and didn't have any time for a rookie. So much for the warm welcome to my first squadron!

THE JUNIOR FIGHTER PILOT YEARS

Aggressiveness was a fundamental to success in air-to-air combat and if you ever caught a fighter pilot in a defensive mood you had him licked before you started shooting.
David McCampbell

Fighter pilot is an attitude. It is cockiness. It is aggressiveness. It is self-confidence. It is a streak of rebelliousness, and it is competitiveness. But there's something else – there's a spark. There's a desire to be good. To do well; in the eyes of your peers, and in your own mind.
Robin Olds

Chapter 5

It was normal practice for a young officer to arrive on a station unaccompanied, present his credentials and become fully operational before bringing the family to join him. This entailed a period living in the Officers' Mess, with all the perils this entailed. The first was falling under the malign influence of the hardened drinkers, many of whom were established bachelors with little else to do in the evenings, especially in such a remote location. Having found my room in the Mess annexe, affectionately referred to as 'Alcatraz' owing to its resemblance to the well-known American penitentiary, I went in search of company before dinner. I didn't have to look far: the bar was full, but few looked young enough to be Lightning pilots; indeed, they turned out to be a mix of the resident Canberra squadron and officers from other branches, most of whom were unaccompanied, divorced or long-term single. Self-consciously, I bought a beer and sidled into a group of the noisier lot, all of whom were wearing 85 Sqn flying suits. No. 85 had enjoyed a distinguished history, but its role at that time was mainly confined to acting as targets for the UK fighter squadrons, a function requiring somewhat boring sorties over the North Sea. The squadron, no doubt as a result of its tedious role, was reputed to be manned with those awarded the CDM (Caught Doing Mischief), sometimes illegally low-flying, more often some social misdemeanour involving an excess of testosterone! Smartly clad, and an obvious first-tourist, I was treated with some suspicion; which rapidly turned to derision when I prematurely mentioned I was a new Lightning pilot. One particularly aggressive navigator (a breed I had previously been advised to avoid at all costs unless I wanted to get hopelessly lost), Mick Mahoney, immediately gave me the benefit of his considerable wisdom on Air Defence. Mick was one of several RAF aircrew from southern Africa; nations which had shed the trappings of colonialism, including the best of their armed forces. He and his charismatic pilot, Dick Buncher, rapidly decided that I needed mentoring in the ways of the 'real' Air Force, which seemed to include a fairly hard hit on my bar book – an omen for the future. Mick made it clear that he had 'forgotten more about air defence' than anyone had learned on 5(F) Squadron; but that nobody came to ask his advice. I later discovered that Mick had completed one tour on the ageing Javelin fighter, and even that had been cut short by the aircraft's early withdrawal from service.

I slowly found my way back to my room in Alcatraz later that evening, resolved to be more wary of the company I kept in the Mess in future; yet another resolution I would struggle to deliver.

No. 5(F) Sqn was one of the RAF's senior units, having been formed from 3(F) Sqn shortly after the First World War. It had served with distinction in outposts of the British Empire, including the Gulf, and was the first to be equipped with the Mark 6 variant of the Lightning, which was fitted with a larger ventral (belly) tank to improve the aircraft's notorious shortage of fuel. Whereas the earlier Marks struggled to achieve forty-five minutes in the air, the Mark 6 could easily exceed an hour, and with air-to-air refuelling (AAR) had a seven-hour-plus clearance. The other major difference to earlier models was the shape of the wing, which had been adapted to make the aircraft more manoeuvrable in air combat. This was my first real squadron, after nearly five years in the RAF; I couldn't wait.

I had to make a good impression, which for a Cranwell officer meant being in No. 1 uniform, with a set of pilots' notes under one's arm. Parking my less than impressive Austin 1100 out of sight of the squadron, I duly arrived at my new unit in 'Best Blue', with a set of Lightning manuals clearly visible in my briefcase. Unfortunately, when I opened the door to the crewroom, there was no one to be seen; not uncommon as I later discovered, as being seen with apparently nothing to do invariably led to some tedious administrative chore. After making myself a coffee (the staple of aircrew worldwide), I ventured into the Ops Room, where there was the usual gathering of pilots clambering to get on the programme, while a harassed Ops Officer and his airman assistant desperately tried to juggle the various strands of aircraft, target availability, weather and last minute changes to everything you thought you had sorted out.

'Who are you?' the Ops Officer bluntly asked, the badge 'Ross Payne' revealing his identity.

'Chris Coville', I replied, somewhat miffed that as a Cranwell graduate I was being treated as an unwanted intruder.

'Go and get your leave pass', Ross retorted. 'We're in the middle of AFCENT and we don't have any spare aircraft.'

I had earlier been warned about AFCENT, which was not only important for national prestige, but also for the Sqn Cdr's career prospects.

'I suppose I'd better check in with the Boss?' I suggested.

'Up to you, mate', Ross replied helpfully, and went back to the jigsaw puzzle that was the daily flying programme. I saw no point in engaging any further with the Ops Officer, so returned to the crewroom to find two pilots, who by the tell-tale marks on their faces from the oxygen masks, had just landed.

'Hello', I said. 'I'm Chris Coville, a new pilot.'

'Tony Alcock', a red-haired, punchy-looking Flying Officer replied, shaking my hand vigorously. Tony was a second tourist, having served a tour at Leuchars in Scotland.

'Colin Cruickshanks', responded the other.

'Ah yes', I replied. 'I remember you from Cranwell; but you were a few Entries ahead of me.'

'That explains why I don't remember you', he added pointedly. He then looked over my shoulder and muttered, 'Oh, shit!' Turning, I was face-to-face with a tall, gangly Sqn Ldr.

'Arthur Tyldesley, you must be Chris Coville? I'm your flight commander.'

'Poor bastard', someone muttered behind me. Arthur glared, but said nothing.

'Nice to meet you, Sir', I replied. Someone snorted. 'I was hoping to start flying this week, but I understand you're still involved in AFCENT.'

'We'll get you a few trips to convert you to the Mark 6, then you'd better take some leave. No chance of flying for a while, I'm afraid.'

I vaguely recalled that Arthur had come to the squadron under a bit of a cloud, having parked a Lightning in the adjutant's office at Coltishall following an undetected, albeit entirely detectable, brake failure while taxiing in. It was rumoured that the only reason he wasn't chopped there and then was that his F5000 Record of Flying was sucked up into the engine of the crippled but still roaring Lightning, and regulations only permitted flying suspensions after careful scrutiny of one's flying history.

'Thanks, Sir, I really do want to get as much flying in as possible; I've already had some leave, and—' I was cut short by the sight and sound of an enraged Cruickshanks, who had disappeared into the Ops room, and re-emerged with a face like thunder.

CHAPTER 5

'For Fuck's sake, Sir, you've programmed me to fly tonight. I've already been flying this morning, and I bloody well told you it was my wedding anniversary today!'

'Well, I'm sorry', replied Arthur, retreating backwards. 'But we are short of pilots, Colin...'

Arthur's discomfort was cut short by the arrival of the squadron's Senior Engineering Officer, Sqn Ldr Jock Tweedie: 'Foxtrot's U/S', (unserviceable) 'overstressed ... at least 7G.'

The Lightning's maximum 'G-force' was six, but the instrument which measured it, the accelerometer, only recorded at five and seven 'G', so allowing a modest amount of leeway. Arthur, determined to re-establish his authority following his bollocking from Colin Cruickshanks, shouted: 'Who was flying Foxtrot?'

'I was', responded a clearly unrepentant Tony Alcock. 'Must have been on the break, Sir.' The break was the hard turn into the circuit from a visual approach; normally conducted at 3 to 4G. Arthur, who was well known for flying timidly, was outraged.

'The b–b–break, Tony! How did you pull 7-G on the b–b–break?' Arthur stammered, which, I came to realise, he only did when under extreme pressure.

'Come on, Sir', replied a now grinning Alcock, appreciating his chance to be the centre of attention. 'If your socks don't roll over your boots on the break, you can't call yourself a fighter pilot!'

'Tony ... how could you ... !?' exclaimed the horrified Arthur, but then ran out of words and retreated back into the relative safety of the Ops room.

The door was flung open, and an officer burst in; this time the other flight commander, George Taylor. He seemed angry.

'Lockwood's grounded ... aerobatics in the circuit.' It turned out that Vic Lockwood had performed the famous 'reheat rotation' take off, and instead of rolling the short way round back to level flight, had exercised fighter pilot judgement and rolled underneath instead – unfortunately for him, just as George Taylor happened to be looking out of the window, which I came to learn he did a lot. There followed a clearly audible shouting match from the Ops room between George and Arthur; the latter claiming that Vic was on his flight and anyway the squadron was short of pilots; the former arguing that flight safety was paramount and Lockwood had to be grounded. Meanwhile, Vic being entirely oblivious to all this clamour, was happily cruising out to the North Sea!

37

'You can take it up later with the Boss', shouted Arthur. As it happened, the Boss, Wg Cdr Ken Bailey, had just shuffled into the crewroom, a cigarette in his hand.

'Morning, Boss', a couple of people muttered. He nodded.

Ken Bailey had flown the Lightning before, but not on an operational squadron, having been an instructor on the then Lightning Conversion Unit at RAF Middleton St George.

He ambled into the Ops room, where he spent the next ten minutes being harangued by Arthur about the challenges of planning the Ops programme, clearly attempting a pre-emptive attack before Colin had a chance to speak his mind. George was more interested in grounding Vic Lockwood; the Boss seemed uninterested in either, and shuffled back into the crewroom. I thought I'd better introduce myself, in a formal style which clearly amused the other pilots around.

'You'd better take some leave; we're too busy with AFCENT to run your operational work-up', he reiterated. I was getting the distinct feeling I wasn't very welcome.

'I understand I might be able to get a few trips, Boss', I surmised. He shrugged his shoulders and retreated to the safety of his office.

I thought I had better go and see the squadron adjutant, a warrant officer called George, who like most of his rank had reached his ceiling, was very comfortable where he was, and had a natural disdain for aircrew generally, but junior ones in particular.

'Leave pass, Sir?' he asked, anticipating my request; more feelings of not being wanted.

'Thanks, George, can you tell me what we're doing over the next few months please?'

He lowered his voice; looking around for Soviet eavesdroppers. 'Quite a lot, Sir. There's Missile Practice Camp at Valley, and we're going to Singapore at the end of the year. We'll be away for Christmas and New Year; about seven weeks in all.'

Christ almighty; this is going to be a difficult one to explain to Irene!

When I first proposed to Irene, I could tell she was unsure about committing herself to this reckless young pilot, who clearly had few real prospects in life. Clutching at a straw, and aware that she was an adventurous girl,

I anticipated her refusal and added that if she married me she would see the world: 'Oh', she said, 'where do you mean?'

'Cyprus, Malta, Singapore; the world would be our oyster.'

'OK', she replied, 'I'll give it a go.'

While some might reasonably argue that I had married her under false pretences, my travel aspirations at the time were not unreasonable, as the RAF was indeed a global force. Unfortunately, from our engagement to the hoped-for delivery on my promises, a succession of savage defence cuts had resulted in severe pruning of the armed forces, and a progressive retreat back into Europe. To make matters worse, the services refused to accept that anyone under 25 could be properly married, so any award of married quarters was conditional on spare capacity. While this may have been available at Ouston, it most certainly was not the case in popular overseas locations. Accordingly, anyone rash enough to take his or her vows under the approved age would be obliged to find their own accommodation off base, which was invariably an expensive business. Most overseas squadron commanders had stated, therefore, that they were not prepared to accept married youngsters; hence Binbrook rather than Singapore, Cyprus or Germany.

Irene seemed fairly relaxed about this, having obviously decided that she had been duped and had better make the best of it. However, not even she could have been prepared for what the RAF had allocated us at Binbrook: a semi-detached, wartime prefab, one of several in a clutch referred to as 'The Leper Colony'! Had the station been bathed in brilliant sunshine, I might have got away with it, but such days in late September are rare in the Lincolnshire Wolds, and our arrival as a family was on a fairly typical afternoon: low cloud, driving rain and fifty yards visibility. As we completed the 'March In', conducted by a sour-faced administrative officer and a local civil servant, both of whom made it clear that we were damned lucky to get anything, I rather lamely argued 'Well, it's not too bad, Darling', to which a furious Irene responded: 'It's bloody awful!' And promptly went to bed, leaving me with baby Peter and a few cases of our belongings. Realising the sensitivity of the situation, I got a fire going in the 'lounge' and made Irene a cup of tea. After a few minutes she emerged from the bedroom, and made it clear that the only reason she had got out of her bed was that it was so cold she was afraid of getting frostbite.

It took only an hour or so to unpack and get our clothes into drawers and wardrobes, and happily I found a bottle of my finest homemade wine, and in front of the fire we toasted bread and drank ourselves into sufficient comfort to make going to bed bearable.

In the morning there was a knock on the door. I looked at my watch: eight o'clock. I was not expected in that day, so who on earth could it have been? I pulled a blanket around my shoulders and went to investigate. A slightly dishevelled, middle-aged woman stood in front of me, a cigarette dangling from the corner of her heavily lipsticked mouth. She looked at me with some disdain. 'Yes?' I asked.

'I'm Mrs Crowe, your batwoman.'

It had never occurred to me that in our lowly state we would qualify for batting, but two hours a week were allocated to each prefab, and this was our morning for Mrs Crowe's services. 'You'd better come in,' I said, and quickly started to tidy up the mess from the night before, which was clearly a little bit ridiculous.

'Can I make you a cup of tea?' I asked, as she scrutinised the kitchen, still littered with the remains of last night's activities.

'Two sugars please, Dear', she replied wearily, shaking her head from side to side.

Fortunately, Irene appeared from the bedroom to take some of the pressure off me, and was soon engaged in girl talk with Mrs Crowe. ''Ow do you like it 'ere?' she asked.

'It's awful weather', replied Irene. 'Is it always like this?'

'In the winter it is, Dear, it's the wind what comes off those big mountains out to the east, the … U … Urinals', she said, struggling in vain to find the right title, and making it clear that winter started rather early in these parts. Mrs Crowe then spent twenty minutes finishing her tea, another ten minutes washing up her mug, and after a quick flit around with a duster announced that we had enjoyed our fair share of her services and she was off to a real officer's house.

Later that day, a few of the girls from the squadron dropped in to sympathise with Irene, and assure her that the prefabs had some advantages over the brick houses. They were cheaper to rent and easier to heat, although the methods of heating consisted of an open fire in the living room and a portable Aladdin oil stove that defied physics by producing ten times as much condensation as it did heat. We learned that collectively those in the prefabs were referred to as the 'Shack Dwellers', and that the residents thereof had acquired a reputation for being hell raisers. It was certainly a lot of fun, especially when Dave and Ann Carden moved in next door. They had just returned from a tour on 74 Sqn in Singapore, and were waiting for a 'proper' quarter to become available. Bringing with them modern HiFi, a Noritake dinner service and a car that started first time, it gave us hope that one day we just might be able to achieve such a level of opulence.

A couple of days later, I pitched up again at the squadron. Before going on leave, I had managed against expectations to get a couple of dual trips in with the squadron QFI, Stu Rance, and a day and night trip in the Mk6. The task now was to get fully operational and ready for the forthcoming detachment to Singapore. In essence, this meant that I had to complete the operational work-up programme, get an uprate to my Instrument Rating, and qualify day and night in Air-to-Air refuelling (AAR). This process would normally take six months, but we had less than three left before the Far East deployment, which I now knew would involve only one stop in the Persian Gulf, and two extremely challenging long legs with lots of AAR.

I arrived to find an old mate from Cranwell days, Alastair (Ali) McKay, sitting in the crewroom, looking as lost as I had been a few weeks earlier. Ali had recently got married to Coreen, a lovely Scottish girl who, like him, was also from Inverness.

'Have you managed to get any flying in, Ali', I asked.

'You must be joking', he replied, 'they're all u/s after AFCENT.'

'Oh gosh, I forgot. How did they get on?'

'Came last', replied Ali. 'Apparently it was a bloody shambles.'

Why was I not surprised?

Over the next few weeks, I flew as I've never flown before or since. My 'mentor', Ross Payne, and I were programmed for three trips a day, often in bad weather and at night. It was exhausting, but exhilarating, and I was making steady progress. There was a minor hiccup during the air combat phase, which was led by a very experienced US exchange pilot, Charlie Neel. Charlie had served in Vietnam on an elite squadron charged with identifying and marking targets before subsequent attacks by fighter bombers. Indeed, he had already ejected from an F100 fighter on such a mission, after being hit by small arms fire. Charlie was, and still is, a real fighter pilot, if perhaps a little too punchy for a peacetime air force, even during the Cold War! He and I had flown two mock air combat sorties, focusing on getting the best out of the aeroplane and its weapons system. Halfway through the third trip, Charlie declared that I had made sufficient progress to go beyond academic manoeuvres to begin real combat, starting from a visual split, where both fighters turn forty-five degrees away from each other, before charging back in to start the fight. Charlie, of course, was clear favourite to win; indeed to give me a real walloping. But he made a near fatal mistake: he turned me towards the setting sun, giving him a problem maintaining visual contact as my aircraft rapidly became a speck. Sensing this, I pulled high, and it was obvious that he had lost contact, although he failed to call it as was mandated for safety reasons. I gradually worked my way round towards a firing position in his six o'clock. Boy, this would keep me in beer for a long time!

'Are you still visual?' Charlie drawled.

'Affirmative', I replied, and then foolishly added, 'Six o'clock.'

'Got you, you little bastard,' he cried jubilantly, and then threw a manoeuvre which I thought must have been beyond the aircraft's safe flying envelope. This turned out to be the case, as almost immediately the nose of Charlie's aircraft pitched up violently and entered a spin. I tried to keep his aircraft in my field of vision, but struggled to do so as it went into layered cloud. I heard a strangled gasp, but no more. Had he recovered from the spin? Very challenging in such a swept-wing aeroplane; had he ejected? Did he stay too long and fly into the sea? In the end, was he alive or dead? Eventually I decided to put out an emergency call to the bemused RAF Patrington fighter controller. He responded that Charlie was a few miles behind me. Of course, he or his spinning aircraft were indeed still visible on radar, but not for long. Only when all trace of the doomed aircraft vanished did the poor fellow actually accept that we were in an emergency situation, requiring an urgent response to find and rescue Charlie; and it was getting dark.

Meanwhile, far below and in twilight conditions, Charlie was entering the North Sea, his back aching from the twenty-four times the force of gravity (24-G) kick up the pants as the ejection seat fired. In pain, and with some difficulty, he scrambled into his tiny dinghy and started the process of survival, covering his shoulders with the dinghy shroud and getting out the locator beacon from his life jacket. Eventually, he was picked up by helicopter and returned to Binbrook, where after a short examination he was taken to the Station Medical Centre. He was subsequently diagnosed as having suffered compression fractures of the lower spine, which meant he would be grounded for at least three months. The Board of Inquiry concluded that he had mishandled the controls in a high workload situation, and as height was not on his side, he had no choice but to eject. An expensive night for the RAF; I claimed a kill and was declared to have finished my air combat phase.

But before completing the operational work-up, we had to complete a live missile firing at the range off the Cardiganshire coast. This required a deployment to RAF Valley, in Anglesey, and a lot of patience, as we waited for the right conditions of weather, sea state and shipping to come together.

As mentioned earlier, the two missiles in service were the ageing Firestreak, and the more modern Red Top. Both used infra-red homing to acquire and pursue the target, which in this case was a flare towed behind an unmanned aircraft, called a Jindivik.

I was designated to fire a Firestreak, no doubt as part of the missile disposal programme. It took a while for the weather to clear at Valley, which as anyone who has enjoyed a summer holiday in North Wales will know well. In addition to sport, card games and technical quizzes, the boys as always found mischief when there was little flying available: too much testosterone and too little adrenaline. The first opportunity to cause mayhem was the traditional exchange of hospitality with the SNCOs in the Sergeants' Mess. They were obviously as bored as we were as we awaited improved weather conditions, so they leapt at the chance to drink young pilots under the table and teach them how to play Mess Rugby – a distortion of the real game, with no rules governing goolie-clutching, punching or tackling off the ball; the ball in this case being a pillow, which normally exploded into clouds of feathers every ten minutes or so. After a while, the poor old Boss, Ken Bailey, loosely officiating from the safety of a mess dining table, decided it was time to leave, as we had a chance of a firing slot the next day and we needed to observe the twelve hours 'bottle to throttle' rule. As expected, the SNCOs were scathing, cat-calling and eventually singing the well-known dirge 'Good night, ladies.' It was more than Ali and I could take. After a brief escape manoeuvre from the rest of the chaps, we furtively climbed back into the Sergeants' Mess through a kitchen window, unravelled a fire hose, and with the water on full stream raced back into the bar, where we succeeded in soaking the scattering SNCOs and the bar furniture.

For this and other misdemeanours too trivial to mention, the Boss called Ali, Vic Lockwood, Tony Alcock and me into his office, and with gritted teeth and shaky voice, announced that it was now a question of survival, him or us. I confess to feeling at the time that he was being a little theatrical, but all that changed when a Meteor aircraft arrived the next morning from Binbrook, collected Ken Bailey, who on arrival was told he was to be posted. It was a sad end to the career of a thoroughly decent man, who was a capable pilot; but who had been left by his predecessor a tired squadron with broken aircraft. In different circumstances, he would have coped well, and I blame the system that put men like Ken Bailey into such challenging roles, without the support they deserved, with inevitable consequences.

Feeling somewhat guilty, I wrote Ken a letter expressing my sadness that he had gone in such a manner. He kindly responded, indicating that in fact it had all become too much for him, and leaving was somewhat of a relief. He was an acting wing commander, so he reverted to being a squadron leader, and as far as I know never regained his previous rank. I never saw him again.

Having successfully fired my missile at Valley, we returned to base to find a seismic change was underway. Ken Bailey's replacement was a well-known, respected fighter pilot called George Black. George had been pulled out of his job as Chief Flying Instructor on the Lightning OCU, where I had briefly met him before the end of the course. He had a reputation as a no-nonsense Scotsman, who kept the Sword of Damocles swishing below his own ankles, leaving a trail of headless victims in his wake. He had already made a statement on arrival: in an effort to improve the dire serviceability of the aircraft he had, in essence, locked all the engineers in the hangar, threatening that they would stay there until he had twelve aircraft on the line, fit to fly. By Friday afternoon, he had his way, and for the first time in over a year the squadron had enough aircraft to fly a Diamond Nine proudly over the airfield. Change was underway; but we hadn't seen anything yet!

The deployment to the Far East was going to be an epic event, not least for those of us who were relatively new on the squadron. On a cold, dark night in December in 1969, we took off in pairs to join three Victor K1 tankers from RAF Marham in Norfolk. In an elaborate and ingenious merry-go-round, the fighters and two tankers refuelled from a single Victor, who after filling us to the gunwales remained off the Norfolk coast to refuel the next wave.

Meanwhile, one tanker and the fighters refuelled over France from the other Victor, who went into the RAF base in Malta. The remaining tanker kept the two fighters topped up, and then headed for RAF Akrotiri in Cyprus, from where two more tankers took off, met up with the fighters, and refuelled them to RAF Masirah in Oman. If it sounds complicated, that's because it was!

Despite the obvious challenges associated with flying for nearly nine hours in a single seat fighter, the trip was largely uneventful. In fact, the only noteworthy incident was the disappointment when we opened our sandwich boxes to discover that the orange juice had syphoned out and the result was chicken and orange porridge. We landed in six waves, twenty minutes apart, and grabbed a beer and a sandwich while debriefing. Little did we know the nightmare that awaited us as we headed south on the next leg to Singapore.

The crew duty rules stated that after a flight of more than seven hours, we needed a minimum of twenty-four hours to recover. As we had to take off for Singapore in the early hours of the morning, for reasons I will explain later, this meant we had approximately thirty-six hours between sorties. Although Masirah was a bit of a hell hole, surrounded by desert and snake-infested seas, we nevertheless decided we were on what today would be called a 'short-break holiday'. Carrying generous supplies of duty-free booze and a picnic of lobster tails and steak sandwiches, we dragged our exhausted bodies down to the 'beach', where we proceeded to do what fighter pilots do best – make a noise. Within a few minutes a group of feral camels had drifted along to see what they could cadge. By then, we were stripped down to our underpants, some had risked snake attacks by swimming, and a few were starkers trying to get an even tan. The Alpha camel for some reason decided to make an approach to Jerry Copp, our Canadian exchange officer, who was one of the naturists, and had only a bottle of Bacardi to conceal his privates. Perhaps because of this, the said camel proceeded to chase Jerry, who must have heard that you should never turn your back on a horny camel, and proceeded to back pedal furiously, frantically bashing the beast's nose with his half-full/half-empty Bacardi bottle. Eventually, realising that the pain was not worth the gain, the bruised animal backed off with a snort of rage. We got to bed late, knowing we had the next day to recover and plan, with take offs from first light the following morning.

Everyone knew, or thought they knew, that the next leg to Singapore was going to be very different to the stroll through the blue skies the day before. For a start, we were going into the notorious Inter-Tropical Convergence Zone (ITCZ) one hour south of Masirah. This area of troubled weather marked the convergence of two air masses, producing storms and very thick cirrus high-level cloud. But there was a greater concern: although we would fly over RAF Gan in the Maldives to pick up another two tankers, we were not landing there, and there were large stretches of empty water euphemistically called 'The Critical Areas'. In essence, if we couldn't take on fuel, we were probably going to end up in the briny, surrounded by thousands of hungry tiger sharks. To be fair, we did have an ageing Shackleton patrolling the areas to drop emergency supplies onto the bits, if any were found, and we also had a shark repellent in the dinghy pack, which several aquatic experts reckon was remarkably similar to a well-known brand of shark food, no doubt to make the ending quick and painless.

With understandable trepidation, we all attended the afternoon briefing before catching a few hours sleep. We would get airborne in pairs again, after our two tankers. Meeting our take-off times was vital. The Victor K1 needed, in normal conditions with a full fuel load, about 8,000ft of runway to get airborne safely. Masirah, assuming the feral donkeys and camels could be cleared, had only 7,500ft, beyond which was the rocky desert. Only by getting airborne at the coldest time of the day, just before sunrise, when a jet engine is at its most efficient, was it possible to calculate a lift off point before the desert tore the tyres off the tanker.

After a troubled sleep, I was woken by my several alarm clocks just after two o'clock; grabbed a quick breakfast and headed down to the flight line. Jerry Copp was already looking at the latest weather charts: 'Not pretty. We'll be into cloud about thirty minutes after take-off.'

After a short review of the complex plan, we walked out, in darkness, to our shiny aircraft. We needed to ensure a spare was available for each wave, in case of an unserviceability in the element before us, so the first batch of six manned up together. All was going well. The mighty Victors started up, and trundled past us towards the runway. We watched, aghast, as the first two lumbered sequentially down the runway. 'Christ', I thought. 'They're not going to make it!' The first aircraft got to the end of the runway, kicking up sand as it lifted off with feet to spare. The second, perhaps because of the disturbed air ahead, was still on the ground as it left the runway, only getting airborne because there were no obstructions to take its wheels off. I breathed out, my pulse racing; this could be an interesting flight. The first two Lightnings taxied past, and took off in a blaze of reheat, soaring easily into the brightening sky in pursuit of their tankers. Jerry and I were in the third wave. After watching our Victors struggle off the ground, we taxied out and took off, the sun now firmly above the horizon, scorching our eyes as we scanned ahead for our refuellers. Radar on; got them ten miles ahead, climbing slowly. We caught up with them, and formated on the lead aircraft until we levelled at 36,000ft.

Time to top up the tanks. Drop behind the tanker onto the starboard hose, Jerry on the port. He plugged in. I moved forward; don't look at the basket – click, fuel flowing. So far, so pretty routine. We settled back in trail formation, the tankers a few hundred yards ahead. It looked fairly clear in front so far; just some wispy cloud in the distance. I engaged autopilot, and made sure my maps were all accessible if needed; but hoping that a dreaded diversion could be avoided. We had RAF Gan as an option; that was about two-and-a-half hours down route. At that stage, our Victors would depart, land there and we would pick up two more as they climbed out of their idyllic coral island airfield. After that, we got into the Critical Areas, with only Sri Lanka airport as a vague possibility, until we were within range of the Malaysian airfields. But that was a long way ahead. The captain of the lead tanker came up on the radio: 'Just heard from the leading flight that they have hit bad weather, with high cirrus and embedded thunderstorms.' Surely not, I thought; it looks fine ahead. But wait, the tanker is starting to fade; quick … close up or you'll lose him. I got there just in time as our formation was shrouded in high cloud. Jerry had slotted in on the other wing; I could just see him.

I started to get the 'leans', a phenomenon known well to aviators, caused by the lack of visual cues, and resulting in strange sensations of banking steeply. I check the instruments; straight and level, but my senses tell me we are banking at ninety degrees. Believe the instruments, and try to slow down your breathing. Jerry Copp pipes up: 'Chris, are you getting the leans.' I affirmed; thank God it was not just me. But a fellow-sufferer did little to ease my growing discomfort. I suggested we should drop in behind the wing, to avoid looking left or right for a prolonged period, which not only results in a stiff neck but also aggravates disorientation.

Jerry agreed; it felt better. But it was getting dark ... very dark. Suddenly there was a bright flash of blue light, followed by a deafening crash of thunder that penetrated the cockpit and drowned out the engine noise. All four aircraft bounced around in the heavy turbulence. We were right in the middle of a vast tropical storm, impossible to see ahead in the thick Cirrus.

The tanker started to fade in the thickening cloud; I closed up as much as I dared. Thank God we had recently refuelled and wouldn't have to attempt a connection in this terrible turbulence. I could see Jerry in my peripheral vision. Like me, he was struggling to keep station on a wing that was flexing under the load of the storm. After what seemed an eternity, but was probably less than half-an-hour, the sky calmed down and the visibility slowly picked up. I suddenly realised that my whole body was tense; my hands clutching too tightly the control column and the throttles; my breathing far too laboured. I checked my oxygen; nearly half used already, and we were only a third of the way down the route to Singapore.

The baskets slowly came out on the lead tanker. With indicator lights on the pod amber, we closed up in turn and with relief saw the tanks filling up. Twenty minutes later we disengaged, and watched the lead tanker move to one side, and give us permission to take up station on the other one, which would now be our tanker down to overhead Gan, still nearly two hours ahead.

Jerry's radio came alive: '564, check your instruments.'

Flying formation on the Victor, I hadn't checked them for a while. With horror, I saw that my main air speed indicator (ASI) and altimeter were wildly in error, and moving around at random.

'Main ASI and altimeter failed', I replied.

'Same here.'

It seemed that in the unprecedented and unexpected icing conditions in the earlier storm, the feeding pipes to our speed and height instruments had iced up, with dire consequences to our ASI and main altimeters.

The tanker captain joined in: 'Just checked with Ops at Gan. Apparently, the earlier waves had the same problem; the word is that you are to continue at your discretion to Singapore.'

Bloody charming, I thought; a standby altimeter that only went up to 5,000ft, and a reserve air speed indicator tucked away at the bottom of the instrument panel that only went up to 300 knots. Both were there to enable a recovery into base, but we still had several hours flying ahead. As long as we could formate on the Victors, we were OK, but we had to meet up with two new tankers coming out of Gan. It got worse: 'Just checked my radar; it's u/s as well,' Jerry added.

To avoid frying the other crew's family jewels, when in formation we always put our air-to-air radar in standby mode. Jerry had dropped back to check his; I did the same and with a gulp realised mine had completely shut down too. We now had no main instruments for the join up with the replacement tankers, and if still in cloud were blind as well. We had obviously been hit by that first burst of lightning, to the extent that it had blown the radar circuits.

Having advised Jerry accordingly, he asked the lead Victor to check the Gan weather, and especially the cloud conditions. If we could stay clear of cloud, we might just be able to pick up the next tankers visually, and when necessary formate on them for the rest of the flight. After a few minutes, he came back with not great news:

'Clear to 5,000ft, then layered up to 40,000, with frequent CuNim.' (Cumulonimbus/storm clouds).

'Roger,' Jerry replied. 'Tell the follow-on tankers that we will need to join up VMC', (Visual Meteorological Conditions i.e. clear of cloud) 'and then climb back to operating height on their wings.'

'OK, we'll get you down to overhead Gan, and then hand you off for the climb,' the tanker lead captain acknowledged.

Thirty minutes later, tucked under the lead tanker's wings, we started our long descent towards the southern edge of the Maldives Archipelago. My mouth was as dry as a sunburned leaf, but I daren't take my eyes off the Victor to have a drink as we went in and out of thick layers of cloud. The tanker captain kept calling out the height every 1,000ft. 'Thirty thousand, twenty-nine thousand, twenty-eight thousand....' It took forever before suddenly, at about 6,000ft, we could see patches of ocean, with small clusters of islands. Oh, to go into Gan, have a shower, an ice-cold beer and a swim, before a supper of fried reef fish. But this was not to be; we had a long way to go before the next beer. A few miles ahead, the airfield at the tiny island of Gan appeared, and at the end of the taxiway waiting to take off were our two tankers. To my surprise, among the other aircraft on the parking area was a Lightning. We later discovered that the Boss, George Black, had developed a technical problem and had to land at Gan awaiting rectification. The 'sweep' Hercules transport aircraft, with an accompanying tanker, were going to pick him up later and get him back on the way to our final destination. But being last on the ground at Tengah was not in George's plan! I could imagine him fuming as he saw the rest of the squadron overtaking him in the skies above Gan.

'OK', called out Jerry. 'Visual, the tankers can get airborne.'

I grabbed a quick drink and a sandwich; we still had over four hours to go before arriving at RAF Tengah airfield in Singapore.

The mighty Victors rolled down the long Gan runway, and clawed their way into the air. Immediately they called us up and made radio contact. As they slowly climbed, circling the airfield, we slotted into formation on the new lead tanker's wings. A quick 'Thank you, guys, to the two who had brought us down this far, and we were back into cloud heading toward the first of the Critical Areas; and the sky ahead was getting darker.

We eventually levelled at 36,000ft, still in cloud, but with no significant turbulence. The descent to overhead Gan, and the subsequent climb back to operating height had reduced fuel margins, and the Victor crews were frantically recalculating whether we still could make it to Singapore.

The lead navigator, normally not heard to external agencies, made an interesting announcement:

> 'We probably don't have enough fuel to get us all to Tengah; the plan is to get the fighters there, and if necessary divert the refuellers into Butterworth,' (an Australian Air Force Base in Northern Malaysia, about one hour north of Singapore).

I have often reflected since those days, what an unglamorous but vital job was done by the Victor crews. Totally selflessly, recognising that it meant another uncomfortable night, and another sortie early the next morning, they were prepared to give the Lightning deployment the maximum priority. But even more adventures lay ahead before anyone's feet touched the ground. After a couple of hours, the lead captain announced – I thought a little too melodramatically – that we were approaching the first Critical Area, so prepare to refuel to full. As if part of a satanic plan, as the hoses started to deploy, the Victors began to disappear in rapidly developing darkness. I had dropped back a little too far to have a quick drink, and to my horror, the rest of the formation disappeared. This was the nightmare scenario – failing to take fuel in the Critical Area; and with no radar to find the formation again, not to mention instrumentation not dissimilar to that of Alcock and Brown!

This is seriously life-threatening. There is only one thing to do. I gently raise the nose, holding a constant power setting. Eventually, I feel a burble on my aircraft from the formation ahead … just a little power, but not too

CHAPTER 5

much … stay in the burble … it's getting stronger … eyes peeled staring ahead … and suddenly there is a Victor a few hundred feet ahead, trailing hoses. But it's getting very dark; again our eyes are temporarily blinded by a flash of grotesque lightning; the aircraft shudders as the accompanying thunder stuns our ears. We are all being tossed around like feathers in a strong wind; I can barely hold formation as we go deeper into the jaws of the storm. The tankers wisely try to change height, but even at 40,000ft we are in the heart of the maelstrom. It's like being in a washing machine. But we have to take on fuel. I look at the baskets: they are corkscrewing wildly, and going up and down about 30ft. As they go above the Victor's wing, they are caught up in its vortex and come smashing back down wildly. Jerry's calm voice comes across the ether:

'We need to be careful, otherwise we'll lose our probes.' I had worked that one out for myself. 'Let's see if we can catch the basket at the bottom of its travel, and take it up to the best position we can hold.'

It made sense, but doing it was not going to be easy. Jerry dropped down, and after a few attempts he pushed the refuelling probe into the basket and rode up with it just short of getting thrown out by the wing vortex. My turn. I dropped down, the basket careering around in front of me. Wait for it to stabilise a bit. Too late it's shooting back up. It's coming back down … now, move forward … I touch the rim of the basket as it flings itself up again … be patient … wait for it to settle a little … down it comes … a momentary halt at the bottom of its travel, and I'm in, but frantically trying to stay connected as the basket is flung back upwards … I fall out, and have to start all over again. I am too high on adrenalin to be tired, or even frightened, but I know I have to get this right next time. I wait … and wait … the basket is coming down … stopped … move forward … probe in, now stay in as it shoots back up. This time I hold it, and the precious, beautiful, divine fuel starts to feed my thirsty tanks. After an eternity, the basket lights flash; I have filled up my tanks, and we will get through this Critical Area after all. I give two fingers to the imagined sharks below!

'Well done, chaps', the tanker captain calls out. 'I thought we'd lose you there.'

Suddenly the clouds vanish, and we are in clear blue sky, surrounded by towering CuNim as far as the eye can see. It's a precious respite, and we can all relax for a moment, grab a drink and a sandwich, and even put the aircraft into autopilot for a while. We seem to be through the worst of the ITCZ; certainly the high-level cirrus appears to be behind us. I try to take the tension out of my arms and shoulders; I must breathe more slowly; oxygen now getting down to a quarter. Christ, is that going to be enough for the next two-and-a-half hours?

We approach the next Critical Area. The tanker lead adjusts his heading to avoid clouds going up to above 40,000ft, lightning clearly visible in the heart of the storm within. We take on fuel; tanks full. I will make it now to Tengah, but only if my oxygen holds out. I need to really calm down … breathe slowly … get my heart rate down. The tanker navigator comes on the radio. 'We can just make it to Tengah, but they are expecting thunderstorms around our arrival time.' Bloody wonderful. But once we get to within a hundred miles or so of our destination, we can accelerate away from the tankers, get down to 5,000ft where the standby altimeters will work, and get a radar feed into a straight-in landing in formation. The time passes slowly. My oxygen warning light has come on; just thirty minutes remaining, but we have about forty-five minutes left to fly at high level. I come clean with Jerry. He replies that he's the same, but providing we can start our descent before the oxygen runs out, we can use the emergency oxygen supply on the ejection seat, which is housed in a separate bottle to cover high-level ejections, but gives twenty minutes supply in extremis. If this wasn't extremis, what was?

The Tactical Air Navigation (TACAN) is still working, and locks on to Tengah. One hundred and forty miles, and we can just make out the sea of the Straits of Malacca below. Jerry calls up: 'Thanks, guys, we're going to leave you now. I think we owe you a beer later.' The tanker captain responds with a chuckle, 'Good luck, see you on the ground.'

I drop the nose; my oxygen runs out, and I frantically feel down for the emergency supply knob. I pull it, but nothing happens, and my lungs cry out for oxygen. Suddenly there's a burst of the life-giving gas; feeling cool as I gulp it down. Tengah approach responds to our radio call:

> 'Roger Rafair; we have you radar contact. Be advised we have thunderstorms on the airfield at present. Main runway is currently flooded, and the wind is gusting up to 30 knots. Do you wish to divert to Changi?' Changi was a transport base on the island, with a longer runway and currently in better weather. Jerry responds:
>
> 'Negative, pairs approach to land at Tengah. Be advised we are on limited instruments.'

CHAPTER 5

'Understood; this will be for a GCA (Ground Controlled Approach); cloud base currently 300ft in rain.'

We drop down to 2,000ft, and reduce speed to 200 knots. Ahead, we can see the vast storm waiting to grip us against its black heart. I close right up in formation to Jerry, and the storm hits us. I can barely see him in the torrential tropical rain. The controller calmly talks us down, and suddenly there is the runway ahead. Jerry touches down and I follow, and immediately we are both fighting to keep the aircraft straight in the violent gusts. Brake-chute out, but that makes the oscillations worse as the wind catches the chute and threatens to pull me off the runway. Gradually, speed decreases, and we drop our chutes on the side of the runway. I look around: torrential rain and flooded taxiways, but I am on the ground at last. My emergency oxygen stops, and I open the canopy to receive a blast of hot, tropical air and a drenching from the rain; nothing ever felt better. I breathe a long sigh in the loneliness of my cockpit.

We taxied in to our designated slots, welcoming smiles from the 5(F) Sqn groundcrew on the advanced party. I closed down, looking across at Jerry. He gave me a 'that was a bit of a bastard' look and I nodded back to him. Suddenly, I felt totally exhausted, physically and mentally. I knew I was close to tears, but some of the resident Lightning Sqn, No 74 (Tiger) Sqn, were waiting at the bottom of the ladder with a few beers at the ready. I struggled out of the cockpit, my legs threatening to buckle under me as I climbed down the flimsy ladder. I grabbed a beer gratefully, shook hands with old friends, and thanked whoever or whatever was up there for getting me through the most challenging eight hours of my life.

That night, we all got drunk, and fell into bed still in flying suits. My restless sleep was punctuated by nightmares of refuelling baskets thrashing up and down, sharks leaping out of the sea towards my aircraft and a constant feeling that I had run out of fuel, in cloud and totally lost.

We were given a day off to acclimatise. As we were non-passenger-carrying aircrew, we didn't merit air-conditioned accommodation, but instead slept under a giant fan which did little more than recirculate hot air. I was sharing a room with John Spoor, who had just arrived on the squadron and so came out with the groundcrew on the transport aircraft. I woke with the mother of all hangovers, a very dry mouth and a feeling that I was in a sauna somewhere. Opening the blinds to let in some 'fresh' air, I found myself face-to-face with the largest spider I had ever seen, or even knew existed. It seemed to be perched on a large fishing net, which turned out to be its web, and was surrounded by half-eaten meals of giant flying insects and a few lesser spiders. Backing away, I was greeted by the sight of a naked Spoor, who, seeing my predicament, had found an insect spray and proceeded to pursue the arachnid across the outside patio. Being equipped with eight legs, and John with only two, it had no trouble outrunning him into the surrounding jungle, at which point the gallant pursuer wisely called off the hunt.

I began to realise that this was a very different environment, not only in which to live, but also to fly. The morning air was calm and relatively cool, but by noon giant CuNims had started to form in the increasing heat, and shortly after the heavens would open, with startling flash floods and vicious, gusting winds. Accordingly, we flew early until noon, then took a few hours off with the aircraft safely in the hangar, and then the night shift would resume operations until midnight.

Flying at night from Singapore was interesting. Immediately after take-off, the world below went black as you flew over the dark sea; but above was a wonderful array of stars. Unfortunately, this delightful blend of dark and light soon evaporated, as you got further out into the fishing areas, where myriad stars blended with numerous fishing vessels, each with a single star-like lamp on the mast. The effect was mesmerising and disorientating, and there is some evidence that more than one pilot met his end confused by the myriad light sources in this treacherous planetarium.

Much of the flying we conducted was international and with several different aircraft types. Tengah itself was home to two Canberra squadrons, one reconnaissance the other bomber, and a Hunter day-fighter ground attack squadron. Together with the small Singapore Air Force and the Australian Air Force contingent at Butterworth, we had plenty of 'trade' as targets, with the Australians being especially tricky customers. On one occasion, having intercepted a low-flying Australian Canberra as it flew over a jungle ridge in Malaysia, I made a call indicating I had shot down the opponent, only to be greeted by an outraged, 'Fuck off, you lying bastard', over the radio. It transpired, as I found out later, to be the squadron commander, who was notoriously aggressive and ate young pilots like me for breakfast!

As I taxied in later, I groaned as I saw four 'Ozzie' Canberras parked next to our flight line. Despite my best attempts to give him the slip in the bar later, the outraged Wg Cdr tracked me down and forced me to admit that my claim for a 'kill' might have been somewhat ambitious. The fact that he was holding me by the throat as I stood on tip toes might have had something to do with my uncharacteristic deference.

For some reason, George Black decided that during the arduous detachment to the Far East, we should have some 'downtime' in Hong Kong, which had a regular Hercules service from nearby RAF Changi airfield to what was then RAF Kai Tak. As we were to go in pairs, Ali McKay and I decided we should look after each other. By then, we had, with some justification, become known as 'the terrible twins', owing in no small measure to our propensity to get into trouble, dragging as many down with us as we could. Indeed, successive Bosses reserved a Monday morning slot to administer a bollocking for weekend misdemeanours. George Black later told me that when I was once on leave, he truly missed our Monday morning encounters.

Our flight was scheduled at 0400 hrs (bloody early in civilian parlance) on a Saturday morning. As we were likely to be in the bar until midnight on any Friday, there seemed little point in retiring to bed, so we stayed until we were thrown out by an angry steward, and still in shorts and flamboyant short-sleeved shirts, picked up our overnight bags and reported to the Motor Transport (MT) section, demanding a vehicle to Changi, some thirty minutes drive away. Not surprisingly, the sergeant who was running the section was somewhat put out to be dragged out of his camp bed at such an hour to transport two bleary-eyed fighter pilots on what was obviously a 'Jolly'.

At Changi, we lined up to check in, only to be told that we couldn't fly to Hong Kong in shorts and party shirts. Had we read the tasking signal, the 'erk' behind the desk said with some glee, we would have known that we needed long trousers and shirts owing to the fire risk. Just then, we noticed what was obviously the Hercules crew checking in at the aircrew desk. After a few minutes discussion with the air loadmaster, we cadged a couple of well-used and rather smelly flying suits, and rejoined the check-in queue. The aforementioned erk, having thought he had got one up on the officers, grimaced and asked for our passports and vaccination certificates. 'Erm...' I replied, 'we didn't know we needed them.' Again, we were reminded that had we read the tasking signal....

Looking across at the aircrew check in, I noticed an ancient Sqn Ldr, who I deduced must be the Hercules captain. It was worth a try.

'Good evening, Sir, I do believe we are accompanying you as aircrew under training to Kai Tak.' He looked suspicious.

'Nobody told me anything about that', he snorted. But as in those days nobody told anyone anything, he didn't seem surprised.

'There seems to be some problem over us not having passports or vaccination certificates, Sir. I wonder if you might be able to help?'

'Wait a minute', he replied. 'Are you two fighter pilots?' We nodded. 'I might have bloody guessed. OK, if you want to come for the flight, you're welcome, but you'll have to come straight back with us if you haven't got passports or vaccination certificates. They won't let you through immigration.'

Ali and I decided it was a better option than an interview with the Boss, having failed to get away from Changi, so we dutifully followed our captain through the aircrew line, as pilots under training! Several painful hours later, we were invited to go to the cockpit to watch the approach into Kai Tak. For seasoned travellers of a certain age, you will remember that in essence the approach was made initially towards a mountain; halfway up was positioned a red and white 'chequer board'. If by a certain height, you hadn't acquired said board visually, to avoid hitting the mountain it was necessary to execute a rapid climbing turn to the right, either to have another go or divert to somewhere with more sensible approach arrangements. If the pilots did sight the chequer board, they then visually followed a set of strobe lights, most placed on top of skyscrapers a few hundred feet below the intended flight path. The strobes were so arranged that they lined up the aircraft with the runway; then the fun really started. Hong Kong airport was notorious for strong crosswinds, squalls, waterspouts and many other meteorological phenomena, all of which made landing on the very short runway somewhat hazardous. Indeed, several aircraft, commercial and military, had in the past found themselves skidding off the end on a flooded runway, or unable to stop the vicious crosswinds taking the aircraft off the side and into Hong Kong Bay.

Ali and I crouched behind the pilots' seats. God knows what the Health and Safety mafia would have to say about it today. It was a pleasant December morning, with just a few wisps of cloud scudding across the hilltops. Transfixed, we watched the captain flying straight towards the chequer board. My God, I thought, he's going to fly us straight into it! But I reckoned it was better to die like a man than show any signs of fear; we were, after all, fighter pilots. Just as I was about to close my eyes and make a last act of confession, the pilot turned sharply right, and sure enough, just a few hundred feet below us and on top of the perilously close skyscrapers, I could make out the beckoning strobe lights, guiding us on a tight descending turn towards the now visible runway. Rows of washing flapped their welcome on either side of the approach lane; people waved out of windows that progressively became higher than our Hercules. The captain made a sharp height adjustment as we cleared the last buildings, and then unceremoniously plonked the aircraft firmly on the concrete. We seemed very close to the end of the runway, but with maximum reverse thrust and a lot of heavy breaking, we slowed to a sensible speed to taxi clear. At this stage, our friendly Loadmaster frantically beckoned us towards the rear of the aircraft.

'I'll open the rear door and you can jump out. The fence is only a few feet high here.'

We gulped, grabbed our bags and with the sort of shove reminiscent of D-Day paratrooper departures, we were bundled out of the door onto the tarmac perimeter track. Amazingly, apart from a few minor bruises and scratches, we were unscathed. The Hercules trundled away towards the airport terminal.

Furtively, for good reason as we were now illegal immigrants, we dashed towards the wire fence which, contrary to the advice just given, was about 12ft high, and looked pretty impenetrable. After a bit of scouting around, we found a weak area of the fence, pulled it up and escaped into Hong Kong, with no papers and dressed for a party. 'Shit!' Ali proclaimed as we emerged from under the fence. We were on a dual carriageway, with traffic speeding by at high speed, most of the drivers coming close to catastrophe as they were distracted by the sight of two bedraggled wretches standing aimlessly by the side of the road. Eventually, no doubt as a result of reports of pedestrians on the highway, a police Land Rover appeared. With blue lights flashing, it stopped behind us and two Chinese policemen emerged and waved cars into the outside lanes. A young European-looking Hong Kong police officer approached us. 'What the hell are you two doing here?' he asked, not unreasonably. We explained that we were fighter pilots on detachment and were on our way to the Officers' Mess. Looking at our clothing, general demeanour and guilty faces, he checked our ID cards, shrugged and announced that he was Roddy Henderson, that he lived in the Mess and was going back there after being on duty. We happily jumped in the back and joined Roddy for a quick jar in the bar, where he spent a few minutes listing the places we should avoid. This turned out to be most helpful in deciding where to go later.

Had we been sensible young officers, which is what our mentors at Cranwell would have expected, we would have had a quiet evening in the Mess, followed by an early retirement to bed, not least considering our paucity of sleep the night before. As illegal immigrants, we should have kept a low profile, in the certain knowledge that any suspicious activity would have resulted in an unpleasant night in prison, our cell companions reeking of strange substances and harbouring sharp knives. We had heard of the Triad gangs, and had no wish to make their acquaintance.

However, being fighter pilots short-circuited the brain's usual defensive mechanisms, so we ordered a cab and set off for the first place Roddy had advised us to avoid at all costs. The one thing he revealed, which made this particular establishment especially attractive, was that as long as you showed interest in the wares, the vendor would keep free drinks coming. The wares in this case happened to be young ladies, and the vendor a charming middle-aged 'Mama-San'. Unfortunately, Ali's thirst got the better of him, and it soon became apparent that, with a stack of whisky glasses alongside him, even had the spirit been willing the flesh would have been weak. We were asked to leave, and rather rudely ordered not to return. This exit might have gone without incident, had Ali not decided that one of the exquisitely padded bar stools would make an excellent souvenir. A short chase reminded us that a young Chinese bouncer can run faster than an inebriated Brit carrying a heavy piece of Oriental furniture.

Chastised, we decided to find a suitable restaurant. Again Roddy's blacklist proved useful, as he had identified a totally unsuitable establishment where we would be served unidentifiable dishes by scantily clad young ladies, who would again provide beer all night as long as we gave the impression of having carnal interests. Unfortunately, Ali's legs seemed to have become disconnected from his brain, so I hailed a rickshaw to take us the mile or so to the restaurant. After bundling Ali into the fragile-looking carriage, I was overcome with pity for the spindly legged driver, who looked as though he would struggle to pull the rickshaw empty, let alone with two well-fed Brits, albeit more slender in those days. With imperial authority, I dismissed the driver and took up position between the two steering handles. Achieving commendable speed in a few seconds, I suddenly realised that I was on a rapidly increasing descent down a busy main road, and without a user manual I could find no obvious braking system. Undeterred, I put self-preservation before camaraderie, and abandoned the vehicle, leaving it weaving and careering between astounded cars and motor bikes, Ali looking confused but totally relaxed as the world spun around him. Perhaps fortunately, a wheel came off the rickshaw as it exceeded its maximum design speed, and after skidding violently to one side it disappeared into a deep monsoon drain, well known for being inhabited by rats, snakes and other vermin. Despite having seen his livelihood turned to matchwood, the faithful driver who had gamely kept up with me until the rickshaw and I parted company, helped me to extract Ali from the filth and rubble, for which he was handsomely rewarded with some loose change and a packet of cigarettes which had been supplied by the once hopeful Mama-San. Realising that a client drenched in sewage would struggle to secure a welcome in any establishment, we decided that a cab back to the Mess would be sensible. After finding the rear entrance, we crept self-consciously back to our shared room, where, with some careful use of sponges, shampoo and hot water, we returned Ali to sartorial acceptability, if not elegance.

Three days later, having established a reputation as trouble-makers in all the bars and restaurants on Roddy's blacklist, we returned to Singapore, leaving puzzled emigration officials wondering why their usually efficient entry procedures had failed; on balance, however, they obviously decided that they were better off without us, and waved us through to our awaiting Hercules.

Ali and I had felt better as we arrived back in the early hours of Thursday with the hope of a day to recover. Sadly, this was not to be; with the Christmas break ahead, George Black had decided to launch a Diamond Nine formation, if only to remind the resident squadrons that we were still there, and still claimed pre-eminence over any other outfit. I groaned as I realised that Ali and I were towards the back of the formation – always the most challenging positions, as minor fluctuations in formation-keeping were progressively exaggerated as they went back. There was worse news for Ali. One of the aircraft had the heating stuck fully on; in Singapore that meant you were flying in a supersonic sauna. Grumbles over, we went back to the Mess for a cold shower, got into our flying suits and made our way back to do our duty. One bit of good news was that Charlie Neel, fully recovered from his back injury, had arrived a few days before and was already flying again; indeed, he was in the Diamond Nine.

The Boss gave his customary curt briefing, which in essence conveyed a simple message: hang on in formation, don't admit to any minor aircraft unserviceabilities, and don't screw up or you'll be on the VC10 home in the morning. After the usual spectacular rotation take-offs, which required each aircraft to take off at ten-second intervals, keeping the nose low until about 250 knots, and then pulling back to a near vertical climb, we were planning to go out to sea for a bit of practice before coming back to do some serious showing off. That was the plan. Unfortunately, Charlie Neel, putting aside his earlier embarrassing misdemeanour, decided to outdo the rest of us with a rotation take-off that left everyone on the ground gasping with disbelief, as his aircraft disappeared in a haze of vapour in the saturated air, before reappearing in what could only be described as an impossible angle. At the time, the Boss was clawing his own way into the blue and was oblivious of the antics behind him, in consequence we all joined up and spent fifteen minutes or so sweating away in close formation – poor Ali sweating more than anyone else. Satisfied that he had a sufficiently tight team around him, George turned the elegant formation back towards Tengah, where we roared around the airfield making a lot of noise and probably impressing nobody. The formation passes complete, we split up to conduct individual 'beat ups' of the airfield, with the Boss's clear instructions of 'nobody to fly lower than me' ringing in our ears. It soon became apparent that Charlie had either not heard that part of the briefing, or judged it to be a challenge not an order, for his aircraft appeared between the palm trees, with dust blown up in its wake, scattering monkeys and destroying any flora that got in his way. An already outraged Officer Commanding Operations Wing, still fuming at Charlie's spectacular take off, was forced to dive for the ground as a silver Lightning bore down on him no higher than 6ft above the ground. It must have been a beautiful sight for onlookers, but one not appreciated by the station hierarchy or George Black, who rightly saw this as not only a threat to his authority, but also his career prospects! Charlie had to go, and the next day we bade him farewell, back to the UK and then home to the USA. We all loved him for the charming rogue he was, for his flying expertise and for the incredible generosity of himself and his wife, Lynda. I met him several times later in the service and after my retirement. Despite the hiccup with the RAF, Charlie went on to become a brigadier-general, and enjoyed a full career in the United States Air Force. Tragically, they lost their lovely son in a flying accident, and when we saw them in the UK many years later, the sadness was still there in their eyes.

We all felt keenly the loss of Charlie's experience on such a young squadron, but life had to go on. After a few more weeks of intensive flying we returned to the UK, enduring similar challenges as on the outbound leg, including my having to divert into Gan with overwing tanks failing to feed. The only real crisis was the unfortunate Arthur Tyldesley, who appeared to be jinxed with fuel venting problems, forcing him to return to Tengah to the dismay of the overworked engineers.

But by the end of January, we were all safely home. Arthur was finally given his marching orders, and being a capable pilot, if not a commander, was posted to be the unit test pilot at the Lightning Maintenance Unit at Leconfield, South Yorkshire, where he settled happily into his comfort zone, and did an excellent job. But back at Binbrook, the preparations started for the next big challenge: the 1970 AFCENT Air Defence Competition, which George Black made clear that we had to win, whatever the cost.

'AFCENT', as it was abbreviated, was a competition between all NATO allies in Western Europe. The stars would normally be the USAF, the German Air Force and the RAF, but having come last by quite a margin the previous year, we were not expected to finish on the podium. George Black had other ideas.

The competition was run along strict lines to avoid the usual clamour over sloping playing fields and Anglo-Saxon favouritism. There were four events: Day Subsonic, Night Subsonic, Low Level and Supersonic. Each had specific requirements, normally involving a pair of fighters intercepting a target from another nation. Points were awarded for accuracy in interception and speed of achieving a 'kill', and were deducted for a range of misdemeanours, for example the two fighters getting within five miles of each other. Nobody understood or challenged the rules, even though many were illogical and incomprehensible; it was, after all, NATO. All declared operational pilots on the squadron prepared for the event, but the week before, only six were pulled out of a hat and allowed to compete. My name was one of those drawn.

Each event started with a scramble from a two minute readiness, which meant we had to have the aircraft primed, the pilots standing at the bottom of the ladder, waiting for the order to go, after which we had just the two minutes to be off the ground. OK, so we were young and fit, but getting up the 10ft ladder, getting strapped in, starting both engines, switching on the radar and instrument array and remembering to close the canopy before roaring off down the runway was a bit of a challenge in 120 seconds.

I was allocated to three events: the day subsonic, the low level and the night subsonic. The first two went superbly well and we got maximum marks for both events, and then the supersonic, which I watched from the ground – again, maximum score. Only the easiest of the lot remained, the night subsonic, which I knew for the Lightning and its capabilities was a complete doddle. It was a beautiful, calm evening, as Ross Payne and I waited for the scramble order. The red light on top of the Ops caravan illuminated, and I scampered up the ladder, and was airborne in one minute thirty seconds; this was going to be easy. I changed to the radar control frequency and checked in with the fighter controller. It was Lofty Wetherall; the best of the lot; still looking good. But then: 'Mission Four Five and Four Six, RTB' (Return to Base). 'Target failed to get airborne.'

Shit. Burn off fuel and get back on the ground as soon as possible. I touched down, streamed the tail chute, and taxied off the runway back to the start point. A quick glug of coffee and a pee and the light illuminated; off again in good order. This time, Lofty called out: 'Mission Four Four and Four Five, target entering the kill zone, range seventy miles. Accelerate Mach 1.4.' Burners in, speed up to 1.4 times the speed of sound. 'Target range five zero; Four Four [me] you are number one; accelerate to 1.6.' Burners in, speed increasing, target appears on radar. 'Four Four and Four Five, Stop, Stop, Stop, target has an emergency!' I pull the throttles out of reheat and see Ross behind me do the same in the night sky. 'Target has hydraulic failure and is diverting into Leuchars (Scotland). You are to RTB.'

I don't believe this; how can so much go wrong at this stage of the competition? Ross and I return and land back at Binbrook. It is late, and we are getting tired and frustrated. The Chief AFCENT judge meets us as we wearily climb down the ladders of our aircraft. 'Sorry about this, but you don't need to scramble next time; just get in the cockpit and we'll make sure the next target is OK before you are scrambled.' Excellent, at least one bit of pressure removed. I climb back in the cockpit, and wait … and wait … and wait. After about an hour the order comes through to scramble again, I start both engines, get the radar on and align the instruments. But wait, the groundcrew are frantically telling me to close down and get out of the cockpit. An order comes over the radio: 'Four Four, you have a brake fire; evacuate now.'

I rapidly close down the engines, unstrap, make the seat safe and get down the ladder, to see the fire crews arriving and squirting foam onto my starboard undercarriage, which is smoking away. No doubt the many take offs, landings and quick taxiing back have taken their toll.

The engineering officer comes running up with a Form 700, which is the book recording all aircraft details. 'Take the spare aircraft, Foxtrot, quickly, sign here.' He holds out a pen in the darkness and I frantically scribble my name to accept the aircraft, and race towards my new mount. Ross is already airborne, but if I don't get a move on, we will lose all our kill points. I start up, taxi onto the runway and get airborne, still switching on the radar and getting the weapons sorted out. It will be a Red Top Missile attack, so I reach down to my right to select GW (Guided Weapons) on the weapons rotary switch. Two clicks; I have done it a hundred times before.

Change frequency – Lofty again.

'Mission Four Four, Buster, Buster,' (go as fast as you can). 'Four Five is intercepting now, you have two minutes before target exits the kill box.' I slam the reheat levers forward, and the beautiful Lightning roars upwards through the black sky: Mach 1.2, 1.5, and I am still climbing. 'Target 35,000ft, range fifty miles.' Even the calm Lofty is sounding edgy. 'You have fifty seconds to complete the kill.' I acknowledge. A blip appears on my radar – got him.

'Contact.' Mach 1.8; really too fast but I have only seconds to intercept the lonely Dutch F104 Starfighter. I lock on, and start a high-G turn towards the rear of the target. The overtake is fearsome, but I have to keep going; nearly there, range five miles; I'm going to do it.

'Ten seconds to kill zone', Lofty's voice is a falsetto. Looking good, any moment now the radar will give me a 'fire' indication, and the interception will be over. But something is wrong; no usual collapsing range circle on the radar, no fire indication; instead the radar tells me to keep tracking the steering dot – what the hell is wrong? Suddenly I see a blur of lights in front of me and instinctively pull back on the stick, narrowly missing the target, who I learn later was severely buffeted by my supersonic wave. What the hell happened? I come out of reheat, and ignoring the requests from Lofty to confirm a 'kill', look around the cockpit. Fuel OK, just; and then it dawns on me. Of the fleet of sixteen aircraft, Foxtrot was the first to be fitted with the new guns capability. The weapons' rotary switch, which I knew so well and didn't need to look down to confirm my weapons selection, had been modified accordingly. The second click was not GW, but Guns. In essence, I had conducted a quarter guns attack at nearly twice the speed of sound. More to the point, my interception had failed and I would get no points. I had let the squadron, the RAF and myself down.

As I taxied back in, I decided I would have to lie and see if we could get anything at all out of it. There were lots of anxious faces around, and I could tell that my squadron mates realised something was seriously amiss. The experts took my film and analysed it. I was interrogated and continued the bullshit, but to no avail. My interception was disqualified, and we lost all the points for what should have been a straightforward exercise. I spent a miserable few days, waiting for the final results. To my relief, we had done so well that we still won the fighter trophy, but losing the 'kill' points relegated my fighter control buddies to second place. I never got over it, and still feel badly about it today, some fifty years later.

In the space of nine months, George Black had transformed the squadron. We had made it out to Singapore and back, admittedly not without drama, we had won the AFCENT competition, despite my best efforts to sink us, and on top of that we had achieved all the statistics needed to achieve a top rating, albeit not without some top-down 'sharp pencilling'. It was enough to win the Strike Command trophy for the best squadron of the year, and to get George Black a well-deserved Air Force Cross. George went to the National Defence College, then at Latimer, prior to promotion, and his place was taken by Wg Cdr Alan 'Chalky' White. The contrast in names turned out to be prophetic. George had been a bluff, no-nonsense charismatic leader, in the air and on the ground. What he lacked in intellect he made up for with sheer determination and a touch of ruthlessness. Chalky had been a late starter in career terms. Still a flight lieutenant in his early thirties, he had realised that he had far more talent than many overtaking him, and had reinvented himself (in today's language), losing his Northern Ireland accent and adopting a far more polished persona. He arrived having done just one tour as a flight commander on 11(F) Sqn, based at Leuchars in Scotland, where he had excelled as a man who understood the intricate politics of success during the Cold War. Highly intelligent, he had just finished Staff College, where he had been identified as a front runner, and despite the pressures of work and a family, he had

CHAPTER 5

signed up for a London University Law Degree. He was handsome, a good pilot and totally ambitious. As any leader recognises, luck plays an important role in success, and Chalky was very fortunate to have two excellent flight commanders: the newly arrived Jerry Seavers, who replaced the hastily removed Arthur Tyldesley, and Barry Holmes, who took over from George Taylor.

Despite being very different people, they were both good leaders in their different ways: Jerry, a natural fighter pilot with a disdain for all things administrative; Barry a quieter, considered man who could be relied upon for sound judgement and maturity. There had also been another stroke of fortune for Chalky with the arrival of a quite outstanding Senior Engineering Officer, Bob Jones, who not only was professionally competent, but also understood the fighter pilot approach to life, and indeed helped us achieve it with pragmatic engineering, sound common sense and a powerful sense of humour.

Alan White made it clear to the officers (he rarely communicated with the troops), that he intended to 'Put 5 Squadron firmly on the map.' We thought we had done that already, but obviously not yet to his satisfaction, or more importantly to his credit. This was the start of a regime of 'stats chasing', getting the hours in at any cost and to whatever purpose, and preparing for the next AFCENT competition, which we clearly had to win again to prove that the last time was not a fluke. We also had to get the squadron ready for the annual external Tactical Evaluation, or TACEVAL, which had been known to make or break careers in the past. TACEVAL at that time was a no-notice exercise, lasting up to four days, designed to test rigorously every aspect of the station's operational capability. Alongside the more administratively and ceremonially focused Annual Inspection by the Air Officer Commanding No 11 Gp, it was the basis of the unit's senior officers' evaluation for promotion, and therefore taken very seriously – at least by them.

Shortly after Alan White assuming command, we welcomed Charlie Neel's successor, Captain William (Bill) Schaffner, who for obvious reasons had been pulled out of his previous job with the USAF at short notice, and after his short Lightning conversion course at Coltishall, arrived with his wife, Linda, and three small boys, all under 5 years old. By then, Irene and I had moved out of the 'shacks' and were in a brick-built house, which seemed luxurious after asbestos and paraffin heaters. Bill and his family moved in next door, and we became good friends, especially as he was extremely generous with his duty-free booze.

65

Bill settled into the squadron very well and was clearly an experienced and capable pilot, albeit new to the Lightning. Sensing an imminent TACEVAL, Chalky decided that Bill should be accelerated through the operational work-up programme, and declared Combat Ready as soon as possible. Accordingly, when the hooter (station siren) duly sounded in the early hours of a September morning in 1970, the paperwork was swiftly completed signing up Bill as competent to take part in the exercise. After the usual 'everyone in as quickly as possible and man up the aircraft' drill had been completed, he and I were stood down to reappear on the night shift, starting at 1600 hrs.

It was a pleasant evening when we reappeared, with good weather forecast throughout the night; it was to be the last sunset of Bill's life. At this stage of the exercise, most of the scrambles had been against probing raids by simulated reconnaissance aircraft, usually Canberras or Shackletons, posing as Soviet intruders. The mission at this stage was to intercept, identify and shadow (follow closely) these aircraft, which had every right in international law to be there, as long as they remained more than twelve miles away from the coast. Bill and I manned up as it was getting dark, and shortly afterwards he was scrambled to take over a shadowing task against a Shackleton, some twenty miles off Flamborough Head, in Yorkshire.

Bill arrived on task after dark at low level, and was reminded by Merv Fowler, who had been shadowing the very slow Shackleton for the past hour, that he would need to select flaps to lower the stalling speed; Bill acknowledged and started a turn in behind the target. Nothing else was heard from him; he disappeared from the view of the Shackleton crew and off the radar at RAF Patrington, where the controller, growing increasingly frantic, called him on the radio. A few minutes later, I was scrambled with a simple order: 'Search for any sign of Mission 45, visually or on the emergency radio frequency.' It was by now obvious that Bill had crashed into the sea, but there was still hope that he had managed to eject, triggering his emergency beacon, which would transmit a series of bleeps on the emergency radio frequency, 243.0 mhz. I stayed on task for an hour, working with the Shackleton, which had now become the lead search asset. But we saw nothing in the inky sea below. I returned to base with a sinking feeling, realising that with every minute that passed without seeing or hearing from him, the chances that he had survived were quickly reducing.

I landed to see the Padre in the crewroom; never a welcome sight on a fighter squadron, where the Grim Reaper seemed to play a more important role than his Divine Master. Chalky and the Station Commander, Group

Captain Mel Shepherd, looked at me. 'Nothing?' I shook my head and the trio that no wife wants to see set off to where Linda Schaffner was getting her three boys into bed, totally unaware that within minutes her life would change forever. Later that night, as I tried desperately to walk past the Schaffners' house undetected, the lounge curtain was pulled to one side, and I saw Linda's frightened, tearful face staring out in forlorn hope that some miracle had happened, and Bill had been found. Irene was waiting for me: 'Have they found him?' she anxiously asked. I shook my head, reaching for something strong and alcoholic. 'Bill's dead', I replied.

Some weeks later, the MOD salvage vessel detected on its sonar a large radar return in 70ft of water. A diver went down, approached the object, and reported back: 'It's an aeroplane, with the letter 'F' on the tail.' He had found Bill's aircraft, and it looked remarkably undamaged. 'Approaching the front; cockpit closed; looking in the cockpit now.' Everyone listening, including the Board of Inquiry officers on board, held their breath, knowing what was coming next. The diver's voice came through, punctuated by heavy breathing as he climbed over the wing. There was a gasp of surprise: 'The cockpit's empty; no sign of the pilot; just a few straps pulled out.'

The aircraft, designation XS984, was recovered with minor damage as it was lifted off the sea bottom, and transported to Binbrook, where it was hidden from view under a large tarpaulin. I couldn't resist the temptation to take a look at it. Despite the covering, it was clearly in remarkably good condition for an aircraft that had crashed into the sea, sunk 70ft and then been pulled back to the surface from the mud below. As it dripped away, the last of the seawater oozing out onto the hangar floor, I was filled with a sense of horror at how quickly a life I had known had been snuffed out; yet another reminder that this was a dangerous business.

The Board of Inquiry eventually drew all the pieces together. Bill was operating at, or even beyond, his limits in shadowing a very slow target; indeed, he had not been trained for such a mission. He got too low and slow, and the aircraft stalled. Despite engaging full reheat, Bill realised that impact with the sea was inevitable, and tried to eject. In the Lightning, a large steel strut divided the canopy immediately above the pilot's head. Prior to the seat ejecting, it was therefore essential for the canopy to detach, and this was achieved by a separate cartridge, triggered as the ejection sequence was initiated. If the canopy didn't separate, an interference link prevented ejection to avoid fatal head injuries. On XS894 there was a negligent servicing error, which stopped the firing pin penetrating the canopy cartridge. At high level, there would have been enough time to separate the canopy manually, but at low level and just before impact this would have been impossible. XS 894 hit the sea, at about 180 mph, almost certainly resulting in severe injuries to the pilot. Nevertheless, he had managed to open the canopy and struggle out, but incapacitated and without his survival dinghy, he almost certainly drowned in the cold North Sea waters. That his body was never recovered was unusual, but not without precedent in the strong currents in the area.

Inevitably, without a body to confirm the Board of Inquiry's findings, UFO experts leapt at the opportunity to construct a story of total fantasy, suggesting that Bill, as an ace USAF airman, had been specially scrambled to intercept a UFO. These stories, which were given far too much media coverage, were most unsettling for Bill's family, and only when the formal findings were released did they achieve closure. Linda married again later, and at the time of writing had enjoyed a good life with her three sons and a new family. Two of the sons, Michael and Glenn, visited the UK and even went to Binbrook, which is now redeveloped as a domestic and commercial estate. However, the hangars remain as they were, with the 5(Fighter) Squadron emblem, a maple leaf, clearly visible on the operations room door. In a sombre and nostalgic few hours, they trod the ground where their father had taken his last steps on this earth, and visited the house where their mother received the terrible news, and where she prayed on her knees all night for the miracle that never happened.

The Inquiry identified the appalling servicing error, and we discovered several other aircraft on the squadron with the same canopy cartridge defect. The responsible airman could not be identified. The TACEVAL Team were criticised for including a target which was not covered in the training syllabus, but there was little criticism of the supervisory aspects; on balance, while a close call, I think this was fair. Captain Schaffner was very experienced on similar fighters, and must have known the dangers of getting low and slow. He had been making excellent progress as a new squadron pilot, and it was sheer bad luck that several elements combined on that fateful night to take him to his death. But any pilot who flew in those days understood the risks, the importance of good fortune and the consequences when things all went wrong. The day after Bill died, we all flew again, perhaps with a little trepidation at first, but soon looking ahead into the blue sky as our beautiful jets flew in a last salute to another lost friend.

CHAPTER 5

Shortly after the turn of the year, we started the long preparation for the AFCENT competition. I was determined to do well after my earlier faux pas, but the team came out of the hat earlier than the previous year, and my name was not among the lucky few. I was distraught, but there could be no appeal, so with the rest of the squadron who were not lucky I resigned myself to supporting the team, including flying the Mk 1 Lightnings which equipped the Target Facilities Flight (TFF). These aircraft were stripped down and much lighter as a result than the operational Mk 6s, and despite being shorter on fuel were real sports cars, and a total delight to fly. Putting my disappointment behind me, I filled my boots with a range of flying, mainly acting as a target for the AFCENT participants. It was, in the end, a happy time. The squadron excelled itself in the competition, and won most of the trophies. Thankfully, perhaps because of my absence, there were no cock-ups and RAF Patrington fighter controllers won the trophy for the best air control unit as well. The squadron won the Dacre Trophy for the best fighter squadron in 11 Group, Chalky got his Air Force Cross and became a Gp Capt, and the Station Commander, Mel Shepherd, was promoted to Air Cdre. I was posted to be an instructor on the Lightning OCU at Coltishall, but before I went I was sent on a two-month staff course, the Junior Command and Staff Course, or JCSS (also referred to as the 'Jackass Course') at RAF Tern Hill, in Shropshire. While there, I was told by a fellow student that a Lightning from Binbrook had crashed into the North Sea. It turned out to be my good friend Ali McKay, who after take-off at night experienced a catastrophic fire and was forced to eject, having stayed with the burning aircraft far too long in order to clear Grimsby before abandoning the stricken Lightning. This time, all the escape systems worked well, and Ali was picked up by helicopter an hour or so later. He had, as often happened, suffered a spinal compression fracture during ejection, but he made a full recovery and was flying again after three months recuperation. In its wisdom, the RAF (perhaps to appease our wives) decided that we should never work on the same station again, indeed in the same country, so Ali was posted to Germany, where he spent most of his career, drinking duty free booze and buying cheap cars that were well out of the reach of those of us destined to remain protecting the UK.

When I look back on my first tour, I do so with mixed feelings. I loved flying the Mk 6 Lightning, which at the time was the finest fighter in the world. We had some amazing experiences, tinged with sadness and tragedy, but it was a life lived to the full; indeed to overflowing. Most importantly, we had been blessed with a second child, a little girl called Nicola, but to us she was always Nicky. But I was aware that we were flying at the edges of our own, and occasionally the aircraft's, limits. We were also burning the candle at both ends, with late nights, lost weekends and flying to total exhaustion at times. Of course, we were young and fit, but not indestructible, and all too often we used alcohol to wind down and caffeine to prop us up. We lived on our adrenalin, frequently surviving by a hair's breadth, although often we kept such close encounters to ourselves. We lost many friends in fatal accidents; a few left the Lightning force of their own accord. Some were posted to be flying instructors on the Gnat or Jet Provost, to give them time to mature their flying and personal qualities before a possible return to the front line. I had ahead of me the ideal second tour, as a Lightning instructor, without the challenges and pressures of the front line. I was looking forward to it.

Chapter 6

I felt very comfortable going back to 'Colt'. The year before I had spent three weeks back there doing the Instrument Rating Examiners' (IRE) Course, which had not gone entirely without incident. The course happened to coincide with the annual AOC's Inspection, at the end of which the great man, in this case AVM Ivor Broome, would fire a Verey Pistol and the whole wing would scramble. Why this totally useless and frankly expensive ritual had been maintained, nobody knew or cared; we just accepted it as part of RAF life. As it happened, the scramble in question turned out to be the last of its kind, for reasons I will explain.

The Chief Flying Instructor (CFI) at Colt was a middle-aged wing commander who did very little flying, but who saw it as his job to lead the gaggle into the air in front of the AOC and, as importantly, to bring all twenty-eight or so back safely. At the chaotic briefing, the Meteorological Officer warned that while the wind remained south westerly, the cloud base would stay above 1,000ft. However, there was a risk that it could shift behind a delinquent front that refused to behave predictably, going round to north-easterly, increasing in speed to over 20 knots and lowering the cloud base to a few hundred feet. There were at least two implications for the mass scramble for this: first, large formations are difficult enough to manage in good weather, but in bad conditions they are impossible; second, all aircraft take off and land as close into the wind as possible to reduce the length of runway used. Runways are designated by their direction: a runway heading west, that is 270 degrees, is designated RW 27; its reciprocal RW 09, and so on. The CFI, totally 'maxed out', briefed that we would take off on the south-westerly runway, RW 22, and stubbornly refused to accept the possibility that we might have to recover to the north-easterly one should the wind change, that is to RW 04. You'll never guess what happened. As the AOC's Verey cartridge rose into the sky, penetrating a cloud base that looked much lower than 1,000ft, the windsock drooped, fluttered and started to move through 180 degrees. As we dashed towards

71

our aircraft (I was flying in a 2-sticker with Flt Lt Bruce McDonald), the USAF exchange officer, looking panic-stricken, shouted:

'Are we Gold or Red Flight?'
'This is going to be a bloody classic,' I said as we were strapping in.
'It'll be good, but it won't be a classic,' Bruce replied, shaking his head.

We got airborne in stream, as single aircraft, following each other on radar as the cloud base was getting lower and the visibility reducing in rain. The thirteenth aircraft to take off was Peter (Oscar) Wilde, who was the station aerobatic pilot and, unlike everyone else, was turning back towards the airfield to do whatever he could in the lowering cloud base. Unfortunately, Ian Rothwell, who was number fourteen behind Oscar, had not taken this on board and led everyone else in the formation back to Colt behind the, by now gyrating, aerobatic aircraft. It was little comfort knowing he was only doing a downgraded flat show under the prevailing weather conditions; it looked, and indeed was, a total shambles.

Meanwhile, out to sea, those who had not followed Oscar were frantically trying to find the CFI, who seemed oblivious to the chaos around him, and was happily heading off towards the Dutch coast as briefed. Eventually, to precise time, he turned round and headed back to base, intent on landing as briefed on RW 22. The sharper readers will have picked up what he clearly didn't: that the change in wind direction meant a change in the runway in use, especially as the wind was, as the Met man had warned, now blowing over 20 knots from the north-east. I suppose the CFI did his best to make it work, but his approach to a downwind runway in marginal weather conditions had the inevitable outcome: he crashed onto the ground, short of the runway, bursting his tyres and hitting the tailplane firmly on the tarmac, so tearing out his best stopping aid, his tailchute. Careering down the runway, with little to stop him and with a raging tailwind, he entered the safeland emergency barrier at about 80 knots, tearing it to shreds and severely damaging his aircraft. The fact that his passenger was the OC Engineering Wing helped him not at all in the subsequent extraction from the wreckage. Mayhem followed as some landed over the top of him, others diverted short of fuel, some declaring emergencies. Bruce and I made it down by the skin of our teeth. He turned to me and said: 'You were right, Chris; it was a bloody classic!'

There were no further mass scrambles at AOC's Inspections, and steps were taken to make sure that executives flew enough hours to maintain currency and competence. Did someone say something about a bolting horse?

But back to my return to Colt, this time as an instructor. My job started when the QFIs had converted the rookie Lightning pilots to the aircraft, which took about twelve trips. At the end of this phase, they were qualified on type, but capable of doing nothing with the aircraft other than fly it around the sky looking pretty. The job of the instructors thereafter was to turn them into productive fighter pilots, able to fly in bad weather and operate the exceptionally complex weapons systems, avionics and radar. The first step was to get students an Instrument Rating, which would extend the opportunities for them to fly in the usual British weather. In essence, the 'White Card' Rating would get them down to a cloud base of 500ft and a mile visibility which, with an approach speed of 200 mph, left just a few seconds to make any flightpath adjustments before landing (landing in the Lightning being a euphemism for whatever happened after the last 3ft of airborne flight). Equipped with a White Card, the students were then handed over to the Tactics Instructors. As an Instrument Rating Examiner already, I had the dual role of White Card training and Tactics instruction.

Largely because of my background on the newer Mk 6 Lightnings, I was posted to 2 (Training) Sqn on the OCU, the unit that prepared pilots for the UK, Singapore and Cyprus squadrons; the other unit, 1 Sqn, focused on initial conversion to type (QFI stuff), and then on servicing the two Mk 2A Lightning squadrons in Germany. My Boss initially was a delightful and very competent leader, Sqn Ldr Terry Adcock, who had the knack of commanding a unit of very experienced, some relatively old pilots, without overdoing the leadership role or appearing patronising. It was a very happy team. Unfortunately for Terry, HQ 11 Gp had decided that the OCU squadrons needed to come in line with the operational ones, with a wing commander Boss and two flight commander squadron leaders; in short order, Terry became one of two flight commanders, with Wg Cdr Paul Hobley as the new CO. Despite our early worries, and with Terry being a perfect gentleman and supporting the new regime, morale rapidly returned to normal and Paul turned out to be an admirable if slightly unorthodox Boss. A large man, with a bluff sense of humour, Paul accepted that his subordinates were all experienced instructors, and kept a gentle hand on the tiller.

My first student was a wing commander, John Hutchinson, who was slated to be the new OC 5 Squadron, after Chalky White. He had no previous experience on the Lightning, was not in current flying practice, and had had a very rough ride with 1 Sqn converting to type. Unfortunately for him, the Boss of that unit, Sqn Ldr Alan Blackley, was posted under the reorganisation as the other flight commander on 2 Sqn.

Although it was obvious that John was rusty, I recognised a maturity and sound airmanship which I admired. I liked him and we got on very well together. After a few shaky moments, and with a lot of hard work from us both, John graduated and became a popular if unspectacular squadron commander. My second student was another wing commander, Martin Bee, also being prepared for command of a squadron. Again, he and Alan Blackley had suffered personality differences, but as with John Hutchinson I very much enjoyed flying with this experienced pilot, who was not only qualified on Lightnings, but who had also flown some 'interesting' missions in the USAF. We parted as, and remain, friends, albeit distant ones.

Just when I thought I had been earmarked to look after future squadron commanders, I was introduced to my next two students, Flight Lieutenants Andy Potter and Keith Hartley, both first tourists. Keith was a natural, and eventually became a test pilot, only blotting his impeccable copy book when he tipped a Battle of Britain Memorial Flight Spitfire on its nose before its first test flight after refurbishment. As the Rolls Royce apprentices who had refurbished the aircraft over six months watched in dismay, the giant propeller dug itself into the ground and the engine was severely damaged. He was lucky to escape a lynching.

Sadly, Andy was not so gifted. His lifelong ambition was to fly Lightnings, and he had worked and struggled through the earlier hoops and hurdles to get this far. But after a few sorties with him, I concluded that he could never manage the massive workload involved, and after an extensive debrief told him that I would be recommending his suspension. His eyes welled with tears, and I left him alone for a while, feeling a real bastard but recognising that I was doing the right thing. Andy was posted to Hunters and eventually became a QFI instructing on the Jet Provost; sadly, he was killed in a Meteor of the Historic Flight some years later. The Inquiry concluded that the most likely cause was pilot error.

Later at Coltishall, and subsequently in command appointments, I had to face up to pilots and explain why they could not continue on their chosen career paths, often when for years they had been working to exhaustion to make the grade. But in the end, the air is an unforgiving medium and especially so in a supersonic fighter. Being brutal might have reduced grown men to tears, but it probably saved their lives and those of others. But I never found it easy, and always spent a sleepless night after telling someone that his dreams could never be fulfilled.

Towards the middle of what was an enjoyable and fulfilling tour, I was given a very special student, Capitaine Louis Eon, of the French Air Force, who was on the exchange programme. Louis had flown Mirage 3 fighters, and was fluent in English, if not in fighter pilot jargon. Accordingly, he was prone to lapse inappropriately into crewroom vernacular. On one occasion, we were hosting a visit by the Lady Mayoress and her Norwich councillors. Seeing an unusual uniform, the distinguished lady approached Louis and engaged him in conversation. Interpreting the extra French braid as signifying senior rank, she asked if he was going to be a squadron commander, to which he innocently replied: 'No, I am just going to be a Gash Shag.' Believing she had misheard him, she persisted:
'Are you finding the Lightning easy to fly?'

> 'No,' Louis responded, shaking his head. He nodded towards me, 'Chris keeps telling me I am making too many cock-ups.' The Station Commander glared at me and steered the Mayoress away to a more decorous group. Louis and his lovely wife enjoyed a most successful tour with the RAF. He went back to France and became a top test pilot, but sadly contracted leukaemia and died in his forties.

About this time, it was fashionable for personalities to come and fly with us to join what was called 'The Ten Ton Club'. This required no more than a few seconds flying an aircraft at over 1,000 mph which, depending on atmospheric conditions, was about Mach 1.6 (1.6 times the speed of sound). One day, the Boss called me in and tasked me with flying a Liverpool-based journalist, Brian Stiff, who had successfully lobbied the MOD to join the 'elite' club. It turned out that he was actually a surveyor, who did a little part-time writing for the *Liverpool Echo*. With his pretty partner, Sue, Brian arrived at Coltishall and went through the extensive preparation before being allowed to fly in a Lightning. After a few days, involving medical, simulator and emergency procedure training, Brian and Sue arrived, he in full kit to fly with me in a Mk T5 two-sticker. The profile was fairly canned for these sorties: fly to 40,000ft; drop the nose and engage full reheat; once at the right speed, let the passenger 'fly' for a few seconds; return and land; glass of bubbly and give them their Ten Ton Club tie. Brian was very keen to see a reheat climb, despite my advising him that it was a bit of a bare-knuckle ride, with the nose nearly vertical, culminating in a roll over to bring the nose back to the horizon. This is where things started to go wrong. The climb obviously exceeded his expectations, and the roll over to level off initiated the first of several retches into his sick bag. Nevertheless, we persisted, to his credit, and reached the magic Mach number, he with sick-bag in one hand and control column in the other.

'OK, Brian, you have control.'

'I have control,' came the retched response.

'Now move the stick to the left,' (retch) 'now to the right,' (retch) 'I have control. Congratulations, you are now a member of the exclusive Ten Ton Club!'

'Thanks, Chris,' Brian retched feebly.

We returned to base where Brian was taken for a medical check-up. He recovered quickly, and went off home with Sue to write up for the *Liverpool Echo* and other well-known journals, a totally fictitious account of the flight, including a final paragraph which resulted in my dear colleagues subjecting me to unrelenting banter and jeering for weeks:

> The Lightning is a wonderful aircraft, but it takes special men like Flight Lieutenant Chris Coville to tame these powerful beasts. As long as such men exist, we can sleep easy in our beds at night. [Retch!]

In an astonishing coincidence, some thirty-five years later, I invited a couple to join our group at a meet-and-greet party in Madeira. After stating that I had been in the RAF, the lady mentioned that her first partner had flown in a Lightning. It was Sue, now married to a very charming gentleman, Keith Jones; she had no idea what had happened to the plucky Brian, and subsequent attempts to contact him have failed.

It's not often that a rat makes an appearance in a book largely devoted to aviation matters. After all, they crawl, run and occasionally swim, but they don't fly. But one such animal did make a name for itself on No 2 (Training) Squadron at Coltishall. The cleaner, who was also responsible for keeping our coffee bar stocked, declared one day that he had found rat droppings among the chocolate biscuits and cheese and onion crisps. This was serious. The Station Medical Officer was called in, and at once closed down the coffee bar, which meant that not only would we be short of essential caffeine for the early flights, but the lack of a quickly devoured 'choccy bar' around lunchtime would leave us low on energy to face the afternoon. Oh to be in the French Air Force, which closed shop for two hours from 11.30am until 1.30pm to enjoy a three-course lunch with wine! The Belgians were reputed to be even more self-indulgent, rarely flying in the afternoon in the interests of flight safety. Meanwhile, RAF fighter pilots, as opposed to their corpulent comrades in larger aircraft, had to be content with a quick snack at best. And now even that had been denied us owing to an infernal, as yet undetected rodent. Drastic action was needed. Oscar Wild declared himself the Vermin Detection and Destruction officer, and drew together a posse of likely lads to bring the miscreant to a swift and well-deserved end. A briefing followed, at which Oscar emphasised that a rat under attack will look for a safe haven, biting anything which obstructs its path. Accordingly, the attack team, who would be armed with hockey sticks, golf clubs and umbrellas, would need to stand on chairs and tuck their trousers into their socks. A sharp-toothed rat disappearing up an officer's trousers was a dreadful prospect. With bad weather forecast for the next day until late morning, an hour was put aside for the hunt. Shortly after dawn, the fun started. Oscar set about flushing out the beast, having laid out a feast of chocolate and biscuits the evening before. A trail of dark brown droppings led him to a large, well-worn and very old settee. Gleefully, Oscar beat the living daylights out of the antique, filling the air with dust and escaping moths until, to our horror, the rat threw itself at him from underneath. Oscar beat at it with his hockey stick, but it gave him the slip and made a dash for the door. Ian Rothwell hacked at it with his golf club (a number five, I think), but lost his balance and fell off his chair on top of the furious rat. Screaming in anticipation of a mortal wound, Ian rolled over and scrambled away, giving the half-squashed rat the moment it had been waiting for; freedom beckoned, and it flew (despite my earlier comments) out of the crewroom door, never to be seen again. An exhausted (with laughter) set of experienced, if thwarted, supersonic killers, turned their attention back to the less dangerous task of defending Her Majesty's airspace.

Every base in those halcyon days was expected to provide an aerobatic pilot, and the competition to become the 'ace of the base' was always fierce. For the first, but not the last time, I joined in with a few other hopefuls to be the Lightning Mk3 aerobatic pilot for Coltishall. Quite rightly, and by a sizeable margin, the Boss chose Flt Lt Peter Chapman as the best man for the job. Pete was like most of us a second tourist, in his case having flown Mk 2As in Germany. He had enjoyed the tactical leadership of several outstanding fighter pilots, including John Spencer, who was in the eyes of most of us the best fighter pilot in the Lightning force at the time. Perhaps in sympathy for my lame attempt to become a Lightning display pilot, Paul Hobley declared me the runner-up and gave me the job of taking Pete's spare aircraft to several national shows. This normally involved beating up the display airfield on arrival and departure, making as much noise and flying as low as possible; those days are long gone, but we enjoyed them to the full at the time, and so did the enthralled audiences. The Lightning was especially suited to hooliganism, being both extremely noisy and incredibly powerful. There are tales a many of windows being shattered by Lightning 'flypasts', especially in East Anglia, where the window replacement businesses did very well patching up the missing glass in vast cucumber and tomato greenhouses.

One of Pete Chapman's first displays was in my home town of Liverpool, at what was to become later John Lennon International Airport. We arrived in the usual fashion, with extreme decibels and at high speed, and after landing had the familiar interview with an enraged airport manager who claimed his phone hadn't stopped ringing since our 'arrival'. Nothing new there.

The next day, Pete put on a truly outstanding display, captivating the audience and earning praise from all who saw it. That evening, still in our flying suits and in the company of fellow display pilots, we revelled in the admiring glances of other hotel guests; the joy of reflected glory. The Red Arrows, then flying Gnats, had been at the show during the day, and we had enjoyed a few drinks with them in the hotel the night before. The then Red leader, Frank Hoare, had been a fellow student on the JCSS (Jackass) course, and we had become drinking buddies. Just before Pete and I were about to get changed, two Scouse girls in dresses that would have jammed a radar appeared in the doorway, and were clearly looking for someone. After a while, and seeing our flying suits, they came up and enquired, in beautifully rich Scouse accents: 'Erm, wer luckin' for Jed and Matt of the Red Arrows.' Now I knew the Red Arrows, and I knew that they didn't include a Jed or a Matt.

'Are you sure they were pilots?' I asked.

'Erm, well they said they were with the Red Arrows.'

The penny dropped, and the next day I phoned Frank, and confirmed that Jed and Matt were as expected in the support team, and had neglected to mention this while chatting up the Liver birds. They were suitably admonished, and reminded of their role in uniform as ambassadors, not playboys.

CHAPTER 6

Pete went on to achieve greatness as a display pilot, and indeed won most of the top trophies at national and international air shows. After his tour at Coltishall, he converted to the Jaguar attack aircraft, where not surprisingly he became their most exceptional aviator. He was, in my mind, the best fighter pilot of our generation. As I clearly wasn't, I never got the chance to be a Lightning display pilot, but my opportunity was to come later in a very different, and very special way.

During the early part of 1973, my new flight commander, Sqn Ldr Alan Morgan, asked me to pop into his office for a chat. He had recently debriefed my annual report, in those days a certain Form 1369, and to my surprise it was glowing. I think it was probably about then that I had started to realise that my real potential was far greater than my old headmaster or the Cranwell hierarchy could have imagined. Alan asked me whether I had given serious thought to my next posting, which I had. There were two main options: stay in the Lightning force or move to one of the new aircraft entering service. I loved the Lightning, but fancied a change.

The sensible options, therefore, were the Phantom, which was progressively assuming the UK air defence role, or the Jaguar, which was entering service as an attack aircraft, and needed at least some single-seat pilots to mix with other 'mud-movers', most of whom came from the Phantom or the Buccaneer. There was always the spectre of the Central Flying School (CFS) and an instructional tour, but I saw that as a backwards step, and thought my patience would not stand the test of flying with pilots who were, by definition, incompetent and inexperienced. As my Chivenor experiences had shown up my inability to navigate at high speed at low level, I reasoned that staying in the same role on a different aircraft type made sense. There was another reason. I had started to become ambitious, not just for promotion, but for command; and more than anything else, I wanted one day to command a fighter squadron. So it was the F4 Phantom that was top of my list. It was, of course, by then, a seasoned weapon of war, having cut its teeth in both the US Navy and Air Force in Vietnam. But the version acquired by the UK had Rolls Royce engines, which were superb at low level, and the most advanced pulse doppler radar, which enabled low-level targets to be detected at long range. I told Alan that I saw the F4 as my best option, and he smiled. 'Good choice; that's where you're going – next Monday!'

It turned out that 43(F) Sqn at Leuchars in eastern Scotland were short of pilots as they formed the first air defence Phantom unit, and the authorities thought that the quickest way to get more was to take a couple of Lightning instructors and give them a short conversion course. One of the pilots was from our sister squadron at Colt, Sandy Davis; I was the other. Irene would really be pleased with yet another short-notice posting, but at least she would be able to stay at Coltishall while I completed the three-month course at Coningsby in Lincolnshire, just two hours away. She was pregnant with our daughter Theresa, and would no doubt see this as another clever ruse to get myself out of the way while she was struggling with the last few months of confinement.

Sandy and I duly arrived at RAF Coningsby the following Monday, and started the usual simulator and ground school phase, which mercifully had been compressed into a week. It was obvious at once that the Phantom had some significant advantages over the Lightning: twice as much fuel, four times the number of missiles, and the option of an amazing SUU-23A Gatling Gun, which fired 6,000 rounds per minute of 20 millimetre High Explosive rounds; that's 100 rounds every second! But there was a drawback, or so I thought at the time: a navigator. As a single-seat pilot, I had always scorned the idea of flying with a 'crew', and pretended that I could cope with anything day and night. In reality, I could not, and soon realised that a good navigator could add 1.5 times the value to a good pilot; on the other hand, a bad navigator could halve it. Inevitably, they turned out to be a mixed group, most having flown in the back of the Javelin some years before. But there were some great characters, who were most professional and good fun as well. The poor man who was selected to mentor No 1 Lightning Short Course was Flt Lt Tom Crockett, a seasoned navigator and superb instructor. Having passed through the hands of the QFIs initially, Sandy and I reluctantly admitted that this was a nice aeroplane to fly, if a little heavier on the controls and lacking some of the agility of the Lightning. At this stage, the ever-cheerful Tom took us under his wing, endured constant jibes about 'bloody navigators', and with some of his esteemed back-seat colleagues turned us round in our attitudes towards the two-man crew.

One of the most memorable characters at the Phantom OCU was Flt Lt 'Middy' Hopper, who was a very experienced navigator in the air defence and ground attack roles. 'Middy' was so called because he had, for a very short period, been a Midshipman in the Royal Navy. During a goodwill trip to Australia, Middy was put in charge of the Admiral's Barge, and was charged with delivering him safely from the carrier *Ark Royal* to the VIP pontoon in Sydney harbour. Once there, the Admiral, in full ceremonial rig, was to be met and feted by the city's mayor and associated entourage. Unfortunately, as the Barge approached the pontoon, Middy became tongue-tied and forgot the important order, 'Full astern both.' The outcome was the Barge striking the pontoon while still doing 20 knots, overturning and depositing the entire crew into the murky waters of Sydney harbour. Holding his breath for as long as he could, Middy eventually rose to the surface to find the Admiral's head, still adorned with ceremonial hat, bobbing up and down alongside him in the briny. Before Middy could utter any words of apology, the Admiral announced with all the gravitas and dignity he could muster: 'Hopper, you're fired!' Middy left the Navy and joined the RAF as a navigator.

It was a tall order to get Sandy and I through a conversion course onto a new aeroplane in just a few months, and we had to work extremely hard, in the air and on the ground, to keep up with the required pace. However, as Lightning pilots, we had a reputation as scallywags to maintain – and we did our very best to achieve this. In the air, we never missed an opportunity to 'attack' any military aircraft that came into sight, resulting in several dodgy dogfights over the North Sea against Harriers, Buccaneers and American F4s. Tom's plaintiff cries of 'I'm not sure we should be doing this', were quietly ignored. We also strengthened the reputation of Lightning pilots as being somewhat excessive socially, and on several occasions were summoned to the office of Wg Cdr Bob Honey, who, as well as being OC No 228(Phantom) OCU, was also the President of the Mess Committee (PMC), and thus responsible for good discipline among officers in our club. On one occasion, Sandy and I had reopened the Mess kitchen after the bar had closed, very much at the request of three wing commanders, who were refreshing or converting to the Phantom before taking command of squadrons, and who had expressed their desire for bacon and egg sandwiches at midnight. As one, Keith Beck, was to command No 43(F) Squadron, and therefore be our Boss, we thought we had better oblige. After a forced fenestration from a side window, we got the kitchen equipment roaring away, opened the doors to the dining room and served up platefuls of 'Eggy Bakes' to the starving senior officers. Unfortunately, when tidying up, one of the future Bosses inadvertently switched an oven on instead of off, resulting in a tropical welcome for the kitchen staff the next morning. In usual military fashion, the junior officers had to take the rap; hence our arrival in 'Best Blue' uniform, outside the PMC's office early Monday morning. As we prepared to receive our bollocking, Sandy realised he had forgotten to bring his leather gloves, which were normally carried in the left hand, leaving the right one free to salute. Hurriedly, I gave him one of mine and we were marched into Bob's office, where he sat behind his desk, trying to look stern. Always believing that one should take the initiative, I blurted out an apology for wasting the taxpayers' money by leaving on an oven. The wing commander looked even more annoyed: 'Well thank you for telling me that, Coville', he exclaimed, 'I wanted to talk about damage to a kitchen window!' Shit. Me and my big mouth.

We listened attentively as he rambled on about un-officer-like behaviour, bad example to the troops and how he expected more from third tourists. We nodded contritely, and after swearing a firm purpose of amendment, until at least the next weekend, we duly saluted smartly and turned to leave. As we did so, the PMC shouted: 'And don't think I didn't notice you've only got one glove each!'

The following week, we were determined not to fall into the same trap, and avoided the three wing commanders at Happy Hour. At least that was our good intention, but one of them found our weak spot: 'Call yourselves fighter pilots!' That was too much; we re-fenestrated into the Mess kitchen and again made Eggy Bakes for the voracious senior officers. Despite our best efforts to conceal the felony, the astute Mess staff detected a shortage of bacon and eggs for breakfast the next morning, and reported the loss to the hapless Bob Honey who, without hesitation, assumed that Sandy and I were the guilty parties. This time the wing commanders came to our rescue, realising that the consequences of a second yellow card could be dire. They wrote confessing 'their' misdemeanour, along the following lines:

Dear PMC,

On Friday evening at about 2359 hours, we detected a strong smell of burning emanating from the Mess Kitchens. Out of a sense of duty, we forced an entry into the kitchens and found several rashers of bacon sizzling in a large frying pan. On looking around, we could find nothing other than bread and eggs to put out the flames, after which we decided to tidy up by eating the contents of the frying pan. We wish to commend the actions of Flt Lts Coville and Davis, who with no regard for personal safety, were at the forefront of this heroic endeavour.

We have the honour to be, Sir,

Your Obedient Servants etc

CHAPTER 6

We were off the hook, and a few days later were debriefed by Sqn Ldr John Allison, himself an ex-Lightning pilot, who commended our performance and good character, but added that Wg Cdr Honey wanted to see us before we left. We gulped, and cast our minds back to our farewell party the night before, but neither of us could remember any particular incident that might have incurred the PMC's wrath. Indeed, he had even dropped in for a drink with us. With some trepidation, we changed into No I uniforms, anticipating another bollocking. His PA looked serious. 'You can go straight in, gentlemen', she declared ominously. We entered, saluted smartly and stood for a few minutes while the wing commander read our reports, making the occasional grunting sound, and raising his eyebrows a couple of times. Eventually, he looked up and smiled: 'Well done, chaps; best reports I've seen for a long time. And it's been great fun having you on the Station. Best of luck at Leuchars on 43.' We saluted and decided to get out while the going was good. 'Oh, by the way….' Oh God, what's he remembered…. 'Congratulations on having a pair of gloves each this time!'

Chapter 7

RAF Leuchars, near St Andrews in Fife, Scotland, was one of the most loved stations in the UK. The weather factor, sheltered as it was behind the Lomond range from westerlies, was usually superb. The only weather which was a constant if infrequent threat resulted from a combination of high pressure, cold waters flowing out of the Rivers Tay and Forth, and a gentle easterly breeze. At any time of the year, this could with short notice produce the dreaded Haar, the local name for a very insidious sea fog. But when Sandy and I arrived on 43(F) Squadron, known as the 'Fighting Cocks', we enjoyed several weeks of splendid weather as we tackled the operational workup programme, which would qualify us to sit on Quick Reaction Alert (QRA): two aircraft, and sometimes more, fully armed and ready to go in less than ten minutes to intercept any unknown aircraft entering the UK's area of responsibility, known as the UK Air Defence Region (UKADR). The crews involved comprised the two pilots and navigators, air traffic controllers and admin support staff at the QRA base, plus fighter controllers at what was called the Master Radar Station, in the case of Leuchars at RAF Buchan, in Aberdeenshire.

Legally, UK sovereign airspace starts twelve miles out from the coastline, but in practice interceptions are made many hundreds of miles away, requiring air tanker support and comprehensive international cooperation. A Soviet/Russian aircraft coming round the North Cape would be intercepted sequentially by the Norwegian Air Force, USAF in Iceland and then the RAF. This was, and remains, essential for the safety of civilian Air Traffic, in case an incursion into sovereign airspace should occur, requiring immediate action, and indeed to demonstrate capability in the complex chess game that is international politics.

The Boss when we arrived was Wg Cdr Jeremy (Jerry) Cohu, who was a charming man, and together with his formidable wife, Sue, made a good couple at the top of the squadron hierarchy. But he was fairly relaxed as a leader, and the two flight commanders, Mike Elsam and Ed Stein seemed to run the squadron. After the youthful nature of Lightning squadrons, this outfit seemed dominated by relatively older men – in fact in their late thirties! Most had come from the Javelin force, a few from Hunters with a sprinkling of Lightning men who had done a full F4 conversion at the end of their first tours. My navigator was Sqn Ldr Bob Rogers, one of the best navigators in the force, but with a strong 'radar will find it' mentality, and unable to comprehend why I insisted in flying below or above cloud to use my eyes as well as the radar. Despite that, we hit it off well and became a good crew. A real character in the navigator world was Barry Mayner, who was a Weapons Instructor, the highest accolade for a fighter pilot or navigator. Unfortunately, Barry and I had a significant clash of personalities, which stemmed from my propensity to decide how best to operate the Phantom, but had other underlying reasons as well; more later.

Shortly after Keith Beck arrived, I was advised that I was to be promoted to squadron leader and sent on the Qualified Weapons Instructor Course (QWI), after which I would come back as the Pilot Weapons Instructor Leader on 43 Squadron. The course was intensive, spread over six months at Coningsby. When I came back, Alan White from 5 Squadron days had become the new station commander. Keith Beck was working up a four-ship formation for a bit of showing off at the Station Open Day a few weeks later. I was told I would be No 2, with the newly arrived flight commander, Alan Winkles as No 3 and Flt Lt Jack Hamill as No 4.

The Boss was determined to put on a good show, and being a punchy character had decided to abandon rules and regulations on flying displays, and do something out of the ordinary. One of his 'out of the ordinary' wheezes was what became known as the 'Canadian Rolling Break'. As explained earlier and in the Glossary, on returning from a sortie, fighters storm into the airfield at high speed and 'break' into the circuit to lose speed, enabling undercarriage and flaps to be lowered for landing. In the 'Canadian' version, the break is conducted from a nose up roll through 270 degrees, going underneath, before turning downwind to land. For Alan and myself, this was a straightforward manoeuvre, but Jack, having come from Vulcans, struggled with its execution; especially the roll underneath.

Concerned that Jack was clearly having problems, the Boss asked if on the next sortie I could fly a hundred yards behind them both, and watch the manoeuvre to see why Jack was having so many problems. That seemed sensible, so the following day we set off as a four-ship, heading North toward Kirriemuir. Once in clear airspace, the two set up for the prescribed practice. The Boss pulled his nose up and started to roll left and Jack started to follow. I could see at once that his rate of roll was inadequate to keep visual contact with the lead, and expected him to just roll out and try again. Instead, Jack's aircraft rolled violently and the nose pitched up. He was in the early stages of a spin, and far too low to recover safely. My navigator, Norman Brown, frantically asked: 'Has he lost it?' But I was too intent watching the disaster unfolding in front of me. I started to scream: 'Eject! … Eject! … Eject!' and kept shouting until in slow motion I saw the navigator's canopy shoot off, shortly followed by Tim Wright in his rocket seat fired safely into the air. Immediately afterwards, Jack ejected, but the aircraft was very low and I had a real concern that his chute wouldn't open. When it did, it initially 'candled' in a big knot, but then opened just before he hit the ground, very close to the exploding aircraft. Barry Mayner, who was in the back seat with Alan Winkles, put out a 'Mayday' call, and we circled round overhead, watching Tim Wright get out of his chute and run across to the prostate Jack, who had suffered a spinal injury on ejection, and some bruising after his heavy landing. Slowly, cars arrived on the scene, and little figures dashed across to the crash site, with Tim frantically trying to keep them at a safe distance, as progressively fuel tanks exploded and hydraulic reservoirs went up in flames. We heard later that one man was found vomiting uncontrollably. The aircraft had crashed in a beetroot field, spreading scorched red bits around the site; and the poor man had thought it was pieces of dismembered people.

We returned to Leuchars, very concerned about Jack; but happily he recovered quickly and after three months was flying again. The principal blame was placed squarely on the shoulders of the Boss, for pushing the boundaries too far, with Jack's mishandling of the controls as another factor. It was a sad conclusion to Keith Beck's tour as a squadron commander; he was in all respects a natural leader and very popular with his people. But in the end, none of us in that formation emerged with credit; we all had the experience to see that Jack was having trouble and should have cautioned the Boss against continuing. Flight safety is a shared responsibility, and in that respect we all failed.

Shortly afterwards, I received a posting to Coningsby as deputy squadron commander of the Phantom OCU flying unit. In due course I would be the CO, which as a squadron leader was unusual, and I knew I would enjoy the command role and its responsibilities. When I look back on my time as a 'Gash Shag' of three tours, I realise now that I made several significant mistakes and errors of judgement, some of which have emerged in the previous pages. For a start, I was too self-confident in the air, and nearly came to grief as a result on a couple of occasions. But I was also too cocky and perhaps even arrogant, characteristics which encouraged bad feelings towards me, especially from those who believed that I was motivated more by ambition than by a sense of duty. That I assessed myself more kindly matters not; it was the perception that I gave to others which lost me respect and even friendships. My ability in the air was not in question, and perhaps as a junior officer in the Lightning force, my character shortcomings would have gone unnoticed. But in the more mature world of two-seaters, and certainly as I aspired to become a senior commander, I realised that I had to empathise more with my colleagues and subordinates, seek less the recognition of my superiors and develop more gravitas in an increasingly competitive working environment.

But I had also learned a lot about leadership, largely from observing others in command appointments. Some had clearly been unsuited to their roles, and most of those had failed. Others who succeeded did so by good luck, strength of character and professional competence. Those who assumed a persona which was not their own fell by the wayside; those who developed their own strengths and overcame – or at least limited – their weaknesses tended to succeed, but with mixed results. It was increasingly evident to me that leadership was as much an art as a science, and even required a degree of alchemy. I would like to say that I had a clear vision of this potpourri as I confronted my first real command tour, but I was to make many mistakes then and in the future; command excellence was to remain a fascinating, elusive and at times overwhelming pursuit for the next twenty-five years.

EARLY COMMAND
AND STAFF YEARS

A true leader has the confidence to stand alone, the courage
to make tough decisions, and the compassion to listen to
the needs of others. He does not set out to be a leader, but
becomes one by the equality of his actions and the integrity
of his intent.

Douglas MacArthur

Chapter 8

I can't say that Irene was enamoured over a return to the fens of Lincolnshire. My promise that if she married me she would see the world had long been discarded as calumny. However, dutiful wife that she was, we packed up and headed south, now with three children. On the way down, as we passed RAF Catterick on the A1, my relatively new Austin 1300 developed a strange knocking sound from the engine area. Fearing a 'big end' failure (whatever that was, but it was spoken of in fearful terms by tech-savvy friends), I pulled into a layby to investigate. As I slowed down, the noise stopped; strange, I thought. I gave the engine a quick rev as we parked, but no matter what I did with the throttle, I couldn't reproduce the quite alarming sound. Putting it down to a transient fault, I set off again, but as speed increased, the knocking started again, but this time much worse. My mechanical knowledge being limited to kicking, scratching my head and swearing, I thought it was time to call the AA again, who by now had a dedicated line for my services. In no time at all, a kind man in overalls arrived, asked me a few searching questions about the strange symptoms, and then proceeded to check the engine, asking me to rev to the maximum; but again to no avail. We both stood there scratching our heads. 'Best I take a look underneath, Sir', he suggested. I nodded gratefully. A few minutes after watching his legs protruding from below the vehicle, I heard him exclaim: 'You little bastard; got you!' Thinking he was referring to me, I prepared to remind him who was paying his wages; but no, he appeared jubilantly holding a large chunk of rusted metal bearing an uncanny resemblance to a car's wheel arch – which is actually what it was. Devoid of original metal, the encrusted chunk had fallen away from the body of the car, and was sitting on top of the front right tyre, so explaining the odd symptoms. We set off again in a virtually noiseless car, with me cursing the salesman who had duped me into believing he was doing me a favour. And he had seemed such a nice man.

We moved into a quarter in the main 'patch' at Coningsby; just a short drive, cycle or walk to the base. Our immediate next door neighbour was Squadron Leader Arthur Vine, who was a 'Specialist Aircrew' officer, and so expected to fly but to ignore requests for other administrative duties. Arthur was somewhat of a legend. He had flown Meteors, Hunters, Javelins and a few other types as well, and had maintained an enthusiasm for flying that put many younger pilots to shame. One of the challenges for programming officers when Arthur was flying was the uncertainty of his return to base. Once established on the fighter control frequency, Arthur would always ask if a tanker was available. As it normally was in those days, Arthur would disappear for a few hours, replete with fuel, no doubt satisfying his passion for low flying in Scotland or North Yorkshire.

The Boss when I arrived was Squadron Leader Ted Edwards, an ex-Hunter and Phantom Ground Attack pilot; he would hand over to me in six months or so. As with most two-seat squadrons, the navigators had a flight commander; in this case Squadron Leader Kip Smith, a delightful man with a puckish sense of humour, who despite being small in stature had none of the hang-ups frequently seen in men who were vertically challenged. Indeed, Kip could give back more banter than he ever received, and young pilots teased his navigator status at their peril. It was, therefore, in contemporary terms a flat organisation, with three squadron leaders, but one a primus inter pares. The entire OCU – flying, engineering and simulator/ground-school squadrons – was commanded by Wing Commander Mike Shaw, who was perfectly content to leave his subordinates to do their jobs, fly whenever he could and only interfere if things were totally out of control. As this rarely happened on an OCU, with all instructors having at least two flying tours under their belts, Mike strolled around in his flying suit, drinking coffee and occasionally dropping into his office to move some paperwork around his desk.

This merry band of casual, flying-suited chums was brought firmly into line, as was the rest of a very busy operational station, by the CO, Group Captain Derek Bryant, who was known only partially jokingly as 'Doctor Death', a name bestowed on him by the many who had come under the ferocious gaze of his liquid blue eyes. Derek was unashamedly a hard commander, in the Captain Bligh mould; indeed, I often felt as though I had been given several strokes of the lash after a one-sided interview with him. On one occasion, when good friend Steve Nicholl, and I were tasked at the end of a sortie with conducting an airfield attack on RAF Binbrook, I slightly overacted in height and speed. The consequence, with Steve hanging onto my wing in appalling weather, was that he and I, plus a pursuing Lightning, roared out of low cloud and 'attacked' the airfield with such ferocity that a local farmer, herding his cattle up the village High Street, was mounted by several of his young bulls excited by the noise and vibration. The outraged gentleman, covered in mud and other unspeakable fluids, forced his way onto the station and demanded the death sentence for the noisy perpetrators. This might have been overlooked, had not my boyish – and some would say attractive – exuberance, become more measured as we left an ear-shattered Binbrook. Sadly, it did not; our return under low cloud the short distance to Coningsby produced a trail of furious phone calls, each following me at high speed down a track back to base. The final straw was my flight over the garden of a Mrs Gilbert, a well-known complainant (something to do with several aircraft having crashed into her back garden over the years), who arrived at Derek Bryant's door with a bill for several shattered windows, aborted calves and premature hens' eggs. Were that not enough, her farrier was just about to shoe a horse when our twenty thousand decibels roared overhead, causing a sudden jerk from the horse and a sudden 'ouch' from the farrier. For some reason all this seemed to irritate the station commander, which was never a pretty sight – or sound, as I witnessed in Number One uniform in his office later.

As mentioned earlier, the job of an OCU was to take a pilot or navigator, two to three years into training and already with their flying brevets, and start the process of turning them into operational aircrew. Flying Training is a long, arduous and expensive process; in the case of pilots, taking up to five years and costing many millions of pounds. At each stage, the constant assessment process erodes numbers, some leaving the service, a few electing to go into a ground branch, and some moving to flying roles other than fast-jet. Most, but not all, navigators start life as budding pilots; most aircrew aspire to fast jets, but some find their abilities or temperaments better suited to less demanding roles. The process of weeding out unsuitable students has its origins in both science and art: objectivity and subjectivity. The aforementioned navigator instructor, Middy Hopper, who, having flown with a particular young pilot, announced to me that 'he wouldn't make a fighter pilot as long as he had a hole in his arse', may have lacked the scientific rigour expected by today's HR professionals, but he invariably got it right, and ignoring his advice only produced wasted sorties and risk to the poor navigators charged with flying behind a dodgy prospect.

CHAPTER 8

A basic Qualified Instructor (QFI) has the difficult task of picking up a very inexperienced pilot, and turning him or her into someone who can fly the aircraft well, day and night, including in poor weather, at high and low level and in formation. By the time a student pilot gets to an OCU, he is competent, but still needs very close monitoring as the margins for error have been narrowed. Let's take a few examples. In air-to-air gunnery, the closing speed on the banner target is over 300 mph. There is half-a-second to fire from 300 to 200 yards before you need to break away to avoid hitting the banner – not a good idea, as it has a steel bar at the front. In air combat, aircraft can be flying towards each other at one-and-a-half times the speed of sound – much faster than a rifle bullet. Getting the geometry wrong can mean a collision, or at best a severe fright. So while advanced level instruction starts from a greater level of trust in the student's capabilities, the consequences of mistakes are dire.

An important part of inculcating a sense of responsibility, a building block of trust, is to take a bit of a chance that people will act in an adult fashion when not being closely monitored. The way this is done in fast-jet training is to allow student pilots and navigators to fly together, normally in a formation including an instructor. Sadly, perhaps predictably, the aggressive qualities required of a fighter pilot do not always chime with a strong sense of responsibility, and when the two clash there can be interesting outcomes. One such clash occurred early in my tour at Coningsby when the then Flight Lieutenant Andy Walton and his navigator, both students, found themselves without a partner when their lead aircraft had a minor emergency shortly after taking off. Using his initiative, Andy decided to do a practice diversion instrument approach to RAF Waddington, a nearby Vulcan base. Shortly afterwards, the phone rang in my office; it turned out to be a bemused wing commander, the OC Operations Wing at Waddington. In his words, Andy had overshot from his approach at about two miles, engaged reheat and flown extremely low across the airfield, causing temporary deafness and some minor damage to windows. 'Ah!' I exclaimed. 'That would be an emergency overshoot simulating single engine failure.' I'm not sure how convinced the wing commander was, but he obviously felt unqualified to refute my lame explanation, and agreed to leave it to me, 'old chap'.

A short while later, Andy and his navigator appeared, signed in their aircraft and were happily heading for the crewroom for what they believed was a well-deserved coffee. I noticed the smirks on their faces slowly evaporating when they saw me, legs astride, hands on hips, confronting them in the corridor. 'My office,' I said. A few minutes into the interrogation on their flight profile, Andy explained in great detail his copy-book simulated engine failure overshoot. Nodding, I said, 'And you inadvertently put both engines in reheat, and kept the nose low to gain flying speed?' Believing he was in the clear, Andy agreed happily, only for me to snort: 'You beat shit out of the place, Walton?' The smile vanished completely.

'Yes, Sir', he stammered. The navigator crept further behind his pilot.

'Right, you're in deep trouble,' I announced. 'Get into your Number Ones and report to Squadron Leader Edwards at two o'clock.' They scurried away. I briefed Ted and Kip; Ted was adamant that he would not be able to keep a straight face during their formal interview, and Kip was certainly not going to get involved. I suggested that Ted should keep them standing to attention outside his office until he composed himself. He reluctantly agreed, and when the hapless pair reappeared in Best Blue I ordered them not to move until the Boss called them in, remarking that he was so furious that they might have to wait a long time. After an hour or so, Ted in need of a pee and a coffee, struggled to contain himself as he left his office, managing only a 'Stand up straight you two', before slamming the crewroom door closed, his face purple from such exertion in self-control.

'I can't do it, Chris', he confessed.

'OK', I said, 'I'll tell them to march in, say, "Sorry, Boss," salute and leave smartly.'

'I'll try', he said, taking a deep breath and returning to his office via an increasingly worried pair of felons.

'OK, you two', I said in my deepest command voice. 'You're to go in, say "Sorry, Boss", salute and get out smartly. If you say anything else, the squadron commander has threatened to blow his top', which was actually true, but perhaps not as implied. 'Right, off you go', I ordered.

They knocked, and waited; knocked again. A slightly squeaky voice called out, 'Come in.' I prayed that these two words hadn't exhausted his sparse self-control. Unfortunately, the pair had not rehearsed their lines, and were unsure who should start. Eventually, no doubt puzzled at why the Boss's shoulders were shaking with such uncontrolled rage, Andy muttered, 'Sorry, Boss.' Ted pulled himself together, at last recognising the gravity of the occasion, and stammered, 'Get out.'

They left, I slammed the door closed behind them, just in time to see Ted 'blowing his top'.

Pride in the squadron is at the forefront of every young aircrew officer's mind. Letting the squadron down is unforgiveable, and is never forgotten by colleagues, subordinates or commanders. Thus, when one Friday night four noisy Americans, having diverted into Coningsby in bad weather in their F111 Fighter Bombers, had the effrontery to claim that 'We own this bar,' it was a matter of honour to see them off. The usual device for so doing was a Schooner Race, requiring two equal teams to consume pints of beer sequentially, the winner obviously being the first to finish their beers. There were, in addition, complex rules covering the starting procedure, to ensure that no one 'jumped the gun', and strict governance on spillage, to avoid claims that 'he spilled more than he bloody well drank'. As I had a strong supporting squad, and as we all knew Americans couldn't drink, I was confident of an early success and consequent departure from the bar in time for the usual supper time on Fridays of eight o'clock. Unfortunately, these were not normal Americans, and it was soon evident, after several calls for 'double or quits', that their claim for ownership of the bar could turn out to be totally justified, and we would have had to admit ignominious defeat on our home ground. I had a brainwave; or so it seemed at the time. 'Right', I declared in Churchillian (slurred) tones. 'Last and final round, Crème de Menthe and Crisps.'

My team looked initially quizzical, then increasingly terrified, as I ordered eight half pints of the green liqueur, and the same number of packets of crisps; salt and vinegar, I recall. The teams lined up, myself looking masterly confident, my team cursing my ancestors, and the Americans wishing they had diverted somewhere else. We started; the crisps had to be consumed first, in their packets – then the Crème de Menthe. I heaved mine down, with a clear advantage over my retching opponent. My stalwart colleagues followed suit, and with a whoop of triumph, we kicked the upstarts out of our bar towards the Gentlemen's room, where they spent the next hour turning themselves inside out. I am hazy about the next few hours, to be honest. But I vaguely recall being despatched to the spare bedroom when I got home. Mike Donaldson, always a strong team member at such times, was arrested by PC Moon, the village Bobby, for being drunk in charge of a bicycle. Les Hurst was picked up by the milkman and deposited with the usual four pints of silver-top at his house. Middy Hopper, always attentive to his wife's needs, had bought a bottle of Bacardi as a peace offering. Unfortunately, the T-junction in Coningsby village arrived quicker than he had expected, and he, the Bacardi and his Vespa ended up in a heap outside the local greengrocers. As people arrived to assist him, they found Middy wiping the blood off his face. With glee and obvious relief, he announced: 'Thank God, it's only blood. I thought it was the Bacardi.'

Thick heads, cross wives, some minor damage. But the reputation of the squadron was intact!

Mike Shaw was posted from the OCU just after halfway through my tour at Coningsby, and his place was taken by an old friend, Wing Commander John Allison; like me an ex-Lightning pilot. John was also a passionate aviator, had a grammar school background and had survived a three-year cadetship at Cranwell, graduating before I arrived.

Mike Shaw's departure initiated reporting action on his immediate subordinates, myself included. The process in those days was through 'Form 1369', which had a range of personal and professional attributes listed, along with recommendations for promotion and an assessment of future potential. Mike gave me a glowing report, including a special recommendation for promotion. Derek Bryant, as Station Commander the second reporting officer, called me to give me his assessments. Not entirely to my surprise, he advised me that he had reduced some of my overall scores and dropped me a promotion notch to highly recommended, but had left my assessment of potential as a positive one. Derek was always fascinated by command, and in his view my performance as a commander fell short of those at the top of the ladder, and he was probably right. I had only been a squadron leader for three years, had not proven myself in a challenging staff appointment, and he argued that I still needed to mature my leadership skills, especially towards the groundcrew. I thought at the time that this particular comment was unjustified, as I always went out of my way to look after the troops, but perhaps not as overtly as was needed to catch his attention. This left me with somewhat of a dilemma: should I adopt a more obviously ambitious persona, having tried since Leuchars to eliminate my tendency to look upwards, and in so doing irritate my peers; or should I maintain a lower profile in senior company and risk being underassessed? It is an eternal conundrum for those with career aspirations, and finding the right balance was a challenge.

A few weeks later, at an Officers' Mess/Sergeants' Mess Games night, a young NCO came up to speak to me. 'I've just spoken to the Station Commander, and I asked him if any of the young officers were destined for the top ranks, and he pointed to you, so I've come to see what you're like.' I looked across at Derek, but he was engrossed in conversation, or at least seemed to be. No pressure then!

I was hoping at the end of my tour at Coningsby to be selected for Staff College, but instead I was posted to the Central Tactics and Trials Organisation, based at Headquarters Strike Command's home at High Wycombe. My job, as the name suggests, was to continue the development of tactics for the fighter community and, where necessary, arrange trials to prove tactics and weapons systems. The organisation was a lodger unit at High Wycombe, so largely left undisturbed by the hierarchy in Strike Command. Led by larger-than-life Air Commodore John Pack, it was a happy and fulfilling tour, despite lacking the regular flying that remained my passion. Inevitably, Staff College followed, at the end of which I fully expected to be given command of a front line Phantom squadron, especially as I was promoted to wing commander halfway through the course, ahead of my close contemporaries. But the RAF had other plans, and I duly received a posting notice to serve in the Operational Requirements division at the MOD. Under normal circumstances this would have been considered a perfect job, working closely with industry and the front line to get the best equipment and weapons for the folk who mattered most. But there were two problems: the first was that I loathed the thought of serving in Whitehall, and the second it kept me away from flying for at least another two years, and possibly longer. Better get some flying in while you can, I thought, and leave Irene to sort out where we are going to live and the children's schooling.

Fortunately, in late October of the course we were given a few weeks off to finalise our major assignment – the Brooke-Popham Essay – which, we were told, would determine our postings and promotion prospects. As I had already received my posting and promotion, I saw no reason to give the essay any priority, so I duly dug out my flying kit and headed back to Coningsby for some serious aviation. Fully expecting to do a dual sortie and then be back to instructional duties, I was a bit peeved when on arrival I was told that the Station Commander, still Derek Bryant, had decreed that as I was officially on a ground appointment, I could only fly dual with a QFI or flight commander in the back – with his own control column. Still better than Brooke-Popham, and I could fly the station Chipmunk solo to have a bit of fun doing aerobatics.

An old friend, Dave Moss, was tasked with conducting my first refresher sortie on the Phantom. Shortly after starting up, there was a loud bang from the starboard engine, followed by frantic indications from the groundcrew that we were on fire and had better get out quickly. Welcome back to flying. Leaving the fire crews to deal with the problem we dashed across to the reserve aircraft, Dave signed for the F700, and we set off into the lovely blue sky, rolling around the clouds as we climbed into clear airspace for some general handling. Suddenly there was an 'Oh shit!' from the back seat.

'What's up, Dave?' I asked.

'When did you last fly a Phantom?' he asked.

'Oh, about a year ago, I suppose. Why do you ask?' I replied.

'There's no bloody stick in the back of this one, and I've only just noticed!'

So there we were, the captain of the aircraft without a control column and the pilot with one but so out of currency that I had virtually forgotten how to fly the aircraft.

'Best we keep quiet and just get on with it', I suggested. Dave agreed, and we landed without incident after a most enjoyable flight.

A week or so later, shortly after landing from another trip, a frantic Station Duty Officer came running up to me and said:

'Sir, the shit's hit the fan. They've discovered you're missing from Bracknell and the Commandant is going Harpic. You've got to get down and see him for a formal interview immediately.'

'Bugger', I thought, 'That's the end of real flying for a few years.'

The commandant at the time was a lovely man called Air Vice-Marshal Mike Beavis, who had been a transport pilot and was both liked and respected in the RAF. I was duly marched in to see him, hat on.

'Ah, Chris, where the hell have you been? We've been trying to find you for two days.'

'Er, Coningsby, Sir', I gulped. 'I thought I'd get some operational time in before going to my new job in the MOD.'

'Jolly good idea', he replied, to my great relief. 'But you're probably not going to MOD now. The new UK MILREP (NATO Military Representative) has just turned down two RAF candidates as his Personal Staff Officer (PSO), and he's insisting on a fighter pilot; so it's you – subject to you getting on with him, of course. You've got to be in his flat in London at six o'clock tonight. You OK on NATO facts and figures?'

'Yes, Sir', I replied, thinking that I had just a couple of hours to cram in a few facts, having slept through most of the NATO lectures, believing them irrelevant to a tour in the MOD. I dashed home, changed into my best suit with crisp white shirt and RAF tie, and shot off to Bracknell station with my course notes on NATO in a briefcase.

The designate MILREP turned out to be Admiral Sir Anthony Morton, a bachelor, who had enjoyed a stellar career in the Royal Navy, including challenging operational tours. I knocked apprehensively on his door in a block of elegant apartments in Pimlico, and was greeted by a white-haired, elderly gentleman, with a broad smile and dressed very casually.

'Wing Commander Coville, Sir', I announced.

'Ah, yes. Come in and have some tea.'

We chatted very amicably for a few minutes, at the end of which he announced that he thought we would get on very well together, and he looked forward to seeing me out in Brussels in the New Year. I left his flat reeling, but elated. At long last an overseas tour, and working for such a kindly and pleasant old man. How wrong I was!

My predecessor as the 'Executive Assistant' or EA (NATO term) to the UK MILREP was an army lieutenant colonel, Ian Townsend, who was very smart, naturally efficient and, after three years in post, fully on top of the job. I was not, as soon became apparent. The Admiral arrived a month or so before I did, and being a clever man immediately became master of his brief. Never having served in NATO, or indeed Whitehall, where cunning and duplicity are everyday tools, I was like a kid on day one at a new school. But there were immediate consolations: there were extra allowances for the 'hardship' of living in Brussels, cars were tax free (I had ordered an Audi) and booze was ridiculously cheap in the military outlets. I at once ordered a lorry-load of wine, spirits and mixers, to be delivered once Ian had left the house and Irene could join me. She, poor girl, was left with the children and the house move to sort out, while I hummed and hahed over Burgundies and Clarets.

Shortly before Ian left, he took me to a 'corridor' party at the Dutch MILREP's wing. There I met some old fighter pilot chums I had come across on a NATO exchange some years before, and they persuaded me to join them in the quaint Dutch custom of Herring and Jenever (strong gin). The herrings were pickled but uncooked, and had to be eaten whole with a large slug of Jenever 'to allow them to swim'. Nothing silly there. I was well into my fourth herring, with accompanying Jenever, when I sensed that someone was pointing a laser at the back of my head. Turning round, with the tail of a herring protruding from my mouth, I saw with dismay that the Admiral had joined the party, and as he sipped his fizzy water was looking at me with total disapproval, even disgust. I swallowed the herring and tried to recover my dignified composure, but gagged as the fish's tail, no doubt trying to swim, caught in my throat. The 'Flag Lieutenant', a Royal Navy lieutenant commander, kindly steered the old chap away to a more couth section of the corridor, and I slipped away into the night, hoping that the dawn would bring forgiveness. It did not, and I received a naval bollocking, and a stern reminder that I was there not only as a representative of the UK, but also of himself. I resolved to improve, and to make things better; but I failed miserably.

The Admiral's 'front office' comprised myself, the hitherto mentioned RN 'Flags', Rowland Raikes, and an army major, Stephen Harris, who was the newly arrived Military Assistant (MA) to the Chief of Staff (COS), a very smooth RN commodore, Ian MacGillivray. Ian had long since decided, correctly as it turned out, that he was never going to be promoted again, and several years into his second marriage was determined to enjoy Brussels to the full, without having to over-exert himself. His example was seized upon with enthusiasm by Rowland and Steve, both of whom obviously believed I was a typically driven RAF fighter pilot, who naïvely thought that a NATO assignment was somewhere to work rather than to play. It was clear from the start that I would be the whipping boy for the Admiral, who recognised that there was no point in being unduly demanding with the others. As keel-hauling, walking the plank and the lash had been outlawed in the Navy some years earlier, the Admiral had to content himself with less effective sanctions. He had a tendency to throw anything near to hand, to push people out of his way and to use incredibly salty language when he felt I had fallen short of his expectations, which was not difficult. He was occasionally a little irrational; even unhinged. On one occasion, when he was angry at a piece of work, he burst out of his office, face ablaze, demanding to know the location of 'SO Sigs'. I should have mentioned that he never used names, only positions: Chief of Staff, EA, Flags, and SO Sigs, who was the staff officer responsible for signals and security, Commander Tony Morrow. Foolishly, I replied ambiguously that Tony had 'just gone to the toilet', to which the Admiral roared, 'What do you mean, just?' I responded meekly that I meant the word in its chronological sense, which he refused to accept, and snorted that I had meant it in mitigation, and that I should never use the word 'toilet', only 'lavatory'. In the ensuing fury at my attempt to conceal a heinous felony, not to mention demonstration of my dodgy background, he threw my overflowing in-tray all over the office, and stormed back into his den.

That evening, I told Irene, who was happily unpacking into our new home on the outskirts of the city, that I didn't think I could tolerate this man's behaviour, and to my surprise she insisted that I confront him and make my position clear. The following morning, I confess with a little trepidation, I asked to see the Admiral privately, closed the door behind me and stared him in the face.

'Sir', I said, clearing my throat.

'Yes, what is it?' he snapped.

'Sir, yesterday you were not only extremely rude to me, but you made me look foolish in front of the front office, who are my subordinates and need to hold me in respect.' He looked startled. 'Another thing, Sir, my father taught me to use the word "toilet", and he is as good a man as you anytime.' The die was cast, and I was on my way back to Blighty.

'Oh', he said, looking embarrassed, 'I didn't realise I was being beastly.'

'Well, I'm afraid you were, Sir.' He nodded, I left, and while he remained irascible and sometimes downright outrageous, he never made me look foolish again.

The MILREP organisation was embedded alongside what was called the UK PERMREP delegation, comprising at the top the Ambassador to NATO, then Sir Clive Rose, with supporting cast from the MOD civil service and the Foreign and Commonwealth Office. Thus it was an interesting (in the Chinese curse sense) blend of military, civil servants and diplomats, all of whom thought they were more important than the others, and who constantly sought ways of conveying this sentiment to lesser mortals. Shortly after getting my desk sorted out, with nameplate and pictures of Lightnings and Phantoms festooned on its surface, the Executive Assistant to the Ambassador entered the office and looked sneeringly at my title: Wing Commander C. Coville BA. I asked Richard what he found so assuming, to which the spotty faced 25-year-old replied:

'I see I outrank you on both counts. I have an MA from Oxford and I am the equivalent rank of a group captain.' I counted to ten, and pointed to a model of an F4 Phantom.

'Richard,' I enquired, 'have you ever flown a Phantom supersonic at night?' He, of course, declared that he had not. 'Well', I went on, 'in which case you're not worth a shit as far as I'm concerned.' He left, his neck becoming increasingly puce by the second.

One of the problems in working for the Admiral was that, not having anyone to go home to, he saw no point in going home, and would sit in his office every night until 7.30, reading the *Times* from cover to cover. Cunning devil that I was, and no doubt encouraged by Irene's threat to nail my supper to the front door if I kept getting home late, I found a solution. Rowland had a few hundred invitation cards. There was always a cocktail party somewhere in Brussels, so we just wrote out an invitation for him whether he had been invited or not. Nobody was going to deny entry to a NATO 4-Star, even if they had any idea who was and was not invited. The consequence was that we got him out of the office at six o'clock, after which we could raid his drinks cabinet before heading off home in good time for supper at seven o'clock. Unfortunately, on one occasion he doubled back to recover something he'd forgotten, to find Rowland, Stephen and myself refilling our gins in his office; thereafter we had to buy our own sundowners.

In 1981, still at the height of the Cold War, Britain was in the financial doldrums, and the new Defence Secretary, John Nott, was charged by Margaret Thatcher to conduct a stringent Defence Review. Among its many conclusions was the substantial reduction in the RN's surface fleet, to below fifty capital ships. Looking at today's Navy, this seems like a generous settlement, but in 1981 it was considered draconian, and indeed the Navy Minister, Keith Speed, resigned in protest at what he described as savage and reckless cuts. The Admiral was a friend of Keith Speed, and was livid when the defence decisions were announced. The Petty Officer who ran his house on the fringes of Brussels phoned to warn us that 'The Admiral's in a terrible temper, Sir.' Well, the Admiral was always in a terrible temper, especially first thing in the morning, so this was obviously a seismic event. We started to batten down the hatches. Rowland had acquired a stuffed cat, which we would throw into the Boss's office, so he had something other than our hides to kick; that was appropriately deposited. A cup of tea was positioned on his mahogany desk, and the *Times* carefully opened at a neutral page, probably the Court section. It was to no avail. We heard the door at the end of the corridor opening with a bang. The poor security guard at the entrance was the first to be assaulted.

'Good morning, Admiral', he declared.

'Good morning, GOOD MORNING? You stupid man, don't you ever listen to the bloody news?' He stormed down the corridor, banging on the closed doors as he got closer. 'I know you're in there', he shouted as he passed locked offices, their incumbents cringing behind or underneath their desks. The MA, Stephen Harris, who worked for the COS, thought he was safe, and was chortling that he couldn't wait to see Rowland and I crucified ... slowly. The door burst open; there was a deathly hush as his eyes went from Rowland ... to me ... and then fixed on a smirking Stephen Harris. He leapt across the room, picking the hapless major up by his throat. 'There'll be no one to pull you out of Dunkirk, there'll be no one to get you out of the Middle East, there'll be no one to escort your tanks coming across the Atlantic'... the list went on, meanwhile Stephen was going a lighter shade of pale.

Rowland and I were thoroughly enjoying watching someone else being garrotted, on the basis that it could easily have been us. Perhaps I let my guard down, for as the Admiral threw the twitching Stephen on to the ground, he turned on me, making a lunge for my throat, and shouted/spat in my face: 'And the fucking crabs...' (affectionate RN term for the RAF) '... didn't support us either.' With that, he shoved me with a force I would never have thought possible for a man of his age, propelling me backwards in to my 'Out' tray, and causing me to roll backwards across my desk, the tray with its contents stuck firmly to my posterior.

Somehow we managed to calm the old man down during the day, not least as we needed to brief him on the forthcoming Civil-Military Exercise (CIMEX), which was one of a series designed to test the top-level decision-making processes and judgements in the Alliance. But the Admiral had other priorities. 'EA,' he shouted, 'get the Chief of Staff to come in right away. The Ambassador is going to make a statement to the North Atlantic Council Meeting this morning about these bloody idiotic cuts to the Navy, and I need to get a note out to all my MILREP colleagues when he does.' We got stuck in to getting the letters ready, got him to sign them all, and then waited and watched the clock. The North Atlantic Council (NAC) was always at 1015, so we had to get the letters out at 1030, but to observe strict protocol not a minute before. It was practically a capital offence for anything to go out to the military before the announcement had been made by the Ambassadors. At 1030 we sprang into action; by 1100 all the letters had been delivered. Feeling very pleased with myself, I was strolling back down the corridor when I met the UK Ambassador coming the other way in his shirtsleeves.

'Good morning, Sir', I stammered. 'Are you not at the NAC?'

'No, it's been delayed until this afternoon', he replied.

A fleet of large trucks drove over my grave; a grave which I would surely be occupying very soon. We had committed the cardinal sin, and I would have to die in consequence. Think … think … what can I do to get a fighting chance to live beyond today? I called in the troops.

'Help!' I announced succinctly. 'We've got to get all the letters back now or I am dead. The NAC has been postponed until this afternoon.'

'You're dead', Stephen Harris agreed helpfully.

'Scramble, now!' I ordered. Five of us shot down the corridor, pushing aside anyone who got in the way. I raced into the US MILREP's office; the letter was still there unopened. I grabbed it and raced on. The Turkish MILREP was the same; great, two out of my three recovered safely. I got to the Greek MILREP's office.

'He's reading it now', the MA shouted as I frantically went through his in-tray.

'Shit!' I ran into the general's office without knocking, grabbed the letter from his hands, mumbled an apology and made for the door. I got back to the office and was relieved to find all copies had been retrieved. I could breathe again, and start preparing the CIMEX brief.

The CIMEX always followed the same pattern: a few border incidents with the Soviet Union (SU); rising political tension; sporadic military engagements; SU mobilise full forces; nuclear forces at heightened readiness; military engagements increase, with SU troops crossing NATO borders; war declared; SU uses chemical weapons; NATO retaliates with a few tactical nuclear weapons; SU launches massive retaliatory nuclear attack; USA responds in same way; game over. It would have surprised the general public then, and indeed now, to know that it would have been NATO that started using nuclear weapons first. But in the absence of a retaliatory chemical response, and with a massive disadvantage in conventional forces, we had no other option. But at least we were thinking about deterrence and de-escalation in those days. Following the end of the Cold War, NATO has been missing several important elements of deterrence, but seems to be unaware or uninterested. Deterrence is like a ladder. Each step must be taken carefully. If one rung is missing, you need to jump a long way up to the next one, and that can be dangerous, or to a potential opponent, incredible; with all the consequent temptations to call the bluff.

The Admiral knew all this, having been a student of the 'theology' of deterrence, but he was often a lone voice among the European Nations, few of whom saw the utility of nuclear power, and several of whom would have left everything to the Americans to sort out. These nations, many of whom littered the periphery of NATO, he referred to in true salty fashion as 'The Begging Bowl Nations': quick to criticise, swift to ask for resources but very slow to provide them. We were, however, to see an event which changed the perceptions of Western resolve, at least that of the UK and the USA, in a most extraordinary way.

On 2 April 1982, Argentina invaded the Falkland Islands. Few in Brussels knew where the Islands were located, and most couldn't care less. But it was an opportunity for some to make mischief and declare the conflict the last of the colonial wars. America, initially on the fence, became a staunch ally, but others remained difficult and some duplicitous. On 5 May, we were preparing for a Military Committee meeting of Chiefs of Defence Staff (CDS), when news came through of the sinking with heavy loss of life of HMS *Sheffield*. The UK CDS, Admiral Sir Terry Lewin, was already airborne en route, and Tony Morton went to the airport to brief him in the car on the way back. CDS's reaction was extraordinary. He nodded, asked for a secure line to MOD when he arrived in the HQ, got the latest facts on *Sheffield*, and then went into a briefing in advance of his meeting the next day. Completely unruffled, despite certainly having a heavy heart, he returned for an update, asked for a whisky and spent an hour talking to the Defence Secretary, John Nott, before coming out to prepare himself for the formal dinner that evening. Throughout, he remained calm and courteous, quietly stamping his personality on the NATO meeting while ensuring he was on top of the conflict issues with Whitehall.

I have never met a more impressive man before or since; such a stark contrast to Admiral Morton, whose blood pressure throughout the tragedy in the South Atlantic was reflected in his red face, bulging eyes and irritability. The poor newly arrived Flag Lieutenant, Alan Adair, a thoroughly nice man and hard worker, was run ragged by the total unpredictability of the Admiral's moods. Alan was especially inept at handling the complex phone system, frequently cutting off MOD officers with an update on the conflict instead of putting them through to the Boss, with the inevitable outcome of an enraged 4-star emerging from his office looking for blood. But the war in a distant place, and tragic loss of life, at least reminded the Soviets of the resolve at the core of the Alliance. The message was not openly broadcast, but it was clearly received in Buenos Aires and Moscow: don't mess with us unless you're happy to get a bloody nose. That's deterrence.

When I look back on the amazing tour in the heart of NATO, it is clear to me that the Admiral was a bad fit for the job. He had a brilliant mind, which was rarely used in Brussels, which he always scorned as 'a Twentieth Century Congress of Vienna', with more attention to menus than working papers. But at times he was the one who found the way through the most difficult political issues, especially where the Greeks or Turks were concerned. He was especially disparaging about the French, who had remained in the political side of NATO, but had removed their forces from NATO Command: 'They're in the Club, but won't pay their subs', he would pronounce. When I asked him why the French seemed so anti-British, he proclaimed: 'They have never forgiven us for saving them in two world wars.' The Americans were a source of exasperation to him, partially owing to their arrogance, but mainly because he saw them as politically naïve, and unable to grasp the complexities of an alliance comprising many European nations. But he was much admired, indeed revered for his clever use of English, and his ability to achieve consensus where none seemed possible. He was a difficult Boss, it was like managing a 20lb salmon on a 5lb line. But in the end, I came to understand that he concealed a deep vulnerability, indeed perhaps even that he was suppressing hidden desires, and I became very fond of him, in the way a performing bear might of his ruthless owner. He assessed me very kindly when the time came to leave, ensuring that I achieved my ambition to command a squadron; and I was to see him later as my career progressed. But when I had finally bid him goodbye, and returned home to Irene, all the tensions I had been containing burst out, and I had an emotional release like few others in my life.

I have often reflected about my time with the Admiral. I learned a lot from him, and in many ways he was a man of immense quality. Many years later, when I was an air vice-marshal, he invited me to stay with him before an RN/RAF soccer match near his retirement home in Winchester. I told Irene that I feared I would wake up in the night with my hands around his throat, saying 'Die, you old bastard, die.' As it happened, he could not have been more charming, and we enjoyed a most pleasant evening and breakfast together.

Chapter 9

I left Brussels and NATO with a posting to command No 23(Fighter) Sqn, flying Phantoms at RAF Wattisham, in Suffolk. After such a long period on ground duties, and despite having flown the aeroplane a few times in the meantime, I needed to do a short refresher course at Coningsby to get back up to speed. Irene was pleased. Wattisham was in a nice location in Constable country, and the quarters were all large and well-maintained. The six months at Coningsby would pass quickly, and then we could look forward to the best tour of our lives. Or so we thought.

A few weeks into a most enjoyable return to flying, the station commander, Group Captain Bob Arnott, asked to see me urgently. Worried that I had been guilty of some social or aviation misdemeanour, I arrived at his door and was surprised to see him at his coffee table, not his desk; a good sign anyway.

'Come in, Chris; you'd better read this.' He handed me a signal, which in essence was deploying 23 Squadron to the Falklands as the permanent QRA force, with aircrew deploying on three-month detachments.

'Any idea what's happening to me?' I asked.

'Yes, I have just spoken to your appointing officer, and you're to go to the Falklands for six months as OC Operations Wing, before taking over Treble One Squadron at Leuchars in November.' I groaned, trying not to show it. Irene was going to be really pleased, having selected our residence at Wattisham and being overjoyed at the location and the many friends we already knew on the station. Worse, I would be away for six months, in the Antarctic winter; in short, three winters on the trot. Bloody marvellous.

'When do I have to go?' I asked.

'You've got to get to Innsworth tomorrow to pick up all your kit', Bob gulped, 'and be at Brize Norton on Sunday night to fly to Ascension Island on Monday morning. From there you get on the SS *Uganda* to sail down to the Falklands. Takes about ten days. By the way, you'll need to make sure your firearms certificates and vaccinations are up to date.' It was Wednesday.

A week later, I was being lowered by helicopter onto the back of the lovely old SS *Uganda*, where I was met by an old friend, Sqn Ldr Piers Gardiner. Piers and I had been on the International Air Cadet Exchange together in 1963. Over an amazing three weeks, we had seen some of the most beautiful parts of the USA and been hosted like royalty by many friendly American families. But we had not seen each other since, and had a lot of catching up to do. Piers was an Air Traffic Control (ATC) Officer, and was going down to be the Senior ATC Officer (SATCO) on the airfield at Stanley. He explained that as I was SBOA (Senior British Officer Afloat), I was last on the ship, and we were just about to weigh anchor and set sail. He suggested that I should get rid of my two vast RAF holdalls in my luxurious cabin, and join him and a few others for pre-lunch drinks in the bar at noon. This was more like it.

My 'cabin' turned out to be a suite, with a proper bath, although the water always seemed tinged a rusty colour. And I had a balcony overlooking the front of the ship, and a steward who would make sure my bed was made and clothes put away tidily. I discovered, on leaving my cabin, that my neighbour was a rotund army major, known as Major Dickie, who at the end of a long but largely unimpressive army career, had elected to spend the last year of service as the Ship's Commandant, trudging up and down between Ascension Island and Port Stanley, from the Tropics to the Antarctic Circle, through some of the roughest seas on the planet.

Piers already had a stiff gin and tonic ready for me, and kindly introduced me to some of the other senior (relatively) people on their way south. Most were RAF, but there was one civilian joining a merchant marine ship, and also a RN lieutenant commander engineer. The twelve of us duly took our seats in the Officers' Dining Room, where we were handed a very nice menu, and I ordered a chicken salad.

'Hmm', grunted Piers. 'That might have been a mistake. See what you think.'

Wine arrived, having been pre-ordered by Piers, who was clearly intent on making a good impression on his new boss. I always admired that quality in subordinates. There was a sudden grumbling sound from below.

'Ah', one of the sailors observed. 'That's the anchor.' Shortly afterwards, the ship started to judder as the engines fired up. We were on our way from thirty degrees centigrade to minus five. Still, everything looked very comfortable so far, and my genial companions would no doubt help the journey go swiftly. Thank you, Your Majesty, for providing such a pleasant cruise.

We started to eat. Wait a minute, the menu hadn't said 'Chicken Salad drizzled with Diesel', but there was an unmistakeable odour and taste of the engine room on the lettuce. 'Told you so.' Thanks, Piers. I pushed the salad to one side, and concentrated on the chicken and the quite reasonable Australian Shiraz. We were moving … and then it started. At first very slowly, and then with gathering momentum. We were in a large Atlantic swell, and the ship was gently rising and falling, the horizon disappearing and reappearing. Everyone smiled, but not for long. Piers was the first to go. I had never seen a man go green before; indeed, I thought it was a myth. But Piers started looking pale, then cadaverous, and slowly his cheeks started to go green. He stood up, unsteadily, his hand covering his mouth, muttering something unintelligible as he ran for the door. The others slowly followed, each heading for the security of the outside deck, where seagulls gratefully received the contents of several stomachs. In no time at all, the dining room was virtually empty, with myself and the two sailors the only survivors at our table. I looked at the six bottles of red wine on the table, and with the approval of my new matelot friends, got stuck in to making the best of a depleted gathering.

Ten days later I awoke to realise that something was different. There was no noise. I looked out of my cabin window and there was Port Stanley, shrouded in mist and low cloud. The picturesque town looked like a child's toy village, with coloured roofs and walls; but not a tree in sight. After breakfast we were given our disembarking instructions, which were quite simple: senior officers first, everyone climbs down the rope ladder, and carry all your own bags. So I was first off, down what I think is called a Jacob's ladder: 100ft down to a bobbing launch, on a slimy set of rungs, holding two massive RAF holdalls, each the size and weight of a baby elephant. I was acutely aware as I went over the side that 300 plus pairs of eyes were watching me, most hoping that the 'toff' would fall into the briny below, or worse (better?) end up in a bruised and battered heap in the boat.

Somehow, to the disappointment of the vultures above, I got down safely, and was ignominiously pulled into the launch, to await the next victims' arrivals. How we escaped without serious injury I shall never know, but in the end only two soldiers fell, probably because they were still inebriated from the last night of cheap booze.

The main base on the Falklands was RAF Stanley, which had been converted from the small airfield that serviced the many small outposts around the two islands, East and West Falkland. Additionally, there was a HQ unit in the town, several radar stations, a helicopter base at the oddly named Kelly's Garden and a relief landing ground (RLG) at Goose Green for the Harriers. The tiny base was crammed, with massive demountable hangars and working areas, several large tents and metal containers connected together as needed for working accommodation. It looked, and was, a shambles, with deep, rutted mud everywhere. Everyone wore combat kit, heavy windproof jackets and boots. This was early winter and the first snows had already fallen. But it was the wind that made the first impression, and explained the absence of trees. It was exhausting, and some found the climate difficult and even intimidating. One minute it could be calm and sunny, with stunning visibility; minutes later it could be blizzard conditions. The most dangerous scenario for the aviators was an easterly wind, which could bring in deep, impenetrable sea fog from the cold Atlantic. It was a nightmare for the meteorological officers (Met Men), who were usually civilians but were given reserve officer status in the Falklands. Despite all the best scientific equipment available at their disposal, they were often caught out by the fickle nature of the local weather, and that could mean loss of lives and aircraft.

The accommodation ranged from tents, to floating 'hotels' (Coastels) and to a ship anchored in Port Stanley – the MV *Rangatira*, a rust bucket manned by Liverpudlians, some of whom had come down with me on the *Uganda*. As they had been totally inebriated for ten days, it was not surprising to discover that the ship only sailed once every six months, and then only when the weather was calm and the swell gentle. We suspected that it went out to empty its bilge and excrement, as it rarely stayed at sea for more than a few hours. The poor unfortunates who resided on her had to endure a ten minute transit each morning and evening, sometimes in atrocious weather. Fortunately, I was in the Coastel, which resembled a cheap motel on a large barge. But it was a haven compared with the other options, and unlike all the other officers, the station commander and I had our own rooms, with a tiny en suite shower. While I was settling in, there was a knock on the door, and I was greeted by my predecessor, Wg Cdr Forbes Pearson, an F4 navigator I had met before. He looked exhausted and had aged in post; barely four months in his case. Together, we drove in an ancient Land Rover down to the operational area, where it was clear a flap was developing. The Station Commander, Gp Capt Pat King, was already in the operations room in the old Air Traffic tower, and he looked worried. 'Argies airborne and heading this way,' he announced. I had not expected this so soon. Forbes spoke to the 'Master Controller' on Mt Kent radar, Sqn Ldr Gerry Dinmore.

'We'd better launch QRA', he suggested. Pat King nodded, and the order was given over the telebrief system to the aircrew.

'QRA, come to cockpit readiness.' Out of sight to us, the two pilots and their navigators raced out to the fully armed Phantoms.

'Q1 cockpit readiness.'

'Q2 cockpit readiness.'

'Roger, Q1 and Q2 Scramble, Scramble, Scramble.' The Ops controller responded immediately. 'Possible hostiles approaching the FIPZ', (Falkland Islands Protection Zone – a 200-mile circle). 'You are to intercept and report.'

We could hear the distant rumble of the mighty Spey engines starting up, shortly followed by a progressive roar as the two aircraft took off, reheat blazing. A few minutes later, one of the two Hercules tanker aircraft started up and took off, to support the Phantoms if necessary. Pat King nodded to me.

'Welcome to the Falklands, Chris.'

'Thanks, Sir', I replied. 'Looks like I'm going to be busy.' He smiled.

Thirty minutes later, the hostiles turned away, just short of the FIPZ, and the Phantoms duly returned to Stanley, followed some thirty minutes later by the tanker.

'Forbes, bring Chris to my office and we'll have a coffee.'

Pat was an ex-Hunter, Swift and Harrier pilot, having recently commanded RAF Wittering, the home of the Harrier. He was immensely popular, well-respected and fun to work with. He confessed that he knew nothing about Air Defence, and although we were to share the Duty Air Defence Commander (DADC) task, if anything serious happened he would call for me and hand over command. The DADC slept on the airfield, actually at the end of the Station Commander's Portakabin. The loo and washroom were a short walk away in the old Control Tower.

'I'll leave Forbes to show you around', Pat added. 'But do come in again tomorrow when you feel you know the lie of the land.'

'I'll show you ATC and Ops first', Forbes suggested. We were joined by a cheerful-looking Flight Sergeant, Jim Patel, who had been on the *Uganda* with me. He was looking very efficient, with a clipboard and a massive bunch of keys. I was introduced to the ATC and Ops staff, and was shown the cramped DADC console, where I would spend a few anxious moments in the coming months. As we were leaving the Ops block, I noticed a steel door in a dark corner, heavily padlocked.

'What's that, Forbes?' I enquired. He shook his head.

'Don't bother; dangerous stuff.' I nodded my understanding.

After a whistle-stop tour of my fascinating new command – Hercules, Phantoms, Harriers, Helicopters and Rapier missile – Forbes headed for the airbridge, the daily Hercules back to Ascension, which would be followed by a VC10 transport aircraft back to Brize Norton and home. I went back to the Ops area, where Jim Patel was waiting with his bunch of keys. After having to find our way past three separate padlocks, we eventually opened the creaky door and put on the light. And oh what a wonderful sight! Stacked to the roof were cases of Wray and Nephew 126 per cent overproof rum; most in litre bottles, a few cases of miniatures. Alongside were boxes of quality biscuits, gourmet tea, coffee and cocoa. The rum had been confiscated by the Liverpool Port police and sent down for 'our boys in the South Atlantic'; the rest was a gift from the *Sun* newspaper. 'Jim', I instructed, 'put a case of the miniatures under the DADC's bed; keep the rest secure. We are going to remove this dreadful temptation from this station over the next six months.'

I headed back to the Coastel, bumping my way gingerly through mud, potholes and rocks. Better check the bar out, I thought. It was hopping, mainly thanks to the Phantom and Harrier Detachment boys (no girls in fast-jets in those days). Several old friends came out to greet me, including Harry Jones, who had served with me as the squadron QFI on 43 Squadron. He very kindly gave me a stiff Gin and Tonic for 'looking after my missus', his feisty wife Adrienne, who lived close to us at Coningsby. The Phantom squadron Boss at the time was Wg Cdr Pete Langham, who I had known before at Leuchars, but also during my cadet days at Cranwell. My first question to him, of course, was how quickly I could start flying with them. He asked two questions: when did you last fly a Phantom – a two weeks ago – and did you bring your flying kit – Yes. 'OK', he replied, 'you can do a check ride with a navigator tomorrow; just get used to the islands and the rather unusual runway approach here.'

What Peter meant was that the runway, which was metallic planking laid over the original concrete, was only 2,000 yards long; much shorter than the usual minimum, requiring every landing to be into the cable, rather like an aircraft carrier. I now had something to look forward to, but I had to check my plan out first with Pat King, who was down at the airfield as DADC. I needn't have worried. By the time I got down there he had discovered the rum, laced his coffee with a generous portion, and was in very good humour.

'That's great, Chris', he slurred gently. 'You fill your boots.' I did.

The following morning, as the sun was rising alongside Mt Kent, I put both reheats in and accelerated down the metal runway. It felt very different, with a sponginess and an awareness of several bumps and lumps as we roared off the ground, very close to the end of the airfield. A magical view opened up, of Port Stanley harbour, with mountains in the background, and visibility rarely found in the UK. As we soared up towards the clouds, the constant pressure of the acceleration pressing into our backs, I rolled several times, relishing the sheer joy of flying again, and in such a stunning location. My navigator, Ian Cassely, commented:

'Yes, Sir, it's quite something else, isn't it?' He sensed my spiritual awareness, a deeply sensual thrill of being up in a world known only to a lucky few.

It was customary for the first flight of the day to 'beat up' the radar station at Mt Kent, where the poor souls were incarcerated for months on end, often unable to get down the rocky road to Stanley owing to heavy falls of snow. I lined up the large radar dome of the station, dropping a wing in salute as we roared across at treetop height – if there had been any trees, that is. A group of heavily clad figures, looking like miniature Michelin men, had braved the freezing wind to give us a wave as we flew past. Like most aspects of RAF life, building team spirit, acknowledging the massive contribution of the others involved in all levels of the mission, was a vital part of leadership. It wasn't just the aircrew, but a whole range of trades, branches and skills that had enabled us to fly that morning; and dipping a wing in salute was the minimum but important recognition by we fortunate ones to those who made it all possible. The radio crackled into life.

'Nice one, Sir, many thanks.' I recognised the voice.

'Pleasure, Gerry.'

Sometimes the personal touch had to take precedent over the usual strict radio procedures.

I rolled inverted, and pulled the nose down towards the plain below. This was a familiarisation sortie, so we flew around the islands, visiting names made famous by the conflict the previous year: Goose Green, Bluff Cove, Mt Longdon, Port San Carlos, which was the base for the initial amphibious landing of UK troops. Not for the first time, I experienced dishonourable and illogical envy for those who had been involved in these famous scenarios; I was, after all, a fighter pilot. After an hour we met up with one of the Hercules tankers and another Phantom, which was already refuelling. I had only before refuelled from large jet aircraft, so this was very different. For a start it was much slower: around 230 knots rather than 300 plus. It also needed to be lower, as the Hercules was fairly limited in its refuelling operating height. The single basket came out of a drum mounted at the rear of the aircraft, and fuel was provided by a large bladder tank in the main fuselage area. It was a typically Heath Robinson British modification, but a great tribute to the ingenuity and agility of our aerospace companies. I took on a few thousand pounds of fuel, which enabled us to conduct a couple of interesting low-level interceptions with the other fighter, before setting off back to Stanley.

As I mentioned earlier, the short runway required each landing to be into the cable, or I should have said *a* cable, as there were five on the runway – two at each end and one in the middle. As part of the normal downwind checks, I dropped the hook down and made sure my harness was tight and locked, and started my finals turn at 175 knots, blinking as I flew over an incredibly bright strobe light on short finals. As going round again was not an option, as you might catch a wire and drag it airborne, at about 50ft I operated the brake parachute, ensuring that it deployed fully by touchdown, minimising the ground roll just in case the hook failed to engage a wire. It did, and we were brought to an abrupt halt. Following a very slick procedure with a ground party, the cable was reset, and we taxied back to the Phantom dispersal. Bloody marvellous!

After the debrief, I was enjoying a cup of coffee with the aircrew when one of them mentioned a problem with the strobe light on the approach. Strobes were being used extensively on USAF airfields, and had been found to be especially effective in poor visibility. Unfortunately, the one at Stanley was, to put it mildly, of the unsophisticated variety, being a massive light on a long pole just before touchdown. As I had just experienced, in good weather it could be a distraction, and I was told that at night it was dazzling and even disorientating. Apparently, turning it off would cause problems with firing it up again.

'Why don't we paint it to reduce the glare at night?' I asked. No one could give a good answer. 'OK', I said, 'we'll fix that today.'

'What about the dazzle in daytime, Sir', someone asked. 'Even painting it won't fix that problem. We need to turn it off, but find a way to get it back on quickly if the weather suddenly changes – which it does here often!'

'We'll put a mail bag over it, and ATC can pull it off when you need it,' I replied.

They all looked astonished, but I spoke to my deputy, Sqn Ldr Dave Vass, and he fixed it that day. The new technologies worked perfectly. I had risen in status and esteem, thanks to a pot of paint and a mail bag!

The HQ in Stanley was run by an army major general, known as the Commander British Forces Falkland Islands (CBFFI). He and the Governor, Sir Rex Hunt, were jointly responsible for representing HM Government's interests on the Islands. The general's wife, a most charming and caring person who took her community responsibilities very seriously, would often come down to chat to us all, raising morale and making us feel special. Unfortunately, she had a rather pronounced lisp, which on one occasion nearly caused Pat King to burst a blood vessel. Having advised us that she would be dropping in to our Ops room for a cup of tea and a chat, I charged Flight Sergeant Patel with breaking out some Earl Grey tea and posh biscuits from the Aladdin's Cave. The dear lady was watching aircraft taking off, enjoying her tea, when Pat asked her if she was going straight home after seeing us, as the weather was closing in. 'Oh, no, Pat', she replied cheerily, 'I'm going to have tea with the other wanks.'

Fortunately, I was standing behind her, but Pat was not so lucky. He first went red, then his shoulders started to shudder; eventually his face started to go purple. I had just managed to get myself under control, so was able to come to the rescue, steering her towards 'a most interesting group' of somewhat bemused air traffic controllers. Later that night, Pat and I took it in turns to mimic her in the bar.

'Would you like another beer, Sir?'

'Will you be in Church on Sunday, Chris?'

Many different questions, but always the same answer:

'No, I'm going to have tea with the other wanks.' Most unchivalrous, I know, especially as this much-loved lady was a force for good in what was in many respects a dehumanising environment. But humour has an important place at such times too, and a good belly-laugh can work wonders for morale.

Life in the Falklands, especially in the winter, was arduous. The constant wind, rapid changes in weather and lack of privacy were especially burdensome, but the mud could get you down most. There weren't any real roads on the site, just rutted mud everywhere. We ate during the day in the SAS detachment, which turned out not to be manned by muscular heroes, but was in fact the Soup and Sandwich detachment. The absolute priority for morale was the quality of the food, which was generally very good, but a close second was the mail, which arrived sporadically on the daily Hercules airbridge. Sometimes there was none, because other priorities prevailed. But even when there was none, the flight manifest would show 1lb of mail, just to keep hopes alive. On one occasion, the weather was appalling, with driven snow and a ferocious crosswind. Reluctantly, I ordered the airbridge to return to Ascension, before it reached the halfway point. The following day, instead of the double amount of mail, there was just the minimum of 1lb. Rumours started to fly. I went into SAS Detachment for my evening meal, and went to sit with the fire crews, as I often did. To my surprise, they stood up and left me sitting by myself. When I went to collect my food in my mess tins, the usually bubbly steward slopped a half portion into my tins, glaring at me as he did so. By the time I got to the pudding, a surly corporal told me it was off. Feeling somewhat aggrieved, not to mention even threatened by all this carry on, I pulled the mess sergeant to one side and asked him why I was being sent to Coventry, ignored and starved.

'Well, Sir', he replied, 'everyone's 'eard about the airbridge, an' you orderin' it to throw the mail overboard to make sure it could get back to Ascension.' I was being castigated for what today would be called 'fake news'! The following day, the mail caught up and I was exonerated, but only after having endured two days of mutterings and vitriol.

One of the challenges of operating in the Falklands in 1983 was the fickle weather. Under normal circumstances, aircraft fly with a couple of diversion options, to cover unexpected changes in cloud base, visibility or wind strength. This was not possible in the Falklands, at least not for the Phantoms; the Harriers, with their vertical landing capability, could divert to a few prepared strips on the Islands. There were a few possibilities for the fighters, but they involved extremely long transits and uncertain reception on arrival. Worse, all weapons would have to be jettisoned into the sea; that was four Skyflash, four Sidewinders and a gun – total cost to the taxpayer over £6 million. As normally the aircraft flew in pairs, that meant over £12 million would sink gently to the bottom of the South Atlantic. Accordingly, we always flew with a Hercules tanker, just to make sure the Phantoms could hold off for several hours to allow weather to improve, or in extremis to divert, with all the above costs. One day I was watching the swirling fog outside my office window, the occasional patch of blue breaking through. The Duty aircrew officer, Chris Hull, knocked on my door.

'Good morning, Sir.' I nodded and smiled. 'The wind is coming round to the west and the Met Man is forecasting good weather for the rest of the day. I'd like to launch two F4s and a tanker now, if that's OK with you.'

I went out onto the roof of ATC, and for sure the windsock was moving towards the east, and occasionally it would twitch and flop. To the north and east, I could still see banks of fog, lurking and waiting to sweep back in on an easterly wind. I went down to talk to the Met Man myself. He was adamant that the change would be stable, and a brisk westerly wind would send all the mist, fog and low cloud out to the east. I went back to ATC, where Chris Hull was on the phone to his Boss. Pete Langham asked to speak to me.

'What's the problem?' he asked abruptly. 'Why are we still on hold?'

I looked again at the windsock; it seemed to be steadying on a westerly wind, and the sky was clearing.

'Pete, I want to give it another hour to be sure this clearance isn't a blip.' Pete uttered an unmentionable expletive, suggesting I was lacking in moral fibre, not to mention questionable parentage.

'Well, I'm bloody well launching anyway', he declared.

'No you're not,' I replied. 'The airfield is closed until I say otherwise.' I noticed Piers Gardener nod; his air traffickers would not give permission to taxi or take off. The phone was slammed down. A couple of minutes later, Pat King appeared.

'Pete Langham's been on the phone, saying you're stopping him flying.'

'That's right, Sir', I replied. 'There's a lot of fog still out there, and I've just got this feeling…' Pat nodded. A few minutes later, the sun was breaking through. Chris Hull had obviously taken another angry phone call.

'Sir, I really can't see why we can't fly now; it's clear blue sky out to the west.'

'Chris', I said sternly, 'I told you, we would wait one hour!' He retreated to the ATC tower, where I could see him on the phone, his face getting very red. Poor chap; he was the fall guy between two wing commanders. My phone rang again; knowing it was Pete Langham, I ignored it. The next thing I heard was two Phantoms starting up on their nearby dispersal. Piers raced in.

'I've got OC 23 calling for taxi; what do I do.' This was getting silly.

'Tell him to hold, the airfield is closed.' Piers dashed back to ATC. The sky above was clear blue, with the weak winter sun brightening up the surrounding landscape. I flipped on the radio on my desk, just in time to hear an angry voice declaring that he was bloody well keeping the engines running until 'that idiot' saw sense. This was not only silly, but getting personal. Then something quite unexpected happened. The windsock slowly sagged, drooping and flapping in a softening breeze. We all watched. It kicked a couple of times … stopped … kicked again, then moved gradually round in a light easterly wind, lifting progressively as the wind increased. In minutes the airfield was enveloped again in fog, but this time even more dense, swirling in the strengthening breeze. I heard the Phantoms close down their engines. Chris Hull came in, looking sheepish.

'I've just spoken to the Met Man, Sir. He doesn't know why this has happened, but he says the temperature's dropping, and the fog is in until tomorrow morning.'

'OK, Chris', I acknowledged. 'Learned a lesson?'

'I have, Sir', he replied. 'Thanks a lot for that.'

Pat King called:

'Well done, Chris. That could have been a bit nasty.'

I heard nothing from Pete Langham.

I mentioned earlier the lumps and bumps I had experienced on the runway during my first take-off at Stanley. The biggest bump was the one right in the middle, when the aircraft was doing about 120 knots – and it was getting worse. This particular bump was the result of the first, very successful, attack on the airfield by a Vulcan bomber. A great success at the time, but an infernal use for future operations, as the 1,000 lb bomb used had dug a large crater which, despite being filled with hardcore, needed to be repacked regularly to avoid a Phantom one day disappearing into the

Cadet Sgt Coville – age 17 – with PPL already! Chipmunk, RAF Woodvale, 1962.

Chipmunk again – 40 years later, flying Air Cadets.

Left: Flt Cadet Coville, 91 Entry Cranwell 1964 – age 19.

Below: No.5(F) Squadron, Binbrook, 1969. Left to right: Vic Lockwood, Me, Ali McKay, and Tony Alcock. Mk.6 Lightning as a backdrop.

Above left: On Instrument Rating Examiners' Course, RAF Coltishall, 1970. Self and Ron Shimmons with Lightning T5.

Above right: The fateful Phantom 4-ship 43(F) Squadron before Jack Hamill's ejection. Myself No.2 in echelon starboard.

Argentinian Lockheed Electra, Falkland Islands, 1983. Photo taken from 23(F) Squadron Phantom.

Above left: 1,000 hours F4 flight, August 1983, 23(F) Squadron, RAF Stanley, Falkland Islands. Left to right: Gp Capt Pat King, Flt Lt Phil Williamson, self, Wg Cdr Pete Langham.

Above right: OC Treble One Squadron, Leuchars, 1984. Phantom FG1.

OC Treble One Squadron, Leuchars, crew room.

Right: Arrival as OC RAF
Coningsby, October 1986.
Irene and myself.

Below: First Hurricane IIC
flight, 4 June 1987.

With HRH The Princess
Margaret, RAF Coningsby,
1987.

Above left: After BBMF public display clearance, 15 June 1987.

Above right: Collecting 100th RAF Tornado F3 from Bae Warton, 22 June 1988.

Right: Solo again on Jet Provost, March 1990, RAF Cranwell, as Air Cdre Flying Trg.

Below: Flying with the Red Arrows, June 1994.

Flying with the Red Arrows, June 1994.

Hawk T Mk. IA landing in Greenland on way back from USA, 19 June 1991.

Above and below: Su 29 'Flanker' flight, August 1991.

Left: With Irene and General A. Antoshkin, Soviet Air Force.

Below: Mirage 2000 Flight with Gen. J.G. Brevot FAF.

Debriefing with Gen. Brevot – 'Oh no I didn't'.

Departure ceremony from NATO HQ Brunssum, 27 February 2001.

Farewell from Gen. J. Spiering, C in C North, 27 February 2001.

Knighthood, March 2000.

Right: After Knighthood, March 2000. Left to right are Nicky, Self, Irene, Peter, Theresa.

Below: After public display authority with Red Arrows 2002. Irene on the wing.

Left: April 2003, after graduation parade at RAF College Cranwell.

Below: May 2003, farewell dinner as C in C Personnel and Training CMD. Self – Ali McKay – ACM Sir John Allison, Coreen McKay.

Rogues Reunited: Ali McKay, George Black, Self.

Author in Spitfire Mk.II on 25 June 1988, formating on BBMF Lancaster from Manchester to Woodford.

Flying a Lightning Mk.3 on 26 June 1973 – my last Lightning sortie.

Spitfire Mk.II.

A Happy BBMF Pilot!

ground. The trouble was that this required the airfield to be closed down for up to twelve hours while the Royal Engineers (RE or Sappers) lifted the metallic planking and refilled the sinking crater. Had the Argentinians chosen that moment to wreak revenge on the Brits, we would have had very little response other than the short-range Harriers and the Rapier SAM. The only answer was to wait for the worst possible weather, when an attack would have been highly unlikely to succeed, and send the 'Sappers' out in the rain, fog or snow to do their work.

I looked out of my window early one June morning on to the airfield, and could hardly see ten yards. The snow was being driven by a 50 knot wind, the windsock stretching out like a Giraffe's neck. I had spoken to the Met Man earlier, and it was obvious that this weather would stay for at least twenty-four hours; perfect for getting the boys from the RE to sort out the crater problem. Suddenly my buzzer went. It was Pat King, as Duty Air Defence Commander.

'Chris, could you come here quickly; there's activity.'

That could only mean one thing. I raced across to Ops, where Pat had the Master Controller at Kent on the loud speaker.

'Yes, Sir', Gerry Dinmore announced, 'It looks like a flight of Mirages and a tanker; they're holding about fifty miles west of the FIPZ.'

'What's the weather like at Cara Cara?' I asked.

'It looks OK', Gerry replied. This was a problem. The new radar (callsign Cara Cara) on the western fringes was obviously vulnerable to attack, and it looked as though something could happen at a time when flying from Stanley was impossible. Or was it? The Argentinians would know that Stanley was in a blizzard, and might have calculated that we could not respond to an attack to the west. Pat looked at me: '

'Chris, what do we do?' I knew exactly what to do.

'Are you happy for me to take control, Sir?' He nodded gratefully.

'OK, I recommend you call the general and warn him now.'

I picked up the phone and called QRA. Harry Jones answered.

'Harry, you know about the threat. I plan to bring two aircraft to cockpit readiness soon, but I will only launch if there's a threat to Stanley, not Cara Cara. Make sure you brief the crews to minimise radio chatter; the Argies will be listening. If I issue a scramble order, Q are to hold at the take off point until they get a direct order from me, and no one else, to get airborne.'

'Got it, Sir', he replied.

Pat had an open line to the Commander in the HQ, who had hurried to his Ops Room.

'What are the chances of recovering the aircraft if we respond?' the general asked. Pat looked at me. I leaned towards the phone.

'I daren't risk getting a tanker airborne, General; I will only scramble QRA if there is a risk to Stanley, but I want the Argentinians to hear that we are prepared to launch. It might stop an attack on Cara Cara.'

'But what will happen to the aircrew?' the general asked again.

I replied as bluntly as I could:

'Without the tanker they will not be able to divert, so they will either have to try an approach here or eject. In either case, they will almost certainly be killed.' The penny dropped.

'Are you telling me that we could lose two aeroplanes and four men?' he spluttered.

'Exactly, Sir', I replied. 'May I suggest that Alan Cushman stays on the line?' Alan was a fellow wing commander at the HQ, and knew both the risks and the complexity of my forthcoming decision. He would let me get on with it. I felt totally calm and in control, but I could see that many of my colleagues were not. 'Lee', I called out to one of the Ops staff, 'Two cups of tea for myself and the Station Commander, please.' It helped.

The buzzer from Mt Kent sounded. I picked up the handset. 'Evening, Gerry, I am now DADC.'

'Thank God', he replied. 'Just heard from Cara Cara; they seem to be heading inbound towards them.' I explained the plan to Gerry, then raised my voice:

'Bring QRA to cockpit readiness.'

The Ops Officer called the Phantom dispersal.

'QRA to cockpit readiness.' Harry Jones acknowledged. Five minutes later, they checked in on the radio.

'Q1 cockpit readiness.'

'Q2 cockpit readiness.'

I picked up the microphone.

'Roger, Q1 and Q2, Sitrep,' (Situation Report) 'potential hostiles to the west; expect scramble shortly.' They acknowledged. I could only imagine the feelings in their cockpits, as they waited for me to decide whether they were going to live or die. Gerry Dinmore called, alarm in his voice.

'Cara Cara have reported high speed, low-level contacts to the west, range fifty miles.'

'Roger,' I replied. 'QRA Scramble, Scramble, Scramble.'

We heard their engines starting up, although the snow was too heavy to see them. The snow-clearing team, pretty ineffective in such conditions, raced off the runway. Slowly, the Phantoms slithered around the short perimeter track towards the take off point. They lined up and waited.

'Gerry, what's happening?' I asked.

'Just heard from Cara Cara; they've turned away and the tanker appears to have returned to base', he replied excitedly. I gave it fifteen minutes to be sure, then told the QRA aircraft to close down their engines; they would be towed back to dispersal.

Four very relieved young men retreated back into the warmth of their QRA accommodation. I winked at Pat and he smiled back. We would never know for sure if the low-level contacts were just a computer glitch combined with understandable apprehension, but the main formation certainly was for real; and they dispersed shortly after QRA was scrambled. One up to the Brits. With the early night soon closing in, and the weather getting even worse, we could now get the poor Sappers on the runway.

A few hours later, the Sappers were furiously re-laying the metal planking. It was after midnight, and they had been working in blizzard conditions for nearly seven hours. I waited until they had finished, making sure I was seen to be enduring the atrocious conditions as well, before gathering them round. 'Many thanks, gentlemen', I said through chattering teeth. 'You are an essential part of our operations here. I've brought you some hot coffee.' Looking only mildly interested, the soldiers trooped round the back of my Land Rover, and started to pour cups of hot coffee from a large urn into paper cups. But suddenly the grim looks on their faces were transformed into wide grins, as the icicles on their noses and eyebrows melted away. The 'coffee' had been generously laced with the overproof rum, and at least in terms of their perceptions, the Antarctic snow gave way to beautiful, warm Caribbean sunshine.

One of the assets available to the Argentinians was an old Lockheed Electra aircraft, converted to conduct electronic surveillance operations. One afternoon, Gerry Dinmore called me. There were indications that the Electra had come inside the FIPZ that morning, probably sniffing around to gather up radar frequencies from Cara Cara.

'We picked up about fifteen minutes of a radar contact about 120 miles west', he announced, 'Going too slowly to be a combat aircraft. By the time we had realised what it was, it had turned away.'

'OK', I said, 'I'll speak to Alan Cushman, but if it happens again, we'll scramble QRA.'

He agreed. I advised Alan, who said he would mention it to the general, and in the meantime we would take a look at our Rules of Engagement for non-combat aircraft.

The following morning, Alan Cushman phoned me.

'Chris, don't ask any questions; get QRA airborne and get them to the western edge of the FIPZ ASAP.'

I picked up the Ops phone; Pete Langham was Q1 pilot.

'Pete, we might have some trade, but you must go under silence procedures. Scramble as soon as you can. Happy?'

Pete agreed and went off to brief the other crews that radio was not to be used; we would use red and green lights as required from the tower.

We saw the fully armed aircraft taxiing out. I nodded to Piers who shone a large green light at them. One at a time, they entered the runway, engaged full reheat and took off, without a word spoken. I phoned Alan in the HQ:

'You'd better get the general in, Alan; we might need some high-level decision making.'

'He's on his way', Alan replied.

The Hercules tanker was just getting airborne as Pat King rushed into the Ops room. I gave him the three-minute brief, and he seemed quite content to leave me running the show.

'Rules of Engagement?' he asked. I nodded towards the open manual on the desk. He spent the next ten minutes reading them. The line to HQ buzzed. It was the general.

'What do we do if he refuses to turn away?' he asked.

'It's not straightforward, Sir,' I replied helpfully. 'We do have a few options. But we should be ready for the worst case scenario, which is that we have to shoot him down.'

'My God', he replied. 'Is that a possibility?'

'I hope we can do everything to avoid it', I responded, 'but if we judge him a threat to our people or equipment, we have to consider our sovereign right of self-defence. On the other hand, if he keeps coming towards Stanley, he could be defecting.' The general went quiet.

'Who decides whether or not we shoot him down?' he asked.

'As things stand, you do, General, unless you delegate to us.' To his credit, he decided not to.

An hour later, the Phantoms refuelled and went back on patrol; nothing had been seen, and we were beginning to wonder why Alan Cushman had been so sure of his intelligence. Then Gerry Dinmore piped up.

'Stanley Ops, Zombie Zero One, radar contact twenty miles outside the FIPZ, heading east, 20,000ft.' That had to be him. A Zombie was an unidentified, potentially hostile aircraft. If he came inside the FIPZ, he would be allocated an X-Ray tag – a confirmed hostile. I had never seen one before, and I could feel my blood racing. The Phantoms headed towards him, planning an interception on his projected track, which would take him inside the FIPZ in six minutes. We all waited, the atmosphere in the room tense. On the plotting board, the Ops clerk had put the unknown's position, with the Zombie callsign. The radio burst back into life; it was Gerry.

'X-Ray Zero One has entered the FIPZ; confirmed hostile.' I had to remind everyone to calm down.

'Total professionalism from everyone, please.' I reported the designation of hostile to the general, who was obviously starting to realise the implications of the next few minutes.

What a surprise the Electra crew must have had when two full-armed Phantoms appeared from nowhere on his wing. Pete Langham broke radio silence for the first time:

'Q1 confirm Argentinian Electra.' He then went through the agreed, international recognised procedures to get the Electra to turn away, including calling him on the emergency radio frequency. But the Electra kept coming. I turned to the Station Commander. 'I recommend firing the gun alongside him. He'll see the tracer rounds and know we mean business.' He nodded. I relayed this to the general, who agreed. Pete Langham flew right next to the Electra, making sure he was in a position where the aircraft captain could see him easily, and fired a two-second burst on his SUU-23A Gatling gun. Two hundred rounds of high explosive shells, every seventh shell a tracer round, streamed out in front of the Electra. He immediately turned, heading back towards Argentina.

We all sighed with relief, but some unworthy souls were quietly disappointed that the incident had ended as it did. If you select and train people to be warriors, you shouldn't be surprised when they want to taste blood. This, of course, is the very essence of the military code: aggression must be encouraged, but strong discipline is essential to constrain behaviour.

The Falklands tour was fascinating, not least because it was intensely operational, in a challenging environment at work and domestically. I hadn't spoken to Irene in over five months, the only contact being through the blue aerogramme; and I missed my children, Peter, Nicky and Theresa very much. The weather could be treacherous, but also exhausting, especially the wind. Living and working in cold and mud was too much for some people, but the majority got on with it, and the companionship was like no other I had experienced. But it was a dangerous place to fly; a few weeks after I left, Flt Lts John Gostick and Jeff Bell were killed when their Phantom flew into the summit of Mt Usborne in cloud. Many other aircrew lost their lives later, often in bad weather and at night. But as I climbed into the Hercules airbridge on the long journey home, I felt a sense of loss, and a realisation that I was leaving a very special place, where I had enjoyed superb flying and made many friends. It had certainly sharpened my leadership skills, which I knew I would need to display in no small measure as I took command of my squadron. I couldn't wait.

THE SENIOR
COMMAND YEARS

'Tout Homme qui s'eleve, s'isole.'

The French Journalist and Writer, Antoine de Rivarol,
1753–1801

Chapter 10

Treble One, or more correctly CXI(Fighter) Squadron, was one of the most famous in the RAF. As well as a distinguished history in the Second World War, the squadron had formed the Black Arrows aerobatic team, well known for its displays in black Hunter aircraft. The squadron to this day still holds the record for the greatest number of aircraft flown in a loop; no less than twenty-two at Farnborough in 1958. I was going to command an elite unit, equipped in 1983 with the F4 Phantom FG1, and based at RAF Leuchars, in Fife, Scotland.

After a bit of leave, and Irene getting used to me being under her feet again, we set off for Leuchars late in 1983. The Station Commander was an old friend, Gp Capt Tim Elworthy, and the 'rival' squadron, my old one No 43, was commanded by Tony Bagnall. That was bound to turn out to be an interesting combination! Treble One were flying the FG1 version of the Phantom; the aircraft, as with 43 Sqn, were ex-RN Fleet Air Arm, designed for carrier operations. This gave them some engine and airframe modifications, which enabled slower approach speeds, and a degree more manoeuvrability prior to landing. But in every other respect, it was no different to the other Phantoms I had flown. Perhaps this made me a little complacent, and in consequence during my operational refresher, I came within feet of meeting my Maker, and taking a young navigator with me to the Pearly Gates ... or wherever.

I was flying with Ian 'Topo' Morrison, a first-tour navigator who had made excellent progress and had been declared recently as Combat Ready. Flying as number two to Flt Lt Mike Wilkinson, we had a successful sortie of air interceptions, before returning to base. It was clear during the recovery, however, that the weather had deteriorated rapidly, with low cloud and driving rain, and after taking a quick look at the options, we diverted to Lossiemouth, some seventy miles north on the Moray Firth. After an overnight stay, we set off for Leuchars, briefing to do some radar interceptions on the way back. As the cloud base was extremely low, Mike briefed a thirty-second radar stream take-off, on the south westerly runway, with us catching him up in the climb. Shortly after lifting off, there was a panicky call from air traffic for us to level off at 1,000ft, as a Nimrod Maritime Patrol Aircraft from nearby Kinloss had just made a late call that he was approaching Lossiemouth overhead at 2,000ft. Raising the undercarriage and flaps, I levelled off as directed and accelerated to 400 knots. We were in thick cloud. Suddenly the low-level warning light illuminated, Topo screamed 'Pull up', and I yanked the stick back into a steep climb. As we emerged from the cloud, there was high ground either side of us. When we came to look at the maps later, it was obvious that we had flown down a narrow valley, surrounded by mountains. Just a few degrees either side of track and we would have been vaporised.

So how did such an incident, so nearly a fatal accident, occur at an RAF airfield, with experienced people involved in a catalogue of errors? For a start, we hadn't done our 'what ifs' (these days a Risk Assessment) as part of our briefing. First, we had assumed that we would just take off and climb to height. Unlike most of the other airfields from which I had flown, departing from Lossiemouth on the south-westerly runway took you immediately towards high ground. Second, the air traffic controller made a near-fatal mistake in levelling us at a height that could well have killed us; and third, the Nimrod left it far too late to advise Lossiemouth of his height and location. Add this to my lack of recent flying, and all the ingredients were there for a disaster.

So what saved us? In simple terms, it wasn't our time; unlike so many others before and since, we were exceptionally lucky. I was able to go on and command the squadron, have a full career and see my children grow up and have children of their own. Like me, Ian went on to become an Air Marshal after a very successful career in the RAF, with a family and a great second career to follow. We often see each other and when we do we exchange a knowing look.

Phew!

So, back to commanding Treble One. Leuchars was a delightful base, near St Andrews on the lovely Fife coastline, with an excellent weather factor, owing to being in the shade of the Lomond Hill range to the west. As mentioned earlier, like the Falklands, the worst weather was during a high-pressure period, when the rest of the UK was basking in glorious sunshine. On the east coast of Fife, the dreaded Haar would be lurking out to sea, just waiting for a slight drop in temperature or an increased easterly wind – just enough to bring a thick blanket of fog over the airfield.

Shortly after completing (or should I say surviving) my operational work-up on the squadron, the conditions for the Haar were perfect, and we could see the mist licking at the approach lights to the eastern end of the runway. But there was something else needed to bring it in, and that can only be summarised as a magic ingredient, a feeling in the air, without which it would sit stubbornly for days just out to sea. As I finished for the day, I sensed that the magic ingredient was missing and that the night shift would get in some good flying. The duty flight commander that evening was Sqn Ldr 'Mac' McNeil-Matthews, a very experienced and capable navigator, but who was still feeling his way with the new Boss. About seven o'clock, Mac phoned me to say that he was worried about the weather, but that he wanted to discuss it with me before scrubbing. Feeling somewhat irritated, I told him that he was paid to make decisions that night, but as he had called me I reckoned the weather would stay fine, so he'd better get his backside into the air and stop bothering me. As expected, all aircraft flew and returned safely.

The next afternoon Mac asked to see me, apologised for being a wimp, and acknowledged that he should have made the decision to fly himself. So far so fine. As I drove home, I got that smell, that feeling in the water; the Haar was stretching its limbs out. Shortly after finishing my supper, I was interested, but not alarmed, to hear four Phantoms taking off into the night. A visit to the garden confirmed my fears: the visibility was slowly reducing. But no problem; the diversion airfields to the west were forecast to remain fine, and we could get the aircraft back tomorrow.

An hour later, the visibility was down to 50 yards; there was no chance of the aircraft getting in that night, so the Duty Aircrew Officer (DAO) would probably direct them to divert on recovery to Prestwick, near Glasgow. I was therefore surprised to hear a Phantom overshooting into the fog, shortly followed by three more at two-minute intervals. A call came through from the Ops Room, confirming that all four were diverting to Prestwick. Sensible. But an hour is a long time in military aviation. Shortly after eleven o'clock, I had a call from Mac, who was by then at Prestwick, to inform me that the fourth aircraft, flown by Flt Lt Mick Mercer, had suffered a bird strike while overshooting in the fog at Leuchars. The only problem was that the bird was in its nest in a tree at the time. Mick, perhaps pushing his luck and going a bit lower than he should have done, had flown through a row of conifers in the back garden of some unfortunate chap living on the approach to Runway 09, the easterly runway. The aircraft was obviously damaged, and would have to be repaired at Prestwick or recovered by road. Mick and his navigator were two very lucky lads; the bird in the conifers less so.

Quick Reaction Alert (QRA), readers will recall from my time on 43 Sqn, was always exciting at Leuchars. The base was sufficiently far north to get quickly into the UK–Iceland gap, a popular transit and patrol area for Soviet shipping and aircraft. As in the Falklands, we kept a few aircraft fully armed, but with missiles only, not the gun, with air and ground crews in nearby accommodation. At Leuchars, surrounded by chilly water, we spent most of the year in rubber immersion suits, with heavy clothing and a G-suit underneath. With this kit, and the dinghy, which was part of the ejection seat equipment, you could expect to survive several hours awaiting a friendly lifeboat or helicopter. Without them you would be dead in twenty minutes. So a spell on QRA could be pretty exhausting, and heavy on flying and sleep deprivation. On the other hand, the food was generally very good, and the opportunity to do a real job intercepting Soviet long-range aircraft was much relished.

I was fortunate to be involved in many interceptions during my two tours at Leuchars. Generally, the Russian aircrew were quite friendly, waving enthusiastically and showing us their mugs of coffee; laced, we suspected, with vodka. Indeed, the poor chaps in the back of the aircraft, dressed in very lumpy clothes against the cold, would very often hold up a bottle, no doubt provided as anti-freeze. If we were lucky, they would even hold up the centre spread of Playboy, which produced some interesting photographs for the intelligence staff. Just occasionally, someone would turn nasty and cause a potentially dangerous situation to develop. There was a brief period when they started pointing high intensity lasers at us; but appropriate diplomatic action stopped that quickly. More common was the aggressive pilot, who would slow down and turn towards us, getting our aircraft close to the stall. At high level this was uncomfortable; at low level it could be fatal.

On one occasion, I had the misfortune to meet up with such a fellow aviator. Unusually, he was alone: a Bear Foxtrot, with four massive turbo-prop engine pods, and a specialist radar dome under the belly. This version of the ubiquitous aircraft was a specialist sub-hunter, and he was obviously not doing the usual transit run to West Africa or Cuba. As soon as he saw me, he started a rapid descent into cloud. I just caught him before he disappeared, and hung on to his wing as he turned, then throttled back and did everything possible to shake me off. I had just taken on fuel from the tanker; the aircraft was heavy and unresponsive, especially when he dropped his speed to just over 200 knots. I lowered the flaps to aid manoeuvrability and decrease the stalling speed, but he immediately lowered his nose and accelerated, forcing me to raise them again. My mouth was dry, my breathing heavy, but I was damned if I was going to let him slip away. Suddenly, the cloud cleared, and there below was a Kirov Class nuclear cruiser of the Soviet Navy. Almost certainly, it was providing acoustic cover for a nuclear submarine underneath him. So this was why the bastard had given me such a hard time! We took lots of photos of the aircraft and the ship, constantly reporting their position, until as we approached the western coast of Ireland, we were ordered back to base. Cutting across the north of Scotland, we landed back at Leuchars after a sortie of over four hours, most of which had been in formation with an aircraft that was trying to dump me in the Atlantic. It may have been the Cold War, but for us it was at times decidedly hot.

Sometimes, because machines and equipment fail, or bits of them do, they will let you down. Anyone who has a car knows this. The same is true of aeroplanes. Despite the most stringent engineering procedures, adherence to maintenance schedules and the like, just occasionally a bit will break, come lose or bend. Just as likely, especially on complex pieces of equipment like the Phantom, something will find its way from where it should be to where it can produce maximum harm. Like my aircraft in the late summer of 1984.

I was planning to do a routine sortie with a young navigator, as part of his work-up programme. As we were taxiing out, my number two reported he had a technical problem, and would have to return to dispersal to get the engineers to check it out. No problem, I would get airborne, and do something useful like a practice heavyweight single-engine approach, by which time the number two should have sorted out his problem, one way or the other. So after take-off, I called that I was simulating engine failure on the left engine, and requested a Ground Controlled Approach (GCA) to overshoot. The weather was bad, with low cloud, and we were on the easterly runway which took us over hills on the approach. Everything was going fine, and I was feeling quite pleased with myself. As we lined up for the final approach, the talkdown controller called, as normal, for me to complete landing checks and advise him when they were complete. I lowered the undercarriage – three greens so all wheels down and locked – then lowered the flaps; at that stage things started to go horribly wrong. When the flaps were lowered in the Phantom, the nose would drop, requiring a backward move of the control column to correct to level flight. But when I started the check back, I hit a solid obstruction, and the nose kept going down. Slightly concerned at the radio altimeter indicating that we were getting closer to the hills below, I shouted to my back-seater to be prepared to eject, raised the flaps and undercarriage, put the in-use engine in reheat and brought the left-hand engine back up towards full-power. The reheat lit quickly, but it seemed an eternity before the left engine reached full power, by which time we were getting very close to an ejection situation. Slowly the speed started to increase, the nose started to rise, and I called the navigator to take his hands off the ejection seat firing handle. We clawed back up to 5,000ft, above cloud, I advised ATC that we had a problem, and I started to think about how I was going to get this aeroplane back safely on the ground. The Duty Aircrew Officer (DAO) came on the radio, we discussed the problem, and he started looking at various manuals for help. In the meantime, I started to investigate how slowly I could fly the aircraft safely, without using flaps, and concluded that at anything below 200 knots I couldn't keep the nose up and the aircraft became uncontrollable. The DAO helpfully advised me that he had no advice, and we should consider ejecting out to sea. I didn't like that idea, so told him we would do a high-speed approach, planning to engage the cable to avoid problems (like dying) if the wheels came off on landing. Normally we would land a Phantom at around 150 knots, so we were asking a lot of the old bird to be plonked down 50 knots faster. I told the young back-seater what we were doing, and told him not to eject unless I went first. The last thing I wanted was the distraction of a massive bang, a rush of cold air and a cockpit full of cordite smoke.

I lined up, as before, and started my approach, using 215 knots to keep a margin of safety. We slowly descended, the calming voice of the talkdown controller advising my position constantly: 'You're on the glidepath, slightly left, converging.' We broke cloud at about 200ft; the big mistake now would be to throttle back and lose too much speed. I was flying a sick aeroplane and if I got it wrong the consequences could be fatal. So, slowly bring the speed back as we approach the threshold … runway dead ahead … must land before the cable … 200 knots … no slower … sinking down and … bang … both main tyres burst as we touch down … the aircraft slews violently … but the hook catches the cable and we abruptly stop. That was interesting.

It was discovered that a bolt had sheared in the tail area, and probably after several flights had found its way into the elevator control mechanism. I was awarded a 'Green Endorsement' for saving an aircraft, and both we and the aeroplane were flying again the next day.

Another Phew!

Commanding a fighter squadron is tremendous fun, while being an interesting challenge. You have to fly as much as anyone else, ideally better than most, and also deal with the myriad administrative and engineering challenges associated with a large number of people and equipment, including aircraft worth over £20 million each. I was lucky to be well-supported by good flight commanders, unlike poor old Ken Bailey on 5 Sqn. I also had a good set of engineers, led by an understated Sqn Ldr Ian Purnell, and utterly reliable administrative staff, as well as great aircrew with bubbly wives or girlfriends. But I could tell from the start that this was not a squadron. It was a set of different entities: aircrew, engineers, administrators, flying clothing workers and so on. The squadron HQ was in the old air traffic tower, and it had been considered the aircrew sanctuary. I decided that this had to change, and insisted that all people on my squadron, whatever their rank or trade, should consider this room their 'alma mater' while they were on the squadron. It was there that we had the squadron memorabilia, the silver from bygone days, the wonderful photographs, diaries, and the shields from other visiting squadrons. Many of the aircrew didn't like this, but they had to get used to the idea. Of course, the aircrew room was theirs alone for normal operations, but for beer calls and briefings to the whole squadron, I got everyone under the same roof. Sadly, it is the only weakness in RAF leadership that I have ever identified: that aircrew tend to form a clique which is impenetrable to others. But not on my squadron, whatever the mutterings in the background. We worked and played together, did our annual fitness test together, and we even flew a number of our groundcrew in the back of the Phantom, including the much-loved 'NCO Discip', Sergeant Dave Lunnon, who kept an eye on the young lads, but was always there for them if they needed a fatherly chat. I flew him myself, and he didn't stop talking about it for months. It was, to some of my officers, an unnecessary use of squadron resources, but I thought otherwise, and I was the Boss.

The payback changed most peoples' minds. TACEVAL, as previously mentioned, was an external evaluation of a station, and it was gruelling. By the time that we had our first one, I had formed Treble One into a single unit, where everyone felt they deserved to wear the squadron badge. After several days of living under war conditions, we had the debrief from the Strike Command team. The team leader was very clinical, but made it clear when debriefing the two squadrons' performance that Treble One groundcrew had given 100 per cent, and had on occasions been seen running between tasks. We achieved an Excellent rating, which was virtually unheard of in the challenging days of the Cold War. Tony Bagnall very graciously congratulated me on our performance, but I suspect that both he and the Station Commander, Tim Elworthy, were bemused that we had done so well. Of course, the simple answer was that we worked as a team, with everyone focused on being better than 43 Sqn.

We repeated the result the following year, and overall did better than any other squadron in the command. But it wasn't all easy or straightforward. My strong sense of duty and total commitment didn't always strike the right chord with some of my aircrew officers, who no doubt saw me as looking upwards to promotion and other accolades. As observed earlier, it had been a constant struggle throughout my career: my energy and belief in total effort had been interpreted as excessive ambition. In reality, I only ever wanted to excel at the job I was given, and I certainly pushed myself in the air and on the ground harder than I pushed anyone else; indeed for the first time, I achieved 'Exceptional' flying ratings in my logbook. But I could not ignore perception from my subordinates and peers; I still had not managed to find the right balance as a leader.

Rather abruptly, and before I was ready to leave, the Air Officer Commanding No 11 (Fighter) Group, Air Vice-Marshal Ken Hayr, called me to say that I had been selected for promotion to group captain, and would be coming to his HQ at Bentley Priory, north of London, to lead the Ops Staff; but in the meantime he wanted me to do a re-run of a Board of Inquiry into a fatal Lightning accident. I had again to go home and tell the long-suffering Irene that I had to leave in a hurry, get down to Binbrook and pick up the Board proceedings. She would follow me down shortly to Bentley Priory. Fortunately, my successor, Phil Roser, was able to cut his refresher course short, and we managed a quick handover, and a brief farewell to my new CO, Ian Macfadyen. Two days later, I was at Binbrook again.

A few weeks earlier, a young Lightning pilot had managed to get into a spin in air combat manoeuvring, but had failed to recover and so ejected, albeit a little late. Sadly, the parachute main cords wrapped themselves around the top of the ejection seat, the parachute failed to deploy, and he was killed on impact with the sea. The original Board of Inquiry had concluded that no one was to blame; 11 Gp disagreed, and wanted me to revisit the whole sad business. It was messy, and I concluded that a couple of people had been negligent in their duties as supervisors of the young pilot. They were both good people, and friends, and it hurt me then as it does now to think back on how it affected them, and possibly their careers. But I did what I was asked to do, and I believe I did it honestly and fairly. At the Coroner's Inquest, I met the parents and afterwards had an hour talking about their son and the accident. It was heart-breaking.

One of the officers involved kindly came up to me many years later and said:

'I didn't entirely agree with your conclusions, Chris, but you were always honest and told us exactly what you had written.' In a tragic and sad affair, I suppose that was all I could expect.

Chapter 11

Bentley Priory had been the original home of Fighter Command, which became No 11(Fighter) Gp as the RAF contracted. It was where Air Marshal 'Stuffy' Dowding had managed his fighters during the Battle of Britain, and it oozed history and heritage. My job was to oversee all the operational aspects of the air defence of the UK, reporting through the Senior Air Staff Officer (SASO), Air Cdre Mike Graydon, to the Air Officer Commanding (AOC). AVM Mike Stear.

It was nice to enjoy the privilege of promotion to the rank of group captain, and I felt comfortable in the HQ of the fighter group. But a priority was to find a way to get some flying. Fortunately, an old friend, Rick Peacock-Edwards, had just taken command of No 229 OCU at RAF Coningsby, where the new air defence version of the Tornado was entering service. I thought that, in my capacity as Gp Capt Ops, it was essential to get checked out on the new aircraft. Accordingly, after four months in the job, I took myself up to Coningsby for a short introductory course. I had a week before the AOC would start asking where I was, so we had to be quick. I did a day's ground school, two simulator rides, three dual sorties, including one with Rick, then was allowed to fly on the Friday morning with a navigator, Andy Lister-Tomlinson. I loved the Tornado. It was sweet to fly, had the great attributes of variable geometry (swing wing), which helped with agility at slow speeds, but with wings swept back meant it went like a rocket, only smoother. Whereas at 750 knots (yes, you read it correctly) at low level, the Phantom was a handful, the Tornado was a dream to fly. There was only one problem: it couldn't do the job owing to significant shortcomings in the radar and associated systems. Thus, at the time, it was a wonderful plaything with little operational capability. I arrived breathless back at Bentley Priory in time for the 1600 hrs end of week wash-up, grabbed the Ops brief from my PA and arrived in the briefing room just in time. I must have looked guilty because Mike Stear immediately asked: 'Where have you been?'

'Liaison visit to Coningsby, Sir,' I replied.

'Hmm,' he snorted. 'And I don't suppose you did some flying on your liaison visit?'

'Just a little, Sir,' I replied defensively. 'But I have come back with a full report on the aircraft; it's not all going smoothly at the moment.' He looked at me sideways.

'I await your report.'

He got it on the Monday morning and called me in. Fifteen minutes later, I left with an arm-waving task to 'sort out the bloody mess with the Tornado F2'. In essence, the radar was wrong for the role, and much of the hardware, especially that operated by the back-seater, had been designed by boffins sitting in armchairs and drinking coffee. In the frantic, high-G, cramped and sweaty environment of a fighter cockpit, it was virtually unusable. Added to that, the design characteristics of the aeroplane were configured for multi-role, with the inevitable compromises: specifically, great thrust and fuel efficiency at low level, but pretty awful above 20,000ft; and a relatively poor turn-performance compared with American counterparts, many of which were cheaper and being bought by nearby European countries. Our aircrew were facing the dreadful prospect of being trounced not only by the Americans, but also by the Belgians, Dutch, Norwegians and many others. It was going to be no use telling them that in the end these were allies, not adversaries. It was our allies that we met on a daily basis for mutual training. Nor did it wash to explain that many British jobs were at stake, and the Tornado kept us firmly in collaborative European programmes, unlike American options, which were largely bought 'off the shelf' with little or no UK content or jobs.

But the F2, which became the Tornado F3, was the replacement for the remaining Lightnings and Phantoms whether we liked it or not, so we had better get on with it. I agreed with Mike Graydon that we would task my old unit, the Central Tactics and Trials Organisation (CTTO), with assessing the capability gaps of the F3, and then we could move on to identify solutions. I secretly thanked the Lord that this would not be my problem, as I had had the nod from my appointing officer that I was pencilled in to command a Phantom base in Germany, RAF Wildenrath, so someone else would have to deal with it. Oh dear, wrong again!

A few months later, I was accompanying the AOC on a station visit, when I was asked to call my appointing officer ASAP. I slipped away, found a phone in a quiet office, and gave Richie Profit a call.

'Chris,' he said, with a "don't shoot the messenger" tone to his voice, 'I know you're slated for Wildenrath, but something's come up.' There was an awkward pause. 'You still there?' I acknowledged that I was indeed still there, still listening. 'Well, you see, Ali McKay was due to take over Coningsby at the end of the year, but we can't get him out of the Falklands for twelve months, and Mike Elsam needs to get out before Christmas—'

'Delighted to take Coningsby, Richie,' I interrupted. He was very relieved.

'Great, I'll get the Air Secretary to contact your AOC today and get the ball rolling. You'll need to do a refresher on both the Tornado and the Phantom, and a Hawk lead-in course. It'll be very tight to get all that in before Christmas.'

'Don't bother with the Hawk course, Richie,' I said. 'I just need a few trips on the F4 and a short refresher on the Tornado F3. I've kept myself fairly current on the Phantom, and I did do a short Tornado course a few months ago.'

'Who authorised that?' he exclaimed.

'I did,' I replied. 'When can I start?'

Coningsby: Phantoms, Tornados and, joy of joys, the Battle of Britain Memorial Flight, with its Hurricanes, Spitfires and even perhaps the Lancaster. All I had to do now was explain to Irene that we weren't going to the land of milk and honey (well, Beer and Bratwurst), but back for a third tour at Coningsby, in a Station Commander's residence that was considered the worst in the RAF, close to the sewage farm and the jet engine test facility. Shouldn't be a problem!

I arrived at Coningsby in the early autumn of 1986. After a short refresher course on the Phantom and the Tornado, I took command from Mike Elsam in October. Irene arrived in the same month, making the most of it as usual, with Peter, Nicky and Theresa already in boarding schools.

Coningsby was built at the outbreak of the Second World War, and officially opened in 1941. The famous Dam Buster Squadron, No 617, had been based there for the second-half of the war. After a period of closure, it became a Vulcan unit, before eventually re-equipping with Phantoms in 1966, following successive cancellations of the medium bombers, TSR-2 and the American F111. Initially designated for ground attack and reconnaissance duties, the Phantoms progressively converted to the air defence role. In 1986 the Tornado F3 began its entry into service on No 229 OCU, with a rapid increase on the station to include two operational F3 Squadrons, No 29 and No 5. It was my job to bid farewell to the last Phantoms on the station, and get the two new units operational; no mean task. For a start, the Tornado still had several issues, some of which had been identified by the aforementioned CTTO trial. In fact, the project officer, Derek Nicholls, had identified no less than forty-one shortcomings which would need to be resolved before the aircraft could be declared fully operational. There was also a shortage of radars, resulting in ballast being carried in the nose of some aircraft. The tag 'Blue Circle Cement' jet was being bandied around, especially in an increasingly curious media. Not surprisingly, the morale on the station was suffering, with the remaining Phantom units disbanding, some of the aircraft moving to Leuchars, but many of the aircrew converting to the Tornado. They, along with a growing number of pilots coming from the ageing but still much-loved Lightning, were horrified that they were leaving proven combat aircraft for something that was clearly not yet fit for purpose. Worse, there were a growing number of F15s, F16s and other superb American fighters appearing in the UK skies, flown by air forces which we deemed inferior to ours, all adding to the misery of those who felt severely disadvantaged in the F3. It was clearly my job to give a clear vision to the station of the challenges ahead, and in parallel, ensure the morale of the whole workforce was raised. Working with me were an excellent set of wing commander executives, including my OC Administrative Wing, Chris Winsland, who had been with me at Cranwell. Despite being a dyed-in-the-wool administrator, Chris had his handle on the detail of station governance that allowed me to get on with my duties; he was also an excellent networker in the local community. Among his many contacts was George Bateman, the chairman of the Boston-based brewery company. Chris arranged for the station execs to visit the brewery around Christmas in 1986, to brief George on station activities and then try some of his excellent beers. During the course of a very convivial evening, I noticed a vast container marked: 'Strong Lager – to be scrapped'. It turned out that this excellent brew had been prepared for an export order, which was cancelled, and to avoid paying duty it had to be poured down the drain. Being a man who hated waste, we came to an agreement to have the lager collected at dead of night, and transported to Coningsby, where we would ensure it was poured down the appropriate drains. As luck would have it, I had tasked Chris Winsland with setting up a training day for the whole station, culminating in an all ranks curry in a large hangar. We now had the perfect liquid refreshment to accompany the Chicken Madras, all in the interests of generating team spirit. It all worked very well, although those passing the station sewage plant the next day did report that it seemed unusually 'fragrant'.

CHAPTER 11

I had secured the agreement of the AOC that, as the senior flying supervisor, I should be current on both the Phantom and the Tornado; and in due course on the Battle of Britain Memorial Flight (BBMF) aircraft, which apart from a little Chipmunk were in winter servicing. Despite the challenges of a Lincolnshire winter, I loved the challenge of the two fighters, which had different capabilities and limitations. Of course, I felt very much at home in the F4, which I had flown for many years, but climbing into a brand-new jet, with a smell like a new car and lots of exotic equipment, was a wonderful experience. One of its major advantages over the Lightning and Phantom, was its modern gun system, comprising a powerful internally-mounted 27 mm Mauser cannon, and an excellent gunsight. I couldn't wait to put it to the test, and the opportunity to do so occurred shortly after taking command. No 229 OCU were deploying to Cyprus, where there was a suitable area of open sea for air-to-air gunnery. I decided to join them for a week. I was not disappointed; the scores all round against the flag target were excellent, and I managed to exceed my previous best by a substantial margin. Feeling rather pleased with myself, I boarded an Air Cyprus flight back to Heathrow, and with my driver awaiting me at Heathrow, I could relax with an evening gin and tonic and a glass of wine with the meal. Or that was the plan. Hardly had I started sipping my aperitif when the gentleman alongside me, having learned I was in the RAF, asked if I had heard about the amazing antics at Cranwell. I confessed that I hadn't, to be told that two Phantoms that morning had flown so low over a graduation parade at the College that several hats had been blown off, the flag poles overturned and the VIP carpet sent flying skywards. With every bit of new information he revealed, my interest level started to rise, shortly followed by alarm bells and eventually panic: Phantoms … Lincolnshire … hell of a stink … oh Gawd!

My worst fears were realised on arrival at Heathrow, where my grim-faced driver had a briefing from Nigel Sudborough, the acting station commander, in his hand, and my Number One uniform and hat in the boot. The facts were worse than the story I had heard earlier: Flt Lts Mike Jukes and Phil Williamson had indeed 'wired' the parade ground at Cranwell, Mike having led the formation past twice, on one occasion getting down to a mere 74ft above the petrified cadets – reheat blasting away. The Reviewing Officer, Air Vice-Marshal Mike Pilkington, had been rendered temporarily deaf, and several spectators were in a state of shock. It transpired that much of this was caused by a rather confused briefing. The Cranwell Project Officer for the graduation had only just arrived, had received a very sketchy handover from his predecessor, and had mixed up two totally separate events. The graduation parade in the morning called for a sedate flypast at 1,000ft. However, in the afternoon, when all the top-brass had finished lunch and departed, the parents, friends and fiancées were invited down to the airfield, where all the local flying stations would put on a show of exhilarating flying, with the instruction 'to fly as low, as fast and as noisily as you like'. In this case, Murphy's Law had applied, and the Project Officer had reversed the instructions, resulting in mayhem in the morning and a series of boring flypasts in the afternoon. To complete the Murphy ingredients, the man who authorised the trips, Wg Cdr Dave Rooum, had himself only recently arrived, and the plan to beat the living daylights out of the parade square may not have struck him as suspect.

Conveniently, HQ 11(Fighter) Gp Hq was on the way back to Coningsby, so my subsequent one-sided discussion with the Air Officer Commanding (AOC), my previous boss Mike Stear, didn't disrupt my journey home too much. The subsequent Inquiry concluded that the briefing and supervision was inadequate, and that Mike Jukes had had problems assessing his height at low-level. Mike was duly promoted and sent to command the RAF's Low-Level Flying Squadron! He was a good man, a sound pilot and, like most of us in our service careers, made an error of judgement rather than skill. The subsequent video, still trumpeted as one of the most spectacular available on YouTube, makes for interesting viewing. My interview with the AOC, had it been recorded, would have been less riveting!

It was soon time for the first of the Phantom units, No 29(F) Sqn, to disband, and we planned a final Officers' Mess dining out night in early March 1987 to give the squadron a fitting farewell. This turned out to be another close call for Coville, but in this case my career prospects rather than my mortal existence.

During my time commanding Treble One, my Executive Officer, Terry Hanlon, had forged a close relationship with Guinness, whose colours of black and gold matched our own. The principal point of contact was Jack Bailey, who arranged once a year for the squadron to brief the Scottish Guinness board on our activities, and then enjoy a most pleasant lunch in their executive dining room. One of the senior managers was Mike Jobson, who later was posted to a senior position in the company's HQ in West London. Early in my tour at Coningsby, Jack called me to say that Mike had tasked him with re-establishing the links in my new appointment. Naturally, I welcomed the idea, and we arranged for a team from Guinness to visit the station in early March, the day of our dining out night for the departing Phantoms and their aircrew. Mike kindly offered to lay on Black Velvet (Guinness and Champagne) to kick-start the evening. Again, naturally, I accepted with enthusiasm. After showing our guests around the flight simulator, flight line and air traffic control, we duly repaired to the bar at five o'clock to enjoy a glass or two. Unfortunately, the glass or two turned into three or four, and before too long five or six. At seven o'clock we all dashed off to change into Mess Kit for the dinner at seven thirty. I should have realised then that there was inevitable trouble ahead, cancelled the whole event and barricaded the windows and doors of the Mess. Sadly, I did not, no doubt owing to the first stages of judgement loss, which turned out to be a progressive ailment.

I arrived back at the Mess, which was already far noisier than most formal Mess evenings, to discover that unlike the usual sherry aperitif, we were finishing off the Black Velvet in half-pint jars. The dinner itself was a riot, with an anxious Mess manager dashing around trying to stop fighter aircrew climbing up the curtains and crawling under the tables. He was right to be anxious, as the relative calm of the meal was shattered when we came to the post-prandial fun and games. Sport is an important element of service life, and one particularly popular pastime is the schooner race; my 'memories' of the evening with the American aircrew should have sounded the alarm bells. To recap, in simple terms (the full rules are complex), two teams face each other, every member of the team facing a glass, normally full of beer, but on this occasion … you've guessed it, Black Velvet. The adjudicator/referee is normally the senior officer present – in this case, me. With my customary sense of decorum and fairness, I lined up the first two teams, explained the rules, ignoring the clamour to 'get on with it, Sir', downed my half pint and slammed my glass down to get the tournament underway. There were eight teams, and as the finalists lined up to do combat, I started to feel a little unsteady, not surprisingly, I suppose, considering I had probably consumed enough Black Velvet to kill a horse. As the last glass of the dark potion disappeared, so did my normal powers of judgement, and when I declared the winners, to shouts of 'fix' from the reluctant losers, I realised that it was time to go home. But that, of course, was impossible, as I had to stay at the helm of an increasingly dodgy ship, come what may.

Calculating that the time was right, the lads brought out their first surprise of the evening. Outside the Mess, revving furiously, were two battered old cars, both MOT right-offs, that had been 'acquired' by 29 (F) Sqn for some fun and games. I was handed the keys to a Ford Granada, and was pitted against Fg Off Rick Offord, whose mount was a rather forlorn looking Austin Maxi. But he was in pole position, and beat the starter's flag before I could react. The circuit around the Mess (NB no public roads involved) had a few sharp bends, a chicane around dustbins and contractors' equipment, and a straight section in front of the Mess entrance. The race was to cover five circuits, or whenever both cars had crashed and were no longer able to compete. I soon realised that the Maxi was better around the bends, but my limo had a distinct advantage on the straight. The key to getting to the chequered flag, therefore, was to keep right behind the Maxi until the final straight, at which time I could streak past him and win the race. Everything went to plan. As he made ground on the bends, I would catch him up on the straight. The strategy was going to work. Unfortunately, as we sped around the final lap, the boys introduced their second surprise of the night: a scrap piano, which they had ignited in front of the Mess entrance, perilously close to the winning line. All of this, of course, was going on as Rick and I were unsighted and concentrating on other things. I was well-placed as we approached the final turn, and anticipating the need to accelerate to full power, put my foot to the floor on the accelerator, only to be greeted as I rounded the corner by the Maxi, mounted across the burning piano. At this stage, I reacted accordingly, but quickly realised why my car had failed its MOT; it had no brakes. With nothing to stop it, my Granada piled into the back of the Maxi, pushing it further into the conflagration. Thanks to the quick reaction and unbridled courage of several chortling bystanders, Rick was hauled unharmed out of the wreckage, insisting he had won as my car was clearly still behind his, although the gathering flames made distinguishing one from the other increasingly difficult. Shortly afterwards, the station fire service and the local fire brigade arrived, called out by distant observers who saw what they believed to be the Mess alight. After giving them all a beer and a sandwich, they left the scene, the burning wreckage safely covered in foam. At this time, Wg Cdr Nigel Sudborough, OC 29 (F) Sqn, kindly summoned my staff car, ordering the driver to take me home and not to accept any orders to bring me back to the Mess. I was deposited at my residence, a patient Irene guided me again into the spare bedroom, where I promptly fell asleep.

Believing that was the end of the story, we went out the following morning to do the week's shopping, although I confess that my participation was limited to producing my wallet from time to time. I was somewhat surprised, therefore, on returning home, to find an anxious-looking Station Duty Officer (SDO), pacing in front of our house, and in the background a couple of shifty-looking characters, one of whom seemed to be sporting a camera with a very large lens. As I climbed out of the car, the camera started clicking furiously. The SDO saluted smartly, and announced that these two fellows were gentlemen of the press, specifically from *The Mail on Sunday*. The one who wasn't clicking from various angles introduced himself as Will Bennett, a journalist, who had picked up from 'a normally reliable source' that there had been antics and mayhem in the Officers' Mess the previous evening, and he was covering the story which he proclaimed would 'hit the headlines' the following day. Indeed, he declared that the first edition was already being printed, but that he had wanted to hang around in the hope of getting an interview with me. I tried charm, cups of tea and chocolate biscuits, but it was clear that Mr Bennett (may he now be rotting in Hell) believed he had a scoop, and could not be persuaded, bribed or threatened with the Official Secrets Act to squash the story. As he stood to leave, wiping the crumbs of my chocolate biscuits from his mouth, he asked for a quote to explain the behaviour the night before. Rather lamely, I responded that aircrew of fast-jets were under enormous physical and mental pressure, and that 'the officers are encouraged to let off steam in a responsible manner'.

He and the man with the long lenses left, and I started to panic. I needed a monumental world event to save me; nothing less than all-out thermonuclear war would suffice, and that seemed unlikely in the next twelve hours. I called my OC Admin Wg, Chris Winsland, and we decided it would be best to advise the MOD duty press officer that there might be some exaggerated coverage of an exuberant night at Coningsby in the morning's newspapers. He duly took note, and announced that he would warn the Chief of the Air Staff and my AOC, Mike Stear. Perhaps it was my cautious wording, but nobody called me that afternoon, and I went to bed confident that I could ride the storm.

The next morning the phone started ringing at seven o'clock. Chris Winsland, an early riser, had picked up a copy of the *Sunday Mail*, and there on page four was half a page, with the headlines: 'Officers on Rampage after RAF Base Party; Man pulled from Blazing Wreck!' The following paragraphs were unfortunately an accurate description of the evening. This being the first edition, the final words declared that: 'The station commander of RAF Coningsby, Group Captain Christopher Coville, was unavailable for comment.' Actually, 'incapable of comment' might have been closer to the truth. The next phone call was from an apoplectic Mike Stear, who demanded to know every detail of the evening, and announced that he had to explain it to the Commander-in-Chief of Strike Command, Air Chief Marshal Sir Peter Harding, at the weekly meeting at High Wycombe the very next morning. In those days there were no emails, so I sat down and drafted what was probably the most important letter of my life, carefully explaining the poor morale on the station, my determination to raise it to get us through the next challenging two years, while playing down what might have been perceived as excessive behaviour, not least from myself. This was faxed down to HQ 11 Gp, and handed to the AOC. In no time at all, he was on the phone again, demanding more detail, the level of supervision, and to what extent I had attempted to curtail inappropriate behaviour; all questions I found difficult to answer without implicating myself further. To add to my misery, the second edition had arrived, including my quote that 'the officers are encouraged to let off steam in a responsible manner'. I spent another couple of agonising hours, crafting carefully the demanded extra detail, realising that with every word I was knocking another nail into the coffin that had been my career prospects. A late-night, one-sided conversation with Mike Stear confirmed that this was a realistic assessment.

The next day Irene started to think about another quick move and life outside the RAF, as I tried to get on with running the station. The local press and Radio Lincolnshire were hounding me, but I managed to give them the slip and left Chris Winsland to handle them. By five o'clock, I still hadn't heard anything; and then the call came through from the AOC's office. I was to report to Sir Peter Harding the next day in Number One uniform, hat on and no coffee. This confirmed my worst fears.

The following morning, I drove myself down to High Wycombe, fearing that sitting in the back seat with my driver would make the journey interminably long. I arrived at the appointed time, and was marched in by his Aide-de-Camp (ADC), who then left. Sir Peter looked at me sternly.

'Seems like things went a bit too far,' he declared.

'Yes, Sir.' I nodded. But then, to my surprise, he invited me to take my hat off and sit down.

'Well, I understand what you were trying to achieve, with all the F3 problems, and poor morale on the station; but keep a better grip on things, will you?' I said that I would, and he then asked me to elaborate on a few technical issues with the Tornado's radar. In fact, he was very pleasant and almost friendly, shaking my hand and thanking me for coming all the way from Lincolnshire to brief him. I left, astonished and very relieved.

CHAPTER 11

It seemed that at the meeting the previous morning, someone had reminded Sir Peter that a similar event had occurred some fifteen years before at RAF Bruggen in Germany; and guess who was the station commander? No less person than the then Group Captain Peter Harding!

Many friends have often been confounded at my apparently natural ability to extract myself from the most dire situations, and frequently gaining some advantage from them. On this occasion, those very few around the RAF who had never heard of me were put right. Moreover, we noticed a surge in applicants in the training pipeline to come to Coningsby, where it was assumed all the spirited aircrew were gathered. I did receive a few letters, not all complimentary, but most tinged with humour. One Second World War pilot remarked that we had become, in his words, 'Incredibly couth, as in my day we wouldn't have taken the piano out of the Mess before setting it on fire!' My infamous quote to Will Bennett became the stuff of crewroom humour for quite a while. In fact, a much-loved RAF cartoonist, Flt Lt Al Turner (Nom de Plume 'Renrut'), produced a wonderful tableau of the evening, in my view slightly exaggerated again, depicting a Bacchanalian feast, with cars and pianos on fire, fire engines in attendance, and the words that would come back to haunt me for years as its headline: 'The Officers are encouraged to let off steam in a responsible manner.'

Mike Stear called me the next day, and announced that I was under his closest scrutiny, but that was a far better outcome than I had expected, or probably deserved. I had survived to live another day. But it was clear that my career hung on a slender, overstretched thread, and I resolved to keep my nose clean and maintain strict discipline on the station thereafter. Oh dear!

As I mentioned earlier, I and my executive team had a massive task preparing the station for its new role as the first Tornado F3 base. In paving the way for a series of external validation exercises, some called without notice, I was given authority to call exercises myself, with internal scrutineers, to help in the transition process. In order to test the recall and personnel recovery plans, it was normal for such exercises to be called in the early hours, when most sensible people were asleep in their own homes ... I will avoid the temptation to dwell on other possible scenarios. Accordingly, to Irene's understandable annoyance, I set the alarm for 0330 hrs one morning, and was getting into my camouflaged combat kit when, to my surprise, the phone rang in our bedroom. As this was an operational extension, fears of a family disaster were quickly discounted. It turned out to be the Station Medical Officer, Patrick Blackford, who advised me of a tragedy in the Married Quarters. The son of one of my excellent RAF police NCOs, had suffered a massive epileptic attack during the night and had asphyxiated. I immediately drove down to the sergeant's house, to find the couple overwhelmed with grief in the kitchen, and Patrick dealing with the poor boy who was lying at the bottom of the stairs. I spent an hour with the sergeant and his wife, talking about their beloved only child, who despite his illness had been a blessing to them. I left feeling emotionally drained, went back to my house for a quick coffee, called the operations room and gave them the codeword to initiate the exercise. A few moments later, the hooters started sounding around the station, and people started pouring in to their war locations.

I wonder if there are any other jobs where the senior executive gets so close to his people that he is called upon to offer comfort at such a terrible time. It is, of course, an awesome responsibility, but one that always left me feeling humbled and privileged.

No doubt following on from the above, I realise that in what is, perhaps more than it should be, a book about my passion for aviation, I have said too little about the great joy of my life, my family. Service life is not for the faint-hearted. There are long periods of separation, frequent frustrations at changes in postings or accommodation arrangements, not to mention for some the dangers of flying aircraft to the edge of the envelope. For the wives, or should I say spouses, these pressures can be overwhelming and occasionally humiliating. Before being offered a command tour in the last century, we were asked two questions, the answers determining whether or not the posting was taken further: will you be accompanied by your wife; and will you live in the official residence? It's hard to believe today that a family could be held to ransom in such a way, but no one seemed to quibble at the time; it was just part of the overall package. We always used to say that the RAF got two for one, especially with officers in command appointments, where the wife was expected to be a hostess, ambassador and head of numerous local service charities. Having a career, at least one with expectations of advancement, was virtually impossible for most wives. But for 'career' officers, and some others, there was another price to pay: disruption of family life. My three children, Peter, Nicky and Theresa, all endured the constant moves, loss of friends, inevitable bullying of the new kids on the block, and eventually boarding school. For some parents, boarding school was a continuation of their own life pattern, but for myself and especially Irene, it was a brutal separation from those we loved most. The alternative, however, would have been a constant change of school every two years, with consequent changes in curriculum, teaching standards and availability of subjects.

By the time we arrived for my command tour at Coningsby, all three of our children were boarding; and at times, especially when they were going back from holidays, it was hard to bear. When we look back on those days, we remain undecided on whether it was the right thing to do or not. Some chose to keep their children at home, and for some it worked, for others it failed. I think it was easier for the girls than for Peter, but we will never know for sure. It is a consolation that we remain a close family, despite some worrying times when we drifted apart. We now have seven lovely grandchildren, all of whom enrich our lives.

But let Irene speak for herself!

> I met Chris in 1963 and we married in 1967, so I'm familiar with the stories and incidents of his life in the air. Added to that, of course, was our complex life 'on the ground'. During this time, we had three children and moved twenty-eight times, all over the UK and twice abroad. We found the RAF community full of bright and sociable people, and were always made welcome to every new station. Each tour of duty lasted about two years, which seemed to go by in a flash. I was fully engaged in childcare, entertaining (chef and hostess!), housework and gardening, a patchy career as a teacher and later a qualified Yoga teacher – not to mention packing and unpacking our home twenty-eight times.
>
> We both consider ourselves extremely fortunate to have lived in the RAF family, despite the 'ups and downs' and hard work. Certainly, we have an abundance of mostly wonderful memories – and we both wish we could start all over again for a repeat experience!
>
> Irene, Lady Coville

Towards summer in 1987, the operational tempo of the station was extremely high. We had already been through one series of TACEVAL, and despite the engineers putting the wrong ammunition in the gun packs, we had achieved a satisfactory result. Inevitably, with a new aircraft being declared and the added attraction of our vintage aircraft, we were inundated with visitors: the UK and French Staff Colleges, the Military Committee of NATO and the SACEUR (Supreme Allied Commander Europe) of the day, who was actually flown in a Tornado by the new OC 29(F) Sqn, Wg Cdr Lloyd Doble, an outstanding CO and pilot, who was to guide the unit through to being the first operational F3 Sqn. I flew with them a lot, and was officially declared operational by Lloyd after a most demanding series of day and night sorties. But there was an elephant lurking in the room, and it would not stay concealed.

Despite my best efforts, and those of many others, to improve the F3's operational capabilities, the aircraft remained essentially unfit for purpose alongside its counterparts and potential opponents. Things came to a head, as so often happens, in the Officers' Mess bar one night. Flt Lts Simon Manning and Mick Mercer (yes, he of bird in the conifers fame), both outstanding fighter pilots, nobbled me after a few beers and berated me for playing down the F3's problems and exaggerating its virtues. Things got a bit nasty when Simon accused me of being more interested in my pension than the operational capability of the RAF, but he bought me a large whisky and I forgave him. Over the weekend, I thought long and hard about what the lads had said, and decided that they were right, and I was losing credibility. Of course, in the background I was writing the sternest letters, albeit in diplomatic language, to my AOC. But I was not communicating well enough – with the aircrew especially, but in fact with the rest of the station as well. I resolved to put that right, and arranged for the entire station to attend a mass briefing. In front of 2,500 of my people, I laid out the good and bad points of the new aircraft, but emphasised that we had to make it work; that was our duty, and it was mine as the CO to make sure we did. I concluded by inviting anyone who could not live with this reality to bring a letter of resignation to my office within the hour, and I would ensure that they were posted forthwith. I sat behind my desk for an anxious period, half expecting a mass of disgruntled aircrew to arrive clutching envelopes, but not a single person did, and we all got stuck into a frantic period of operational training and exercises. During this challenging time, my old unit, No 5(F) Sqn formed under the command of Wg Cdr Euan Black, another excellent CO and pilot, with a puckish sense of humour. It was a great relief to me that I had such outstanding wing commanders at a time of great stress. My OC Ops Wing, Ron Shimmons, was a safe pair of hands running the core of our operational function, and Les Walsh, my OC Engineering Wing probably had the most complex organisation in his area of responsibility, with mechanical, general and electrical engineering squadrons to oversee. Probably totally exhausted, he handed over to Gerry Woodley, who steered the Wing through the final stages of the operational preparation for the station. These were men in their thirties, who had massive personal responsibility, and with it the accountability if things went wrong. In my experience, most people will say that they want more responsibility; some even argue that they deserve it. But put them on the spot when things do not go to plan and they so often dive for cover.

By the time I finished my tour, the much-loved Rick Peacock-Edwards was posted to the Ministry of Defence, and had been replaced by Peter Hitchcock, another Lightning pilot, with just the right calm touch to manage an Operational Conversion Unit. I mention all these people by name because they supported me at a very special period of this famous station's history. Together with their wives, they made the two years at Coningsby the most memorable in our lives in the RAF, even though occasionally pressures of work, or from top down, forced me to push them to their own limits. It was a sad day when I flew my last trip in the Tornado F3 and moved on to a very different future. But there was something else that blessed my tour, a unique experience enjoyed by so few very lucky modern pilots. I had displayed Hurricanes and Spitfires of the Battle of Britain Memorial Flight. I had also set my sights on being the first station commander to qualify on the beloved Lancaster, but that was impossible I was told. Hmmm!

Chapter 12

In the years following the Second World War it became traditional for a Spitfire and Hurricane to lead the Victory Day flypast over London. From that event, there grew the idea to form a historic collection of flyable aircraft to commemorate the RAF's major battle honour, the Battle of Britain. Thus in 1957, the Historic Aircraft Flight was formed at RAF Biggin Hill with one Hurricane (LF363) and three Griffon-powered Mk XIX Spitfires, which had flown in the RAF Meteorological Flight at RAF Woodvale, near Liverpool.

After a short period at RAF Coltishall, in Norfolk, the Flight was renamed the Battle of Britain Memorial Flight (BBMF) and moved to its present home at RAF Coningsby in 1976; it subsequently acquired several more aircraft, including the first Chipmunk in 1983, and a De Havilland Devon, used for multi-engine training and as a 'comms' aircraft to ferry air and groundcrews, together with essential ground equipment.

The Lancaster bomber, PA474, but for much of her life known as the 'City of Lincoln', was acquired by the BBMF in 1973. She was built in mid-1945 and assigned to reconnaissance duties after being delivered too late to take part in the bombing of Japan. After various duties, she was adopted by the Air Historical Branch for display work, appearing in two films: 'Operation Crossbow' and 'The Guns of Navarone'. Until the late 1980s, when the Canadian-restored Lancaster took to the skies, she was the only 'Lanc' still flying in the world – of a total build of over 7,000.

In the 1980s, the Flight had five fighters: two Merlin-powered Spitfires, the original Mk XIXs, and two Hurricane 2Cs. One of the Spitfires, a Mk 2 P7350, had flown in the Battle of Britain; the other, a Mk 5, was flown by the Eagle Squadrons, a brave group of young American pilots who made their way to the UK, often via Canada, to join the RAF before the United States formally joined the Allied effort after Pearl Harbor in December 1941.

CHAPTER 12

Becoming a BBMF display pilot was every fighter pilot's dream; but you had to be at the right place at the right time. I had flown a few piston-engined aircraft, like most pilots of my time. But the 'Hurri' and 'Spit' were a different breed to my Austers and Chipmunks; the comparison between a Ford Focus and an E-Type Jaguar was appropriate at the time. Both historic aircraft were extremely powerful – over 1,000 horsepower – and they could bite you if you let them off their leash. They were well-known for killing young pilots, especially during take-off and landing, where their large noses interfered with forward vision. Additionally, the Spitfire's narrow-track undercarriage left little room for error, especially when landing in a crosswind.

To prepare pilots for the challenges ahead, we were required to fly a couple of trips in a Harvard trainer, two of which were used for filming at Boscombe Down, the flight test centre. Accordingly, when the weather conditions were right, that is with a challenging wind blowing, I drove down for my introduction to flying a big, beefy prop aircraft; and the Harvard was exactly that. Designed as an advanced combat trainer, it first flew in 1935; over 15,000 were built, and over the next ten years were used by a host of air forces around the world, especially in the USA and the UK. Powered by a Pratt and Whitney Wasp radial engine, it produced over 600 horsepower, and had a top speed exceeding 200 mph. It was a beast.

The first trip I flew was in the front seat, concentrating on take-offs, circuits and landings, using the main into-wind runway. We then had a cup of coffee, and I was invited into the rear cockpit. But wait a minute; I can't see out! Just like the Spit, I am told. We then set off on one of the most challenging sorties of my flying career, concluding with several take-offs and landings on a runway with a substantial crosswind component. On a couple of occasions, I had full rudder and brake to stop the aircraft veering off the runway. In the debrief, I was reminded that I might get away with using brake to keep straight in the Hurricane, but if I used too much in the Spitfire, I would end up with the nose buried in the ground. I drove back to Coningsby with some apprehension; the next day I was programmed to fly the Hurricane.

★ ★ ★ ★ ★

On 4 June 1987, I donned my BBMF black flying suit for the first time and, after giving myself an appreciative wink in the mirror, reported to the Flight for my first sortie. BBMF was commanded by Sqn Ldr Tony Banfield, who flew the Lancaster, but the Fighter Leader was Sqn Ldr Paul Day, who was an instructor on the Phantom OCU at the time. Paul was a well-known character in the close-knit fighter community, having flown Hunters before the F4. He had also done a Phantom exchange tour with the USAF, earning the title 'Major' Day.

We sat down and he quizzed me on the checks for the Hurricane, which I would have to fly for fifteen hours before moving to the Spitfire. We then spoke about the sortie itself: cautionary words on the tendency to swing to the left on take off if you used too much power; changing hands on the control column to raise gear and flaps; turning and stalling; approach and landing; and, crucially, fuel tank management, which could catch you out and result in fuel starvation, even with lots of fuel in the tanks.

We walked out to my aircraft: PZ865, the last of 14,533 Hurricanes built. After doing the usual external checks, I climbed in. It was wonderful; that evocative smell one experiences in a vintage car, a mixture of leather, old cloth and fuel, but somehow producing from these ingredients a fragrance like no other. I was stepping into history. Paul stood on the wing as I started up, then after a thumbs-up he vanished, leaving this beautiful, precious aircraft to me, alone. I called for taxi clearance: 'Hurricane 01 taxi.' I took my time, remembering to weave around, enabling me to see clearly ahead. I lined up on the westerly runway, completed my engine checks, moved the throttle forward and released the brakes.

She leaps forward, but is drifting to the left despite full corrective right rudder; I'm going to hit the runway lights if I don't do something quickly … too much power … throttle back a bit … ah, that's done it. The nose slowly comes back to the centreline … tail wheel off the ground … slowly ease her off the runway at about 75 mph … change hands and raise gear and flaps … hold the nose down to gain speed … my God, I'm flying a Hurricane!

I look down at the houses below, and many people are outside waving towels, flags or anything that comes to hand, so much is the affection of the local people towards the historic aircraft.

I climb to 5,000ft. The roll rate is slow, with the small ailerons and flexible wings, but the pitch rate is good. I do a few steep turns, increasing power as the speed starts to come back. We are limited to '3-G' to preserve airframe life, so I back off the turn as the accelerometer shows me reaching the maximum. Now let's try a stall … nose up … throttle back … 65 mph and the nose slices down … a bit of power and relax the back pressure and she's flying again. Time to get back and do a couple of circuits; and then I have to land, knowing most of the Station will be out to watch me. No pressure then.

The first circuit goes well ... downwind at 140 mph ... checks complete ... gear and flaps down ... turn finals at 100 mph, reducing to 95 ... OK, overshoot, but watch the power ... keep the nose straight with rudder ... watch the speed doesn't drop off ... back to 140 mph downwind and repeat the process. I realise I am hot and sweaty ... my pulse rate high ... slow down and relax and you'll fly better. Fuel getting low, so I need to land this time. Round finals ... looking good ... speed reducing to 75 mph as the runway approaches ... can't see much over the nose now, but keep the sideways scan going ... flare into the right landing attitude and bring the power back ... she's down, but need to keep straight and gently on the brakes ... she comes to a halt off the runway and I complete the after-landing checks and taxi in ... Paul and a photographer are waiting in dispersal. He gives me a 'thumbs–up' and I feel very happy. I climb out and he gives me the BBMF badge for my flying suit; a few photos are taken, most of which make me look exhausted, which I probably was. But I was also elated; a dream had come true.

After another couple of trips, I am cleared by the AOC to join my fellow pilots and Lancaster aircrew on the display circuit. With running the Station, and staying current on the Phantom and Tornado, I decide to wait to convert to the Spitfire until the following season, but enjoy participating in several airshows and flypasts in the lovely 'Hurri'.

We rarely flew anywhere in a straight line, as we were inundated with requests to overfly village fairs and town events. On one occasion, I was returning from a display at RAF Manston in Kent, with a request to overfly the RAF Hospital at Ely, in Cambridgeshire, where they were opening a new surgical theatre. I was given a time bracket to coincide with the cutting of the ribbon, and was precisely on time as I lined up with the hospital main building clearly visible ahead. Suddenly, I became aware of the unmistakable trademark of the Red Arrows aerobatic team, red, white and blue smoke – and they were dead ahead, coming straight towards me. The only thing I could do was to dive down to treetop level, hoping the turbulence would not send me out of control. The nine red Hawks roared over me, sending a fine mist of patriotic smoke over my windscreen. The subsequent landing was interesting, and I had to roll my sleeves up with the lads to clean the aircraft before its next flight. Later, I had a word with the team leader, Richie Thomas, who confessed that he had no idea I would be joining them in the flypast, and only saw me as I streaked under his nose; a major communication blunder. Looking on the bright side, the air commodore medic in charge of the hospital sent me a very nice letter congratulating me on the precision with which I had crossed under the Red Arrows exactly over the opening ceremony!

As the season drew to a close, I tackled Tony Banfield about getting checked out as co-pilot in the Lancaster. He reminded me that there was no precedent for a Station Commander to do so, that it would need the AOC's approval and that I would need to fly a couple of trips in the venerable Shackleton first to prove I could handle such a large, four-engine bomber. I told him I would do what I wanted on my station, that I would speak to the AOC (which I never got round to doing), and that I would complete the necessary flights in preparation.

The Shackleton was still in service with No 8 Squadron at Lossiemouth, in north Scotland. The Boss at the time was an old buddy of mine, Wg Cdr Dave Hencken. A quick phone call revealed that he would be operating out of Leuchars the following week, and that he would be delighted to give me a couple of trips in the circuit. Accordingly, I took a Phantom up to Leuchars, flew with Dave twice, concentrating on approaches and landings, got him to certify that I had satisfied him with my handling of the aircraft and pitched into Tony Banfield's office the following day. He looked perplexed; defeated.

'OK, Sir,' he eventually conceded. 'We've got a couple of hours left on the aeroplane before she goes into servicing, and a bit of that is for the display on Saturday to the BBMF Association Reunion.'

'That'll do very nicely,' I replied, and spent the next few hours getting briefed on the aircraft, its handling and its checks.

That evening, I sat down with a whisky, and started to think about the implications of the next day. If I crashed a Tornado I would probably be forgiven after a year or two. But if I bent the RAF's only flying Lancaster … it didn't bear thinking about. I had a quick look at my copy of Queen's Regulations to ensure that the death penalty wasn't still available for gross military misdemeanours, and went to bed full of anticipation.

I woke up at six o'clock on the morning of 1 October 1987. If the weather was bad, I was scuppered, as the Lanc had to be in winter servicing the following week. It was glorious. I donned my black flying suit, kissed Irene goodbye after a quick breakfast, and headed down to the Flight, where PA474 was being pushed out onto the dispersal apron. She looked magnificent in the morning sunshine. After a coffee and a briefing, Tony and I, with a rather apprehensive-looking crew, climbed into the aircraft – itself no mean feat. In the operational Lancasters, the single pilot sat in the left-hand seat, with the flight engineer alongside on his right. In PA474, as in other training versions, the engineers place had been replaced with a rather cramped co-pilot's seat, with a control column and access to the throttles which were positioned in the centre console. Tony monitored my checks and, one at a time, we started the four beautiful Merlin engines. If they had sounded sweet in the Hurricane, all four purring away was like a choir of angels. We taxied out to the easterly runway, the wind on the nose at 10 knots, the visibility superb. Engine and pre-take off checks complete.

Tony looks at me. 'You have control, Sir.' The engineer slowly moves the throttles forward, monitoring each engine's performance and synchronisation. I concentrate on keeping straight. Tail wheel off the ground and then slowly ease back on the control column. She rises majestically into the air … undercarriage and flaps up. We climb like a giant raptor into the clear blue sky. I am mesmerised by the beauty of the aircraft, its wonderful sound and the sight of those giant propellers turning together with a gentle hum.

Tony takes control and we fly towards the airfield for a practice display. A Hurricane and Spitfire have followed us airborne and join in close formation. Together, we fly over Coningsby, then the fighters split off and we do a series of flypasts, demonstrating the immense grace of the Lancaster. We then hold off for ten minutes while the fighters do individual displays, after which they race up to join us for one final flypast before they break off to land. It's now back to me for the landing. We reduce speed downwind and lower the undercarriage and flaps. I turn finals, with speed stabilising at 120 mph. Over the threshold, slowly sinking and raising the nose into the flare for landing … I call for the engineer to 'slow cut' and he gradually brings back the power. We sink gracefully onto the runway, and ever so carefully apply the brakes. We are down safely, and with a good landing; I am now qualified as co-pilot on the Lancaster. As we walk back to leave the aircraft, I can sense the spirits of the 55,000 men who lost their lives in this magnificent machine during the war. I feel honoured and humbled, and not a little emotional.

★ ★ ★ ★ ★

During the winter season, the Flight's aircraft go through an extensive servicing, and sometimes a change of colour scheme. The Chipmunk (only one in the 1980s) remains available for the pilots to keep their hands in on a piston 'tail dragger', and it was a great joy on a busy day, when the time needed for a Tornado flight was impossible, to take thirty minutes in this lovely little aeroplane to do some low-level aerobatics. But all the time we were watching the days go by, anticipating the moment when we could bring out the precious fighters and start a new season. Of course, my time was adequately filled with completing the operational work-up on the station, and flying with the OCU and the new squadrons as much as I could. We also had a contingent of Saudi pilots and navigators converting to the Tornado F3; an interesting mix of very experienced pilots and young first tour navigators. The constant visits by VIPs continued, including a day when the Station's Honorary Air Commodore, The Princess Margaret, graced us with her presence. In the past, some of my predecessors had found her difficult, but I liked her very much and we got on well together. My experience of the Royal Family has been extremely positive, and it is all too often the fawning flunkies who accompany them who place absurd conditions on how they should be greeted and entertained. One of HRH's acolytes insisted that once she had put down her utensils, everyone else had to stop eating. On the day, Princess Margaret nibbled a few pieces of chicken before the rest of the hundred or so guests had been served, then put down her knife and fork, resulting in the Mess Manager halting service. Understandably, as they had all paid £20 for their meal, there was visible annoyance. I boldly asked HRH if we could continue serving, to which she expressed astonishment that I had asked. 'Of course they must have their lunch,' she insisted. A very relieved Mess Manager opened the kitchen doors and the plates reappeared.

We always left the Princess alone for a while by the Hurricanes when she visited the BBMF. One of them had been flown by Group Captain Peter Townsend, arguably the real love of her life. For a few moments, she was lost in personal thoughts and memories. She was a wonderful supporter of her Station, and we were all very fond of her.

Shortly after Easter in 1988 the hangar doors of BBMF opened again, and the fighters and the Lancaster were brought out in all their glory. On 25 April I started flying the vintage fighters, with a practice display in the Hurricane overhead Coningsby. It was so exhilarating to feel the joy of flight in such a thoroughbred again. But I had my sights on something even more special; a machine that still evokes memories of knights of the air, of an aircraft that the entire world stills speaks of in awe – the Spitfire.

After a season flying the Hurricane, the preparation for the 'Spit' was relatively short and straightforward. In no time at all, I found myself in the cockpit of one of the two Mk 5s, AB910. There were a few obvious differences

CHAPTER 12

between the two fighters, but the most significant was the decreased view over the nose. Additionally, I had been warned and warned again that on the ground the Spitfire was an accident waiting to happen. The nose is huge and heavy, the tail is light; so any sudden use of the brakes is likely to lead to the aircraft tipping over. Moreover, the very narrow track undercarriage makes the aircraft prone to 'ground looping' if too much rudder is used, if a crosswind starts a significant yaw or if the pilot is too exuberant with the throttle. But there is another trap awaiting: when the undercarriage is down, the right leg obscures the air intake to the cooling system, quickly resulting in the coolant boiling and requiring engine shutdown. So, from taxi to take off, and from putting the undercarriage down before landing to shutdown, there was a risk of overheating and potentially damaging the engine. This became an issue for me in a future sortie!

There was that familiar feel of a vintage machine, but there was something else: this was a Spitfire, the most famous aircraft in the history of the RAF. It was almost a spiritual experience to feel that wonderful aircraft enveloping me, being surrounded by machinery that had been honed to sheer perfection. But more than that, I felt I was in the company of the souls of those hundreds of pilots who had sat in Spitfires before me, many of whom had lost their lives or suffered terrible injuries.

Paul Day, in his usual laconic way, had told me that, with a fuel tank just forward of my legs, if I had an engine failure after take-off I was probably going to die, burned into oblivion before help could arrive. But as I taxied out, I felt no fear, only tremendous exultation.

I lined up on the runway; take-off checks complete.

'Spitfire 01, you are cleared for take-off. Surface wind 280 degrees at 10 knots.' Perfect. Release the brake lever … slowly ease the power forward, feeding in right rudder to counter the swing from the engine's torque … a little more power, but only a little as she is already wanting to drift left with full right rudder … tailwheel off the ground and gently lift her off at about 85 mph … keep the nose low to gain speed. Now the tricky bit … change hands on the control column … move the right hand over to raise the undercarriage, then the flaps … change hands again and left hand back on the throttle … 140 mph, start to climb. Joy of Joys … I am airborne in a Spitfire and she feels beautiful. None of the heaviness in roll of the Hurricane … the Spit is perfectly harmonised, totally responsive to the pilot's inputs … I feel that I am part of this beautiful aircraft, not something separate. I climb to 7,000ft and try a few steep turns … such a delight. Now a stall … apparently more interesting than the stall in the Hurricane

… throttle closed, speed back … keep ailerons and rudder central, wings level … at 65 mph … oh my goodness, the nose pitches up and left … I am nearly inverted … ease off the back pressure and recover … a quick surge and splutter from the engine … all perfectly normal. I bring the Spit back to level flight and do a few basic aerobatics, soaring high above the clouds, the world below a patchwork of green and brown, tiny fields and houses as I rejoice in my own world in the blueness of the sky.

All too soon, I have to turn back towards base; now the heart begins to flutter. No Hurricane this; the Spitfire is more challenging to land, and I will not be able to relax until the chocks are in place and the engine closed down. I turn into the circuit and bring the throttle back … speed back below 180 mph … change hands again and lower undercarriage … check undercarriage indicator has gone from red to green, confirming gear down and locked … speed decreasing below 140 mph … select flaps down … start turn onto final approach … keep the turn going, speed reducing to 95 mph and line up with the runway … oh my God, I can't see anything over the nose … look down the runway and use your peripheral vision sideways as the ground gets closer … 75 mph … now forget everything else but getting the landing flare right … slowly close the throttle, stick coming back … she's down … a little bump, then she settles … keep looking ahead … keep straight and very gentle on the brakes with stick fully back … carefully taxi off the runway, complete after landing checks and slowly, weaving from side to side, return to dispersal … close down … chocks in … I remain in the cockpit for a while, the groundcrew quizzical … but I am feeling so emotional. Eventually, I unstrap and climb out. I stop and look at this beautiful aircraft that I have just flown, and glowing with pride, head for a coffee and the debrief.

Shortly after converting to the Spitfire, I flew to Duxford Airfield to attend the annual Spitfire Society gathering, a meeting place for pilots young and old (or perhaps old and very old) who had had the joy of flying this renowned aircraft. After doing a short display in the Mk 5, I landed to refuel and have a coffee with attendees, all of whom were sitting on bench seats around large wooden tables, drinking tea and telling aircrew stories. I sat next to a diminutive elderly lady, whose name I didn't quite catch in the ongoing banter. 'Nice display,' she said, smiling. I thanked her. 'I like the Mk 5, but my favourite was the Mk 9.' I suddenly realised that this was

Diana Barnato-Walker, one of the wonderful Air Transport Auxiliary pilots. I listened fascinated as she reeled off story after story about their amazing escapades, ferrying a range of aircraft between depots and operational airfields. Contrary to popular belief, they weren't all privileged young women; there were men as well, the majority being either too old to join the RAF or had a disability which prevented them from doing so. One had only one arm; another used to navigate on Woodbine cigarettes, with a line on his map marked at every 4 minutes 30 seconds – the time he took to smoke one, stub it out and light another.

Very often, two girls would fly a bomber to an airfield, and be greeted by bemused groundcrew who would ask: 'Where's the pilot?' Diana was telling me that on more than one occasion, in disbelief, the airmen would go in search of the 'real pilot'.

A few years later, Diana invited me to attend the ATA annual dinner as the guest speaker. It was a wonderful evening, at the end of which she gave me her pilot's notes, which covered every possible aircraft type, some with only a page each. Sadly, most of the pilots are now gone, but we owe them a lot, as every RAF pilot was needed for operational duties, and that they were not diverted to ferry duties was entirely attributable to the work done by the ATA. Wonderful people and very gallant pilots.

I enjoyed several weeks of display flying, intermingled with running a busy station and keeping up to scratch on the Tornado. Sometimes I accompanied the Lancaster, but often flew alone, with only stopwatch, map and compass to arrive at the right locations, precisely on time. And some locations were especially challenging to find, resulting on one occasion in an embarrassed BBMF pilot being told on landing that he had displayed over a most appreciative crowd in one village, while the one that had paid for the display a few miles away could only enjoy the occasional murmur of a distant Merlin engine. Just now and again, the consequences of getting the navigation wrong could be dire, and they seemed to crop up at the most unexpected times.

On 6 June 1987, I was looking forward to a pleasant early morning flight in the Chipmunk down to Bournemouth, where the Flight had pre-positioned for a ceremonial event in Caen, France. It was only the evening before that I had realised the full significance of the occasion, when I saw on TV the preparations being made on location. The vast memorial, together with a museum, had been constructed to celebrate the anniversary of D-Day, and it was to be formally opened by the French President, Francois Mitterand, in the presence of eleven world leaders, including Prime Minister Margaret Thatcher. Getting it wrong risked a Surface to Air Handbag response. My AOC, Mike Stear, phoned me to make sure I understood that this was to be a perfect flypast in every way; no mistakes would be tolerated. I assured him that the best BBMF navigator was in the Lancaster, so he needn't have any concerns. Oh dear!

The following morning, the sun was shining, and the weather forecast for the sortie was excellent. I climbed into the Chipmunk at 0730, with a member of the BBMF groundcrew in the back seat. We had an uneventful flight, and arrived in good time for a briefing before setting off. To my horror, there on the flight apron was the Lanc with an engine missing. I scrambled out to find an anxious-looking Tony Banfield shaking his head.

'Sorry, Sir, we had a minor problem on the way down last night, and when we did an engine run this morning, we had a major failure. I'm afraid she's U/S.'

'Who's leading the flypast,' I asked, feeling just a little concerned, as we had to be airborne in less than an hour.

'Well, I guess it's you in the Spit, Sir,' Tony replied. I gulped, the words of my AOC ringing in my ears.

We had little time to get organised. Jack Hamill (of 43 Sqn ejection) was on my wing in the Hurricane, and he had thoughtfully completed the necessary flight plan and prepared two maps. But they were photocopies, and the quality was dreadful, with the essential detail virtually impossible to discern.

'Do we know where the monument is exactly?' I asked.

'We think it's about here,' he replied, with a big sweep of his hand. 'Somewhere to the northwest of the city.' Very helpful. 'We do know that the French aerobatic team, the Patrouille de France, are flying over just before us, as the President takes the stand. Apparently, we have to fly over exactly at noon, at the moment he presses a button and the monument is unveiled. I'm bloody glad I'm not leading this.' Thanks, Jack.

We sat down and studied the route, which was going to be interesting, as there was a fair amount of controlled airspace to get through, not to mention crossing the French border and negotiating any fine detail in French, rather than the official air traffic control language, which is English. Fortunately, my French was quite reasonable, so I reckoned we could probably get by if we encountered any stroppy Gallic controllers. We had to wear Mae West lifejackets as there was a good stretch of water to cross, which reduced the cockpit elbow room considerably, with consequent challenges to handling maps and managing radio changes. Fuel was going to be tight, but I wanted to give us at least ten minutes in a holding position in case we were delayed by air traffic or weather.

It was about eighty miles to the tip of the Cherbourg peninsula, after which we would fly around the coast to the estuary leading into Caen, at the port of Ouistreham, and hold there for as long as necessary. It was ten miles from the holding point, with a heading of 197 degrees to our best guess at the museum's location. I could see on the map that at about a mile to go there was a patch of green, with a small lake at the end. If I flew right over that lake the site should be right ahead; or not if our assumptions on its location were wrong! I intended to fly the run-in leg at 240 mph, so it would take two minutes thirty seconds from the port to overhead the likely position of the monument. It could be the longest two-and-a-half minutes of my life!

We climbed into the cockpits at 1100 hrs, started up ten minutes later and took off at 1120. The weather was good, with tufty cumulus cloud beneath us as we climbed to 5,000ft. After thirteen minutes, I picked up the tip of Cherbourg, and dropped down to 1,500ft, just below the cloud. A quick call to Cherbourg airport and we were cleared to proceed; amazingly, they seemed to be expecting us. We followed the coastline round and at 1145 I picked up the Brittany Ferries ships docked at Ouistreham. So far, so good, and the weather looked excellent down towards Caen, the northern outskirts of which I could make out clearly. The run-in would be into sun, but hopefully that would not be too much of a problem. I rechecked my stopwatch against my wristwatch, and started to circle over the port, giving Caen airport a warning call. They acknowledged cheerily, and asked if we could overfly them after we had completed the ceremonial bit. 'Avec plaisir,' I responded. 'One minute to run-in,' I called on the radio. Jack acknowledged. I rolled out of the turn. 197 degrees, 240 mph. This was it. Descend to 1,000ft. Over the port at 1157 and 30 seconds exactly.

Now concentrate on absolutely accurate flying … the river is on my left, slowly diverging … one minute … I can see the patch of green ahead; it's a golf course … and there's the lake at the end … I need to be overhead that lake at precisely 2 minutes 10 seconds … slightly early … throttle back a little … suddenly to my left I see the Patrouille de France, trailing Blue, White and Red smoke … down to 500ft at the lake and look ahead … shit, there's coloured smoke everywhere … but then I can see lots of flags …

now the monument and lots of people … we fly over as my stopwatch goes through noon. I pulled up to 1,000ft, picked up Caen airport to my right.

'Caen, Caen, Spitfire and Hurricane, thirty seconds to flypast.'

'OK, OK, as low as you like. All traffic holding clear at 2,000ft.'

Nod's as good as a wink. We dropped down to … ermm … well, you can guess, and scorched across the airfield.

'Formidable! Formidable!' the controller called out excitedly, as we pulled up and rolled our aircraft into the clear sky above.

I converged back towards the coast, and soon picked up the unmistakable shape of the Cherbourg peninsula. Thirty minutes later, we were closing down our engines at Bournemouth. Jack climbed out first, and a worried-looking Tony Banfield asked him how it went. Jack smiled: 'He was half a second early and I was half a second late.' We all burst out laughing, somewhat nervously, I recall.

The following morning, the *Times* newspaper covered the ceremony. The last paragraph read: 'With perfect precision, as the Memorial was being unveiled, two aircraft of the RAF's Battle of Britain Memorial Flight flew over the world's leaders, all of whom burst into spontaneous applause.'

Phew!

Around mid-September each year, the RAF celebrates its most notable victory: The Battle of Britain, fought in the skies over England in 1940. In halting further German expansion at the Channel coast, The Battle of Britain was not only the saviour of the UK, but arguably of the free world. Had a Nazi invasion taken place, it is hard to imagine how the United States could have entered the war in Europe. Hitler and Stalin, two of the most evil men in human history, would have dominated Europe, and with nuclear weapons emerging from accelerated research, the consequences could have been catastrophic.

As well as a service in Westminster Abbey on Battle of Britain Sunday, many events take place in towns and cities around the country, especially on RAF stations. Celebrations range from air shows on major bases to cocktail parties, giving an ideal opportunity not only to celebrate the famous victory, but also to host local people who have been supportive and hospitable to the unit and its servicemen and women. A special attraction to mark the end of cocktail parties was a flypast, especially if it were by a BBMF aircraft. This kept us very busy most evenings in mid-September!

On 9 September 1988, after a hectic day, I was scheduled to fly a Spitfire over three stations, Binbrook in Lincolnshire, followed by Staxton Wold and Fylingdales, both in Yorkshire. The displays were timed to give me adequate time for transit between the units, but absolutely no slack, as I had to land before it got dark; night flying was not practised on the flight, owing to the additional risk to such precious assets. I had to be on the ground by 1845 latest.

I was feverishly sorting out my maps in my office prior to setting off when Sharon, my PA, knocked on the door. I looked up, showing my annoyance at being disturbed during flight preparation.

'Sharon, you know….'

'Yes, I know, Sir, but there's a gentleman on the phone says he must talk to you urgently. It's about your flight, Sir.'

'OK,' I replied acidly, 'Put him through.' I heared the click. 'Chris Coville.'

'Group captain, I'm so sorry to interrupt you, but I've been trying to contact BBMF for an hour to see if anyone is flying near Bridlington. I'm speaking from there with my brother from a phone box. Our mother is waiting outside.'

He went on to say that his mother had been married for just a few weeks to a young airman, who was killed in a Wellington bomber in 1940. He was 20, and she was 19. She married again after the war, and her husband, their father, had died the previous year. After much persuasion, she had agreed to visit with them the resting place of her first husband, who was buried in the Commonwealth War Graves section of Bridlington cemetery.

'Would it be at all possible for you to do a flypast over the grave for her?' he pleaded. I looked at my watch.

'Can you get her there for six o'clock?' I asked.

'Yes, Yes,' he replied.

'No promises, I'll do my best.' I put down the phone. Maps out again; OK, I thought. Binbrook, then out to sea at Bridlington, and come in from the harbour. 'Sharon, get me an exact position of the cemetery at Bridlington, please; and quickly.'

I can go straight from there to Staxton Wold, and then on to Fylingdales. Could be dodgy getting back before dark. I bundled up my maps and Sharon passed me a photocopy of the cemetery's position. 'Tell Staxton and Fylingdales I'll be ten to fifteen minutes delayed. Sounds better than late.' She nodded and picked up the phone as I headed toward the Flight, where Paul Day was waiting. I told him the revised plan and, typically, he agreed without argument. 'Make sure you know where all the light switches are in the cockpit before it gets dark,' he warned. Good advice.

I get airborne and head north towards Binbrook. No need for maps; I know my way there. But the visibility is poor. Farmers are stubble-burning, and it's getting misty. The visibility west, into sun, is terrible. Could be interesting. I pick up the base easily, do a few circuits of the Officers' Mess, where I can see a hundred faces staring up into the sky. Job done, now north-east and pick up the coast near a big promontory, Flamborough Head. I see it a few miles away, and adjust heading towards Bridlington. Visibility is getting worse as the sun sinks, putting its glaring rays through the gathering mist and stubble smoke. It's five to six; but there ahead is the harbour at Bridlington, on the nose a couple of miles away. I look again at the cemetery position; a quick turn to the left over the harbour and it should be there … somewhere.

The harbour flashes by underneath, and I jink towards where I think there should be a green patch. Suddenly, it's there; just right of the nose. I slam the bank on and put maximum G-force on to correct my heading. And yes, down there, I can see three people waving furiously … it must be them.

No time to relax. I turn onto a westerly heading towards Staxton Wold. Immediately the visibility into sun drops right down. I'll never find the tiny station like this. Look at the map. Turn back up the coast and follow it up to a small town, Filey. I can then at least follow a road down to just north of the base. I pick up the A1039 … watch out for a roundabout with the A64 … I call Staxton … they reply 'We've put the boundary sodium lights on. Clear to display.' Why didn't I think of that?

Roundabout ahead … over the top and hard left on to south. Yes, there are the lights encircling the base. You clever people. I roar over the small Mess, and do a few wingovers and flypasts, before turning north towards Fylingdales, one of the Ballistic Missile Warning Sites, with massive, circular radomes up on high ground on the Yorkshire Moors. But it's starting to get dark, and the ground is rising in front of me. No future in this. Find a big road to follow. Back to the map. I'll head to the big town of Pickering and from there follow the main road north up towards Whitby. If I stay just to the right of the road, I should see the giant white balls out to the east. I pass a small town, Lockon. Then there's a jink in the road. Just another mile or so, and there they are to my right. I turn hard in a climbing turn over the radomes, picking up the Mess with the assembled throng, and dive back down towards them, my Merlin engine singing gloriously. A few passes and it's time to go. But my God it's getting dark.

I fumble around and eventually get the internal and external lights on; but the cockpit instruments are really badly lit. Up to 2,000ft heading south. It's deceptively light up here, but I can see the car lights coming on below me. I fly over Binbrook and call Coningsby for rejoin, descending into the darkness. They respond at once. 'Roger, Spitfire 01, clear to join Runway 27, QFE 1015; circuit clear.' I set the altimeter to 1015 millibars, which will give me the height above the touchdown point. It is bloody dark. I can see the flames spurting out from the exhausts in front of me, a translucent blue colour. In normal circumstances quite beautiful. I turn downwind, selecting undercarriage down ... turn finals and select flaps ... roll out and stare at the runway lights, but keeping an eye right and left to judge height ... over the threshold ... looks about right ... close the throttle and flare ... nothing, just blackness ... hold it a little longer with a tad of power ... and I'm down. A bit of a bounce, but probably no one saw, as it's definitely night time; 1855 hours!

I closed down, and Paul Day was standing there with a grin on his face.

'Bet that frightened you a bit, Sir?'

'Not at all,' I lied.

'Anyway,' he said,' 'Just had a gentleman on the phone, saying that just as they arrived at their Mum's first husband's grave, you flew right overhead. They asked me to say thanks; it made a sad event joyful and very special for them all.'

I went home and pulled myself a beer. I was knackered, but it had all been worthwhile.

★ ★ ★ ★ ★

Air Chief Marshal Sir Hugh Dowding was Commander in Chief of RAF Fighter Command in the early part of the war and the Battle of Britain.

A veteran of the First World War, in which he was a fighter pilot and CO of 16 Squadron, he created the world's first integrated defence system. Before the Second World War, he oversaw the introduction of the Spitfire and Hurricane fighters into RAF service, aircraft which became pivotal to success in the coming air war. He also championed the case of radio direction finding (RDF), which became better known as Radar.

Dowding's complex system of defence included Radar, the Observer Corps, sector operations' rooms, and finally squadrons of modern fighter aircraft which could be accurately directed towards the incoming enemy aircraft. Despite having been an enigmatic character, with a nickname of 'Stuffy', he was nevertheless liked and respected by the men of his command. It was his vision and leadership that, above all other factors, determined the outcome of the Battle of Britain.

Dowding was born in 1882 in Moffat, a small town in Dumfries and Galloway, Scotland, where the local people raised the funds needed to erect a striking memorial in his honour. Every year, during Battle of Britain week in September, there is a service at the memorial, at which a solitary Spitfire flies over the site to break the observed two-minute silence, and then puts on a display to complete the event. At least that's the theory. In practice, getting across the high ground running down the spine of England had proven challenging, and for three years a flypast had been impossible owing to low cloud over the hills. On 11 September 1988, I was given the job of making sure it wasn't four years on the run. On the 6th, I flew a low-level exercise in the north of Scotland in a Tornado F3, and made sure we had enough fuel to do a recce of the memorial area before doing it with only a stopwatch, map and compass in the Spit. It looked daunting, as the final run-in from the west was into rising ground, with Moffat itself in a bowl in front of mountainous terrain. The A74 Motorway would take me within a few miles of the town, but thereafter it would be very weather dependent. To add to the challenge, the trip was right on the limit of the Spitfire's range, so to cover all eventualities we were going to position a couple of the BBMF groundcrew at RAF Leeming, in Yorkshire, as a possible diversion and refuel option.

The service was at three o'clock in the afternoon, and the senior RAF officer attending was AVM David Brook, Air Officer Scotland. I had known him from my Leuchars days, and always found him a most charming and cooperative gentleman. On the morning of 11 September, he called me in my office to see what chance we had of making it this time. I had looked at the Met forecast, and I had to tell him that it didn't look too good, with low cloud over the Pennines high ground and in the Moffat area itself; in fact there was a good chance of rain from midday onwards. I told him I would do my best.

I climbed into the cockpit of the Mk 5, AB910, at 1330, and was airborne twenty minutes later. The first part of the flight was uneventful, but as I headed north into Yorkshire the weather, as forecast, started to deteriorate, and to my horror I could see that the cloud was already on the hilltops between me and my destination. No chance of just flying a straight line; I would have to find a valley and see if I could sneak through. There is a road that goes across the Yorkshire Dales from Bedale in the east to Kendal in the west. I thought it was worth a try, and dropped down to low level up into the rising ground ahead. It was getting a bit marginal, and for a moment I thought I'd have to pull out and admit defeat. But there was just a glimmer of light ahead under the cloud; what pilots call a letter box, and perhaps just enough to get through. I was down at very low level, the cloud just a few feet above my canopy, and the lorries trudging up the steep incline getting ever closer. Decision time; go for it.

I scorched through the letter box, no doubt giving the vehicles below quite a surprise, and the ground started to drop away below me. Definitely worth an interim 'Phew!'

I picked up the M6 motorway ahead, and to try and claw back a bit of time, cut the corner and headed north, easing on a little more power, but always mindful of the fuel situation. After nearly an hour's flying, I approached Carlisle and asked for permission to pass down the western side of their control zone. They replied: 'Negative, Spitfire 01; we want you to do a flypast. All traffic will hold clear at 1,000ft minimum.'

Gawd, and I'm late; but can't disappoint the taxpayers, so I jinked right and flew across the airfield at, errm … again, minimum height and maximum speed. I pulled back up to 1,000ft and overflew Lockerbie, soon to become infamous a few months later. I was still slightly late so increased speed a little.

It was starting to rain, lightly, but enough to bring the visibility and cloud base down. I could see the service station on the motorway coming up … lake on its right. It was three o'clock; the silence would be just starting. I turned hard at the junction and headed up into the high ground.

Viz not good … hardly see the hills ahead … I wipe my brow and stare ahead … I can see the small town now … stay low, below the threatening cloud base … there's the site ahead … I streak across … it is 1402 and ten seconds … Damn, ten seconds late … a few quick passes and orbits at very low level under the cloud and I head back towards the motorway, gradually climbing away from the ground.

I settled down and rechecked fuel … a bit marginal for getting back to Coningsby, so I throttled back a bit and concentrated on saving every gallon of fuel I could. The letter box was still there, and even higher, so I went through without alarming too many motorists. As I approached RAF Leeming, I calculated that I could just make it back to base with minimum fuel. I called Coningsby and the weather was improving; home it is. After a quick call to Leeming to tell the groundcrew to head back to base (sorry lads), I set a direct heading to the overhead, and landed back after a sortie of nearly two-and-a-half hours. When I got back to my office, the phone was ringing. It was an exultant David Brook.

'Bloody marvellous,' he said. 'I was just about to say, as you can see the weather is too bad for a flypast, when we heard the wonderful sound of the Merlin in the distance. There wasn't a dry eye to be seen!'

That's what BBMF was all about. We had to work very hard at times, without the benefit of modern navigation aids, but to hear or to see the joy at what we had done was humbling, and I was honoured to be part of a great bunch of dedicated people, albeit for a short time. My flight over Moffat was my last one in the Spitfire, and it was also my most memorable.

Before leaving Coningsby, I had one last great flying experience. No 29 Sqn, led by Lloyd Doble, had been tasked with a round-the-world trip in their Tornado F3s, supported by tankers and Hercules transport aircraft. It was a truly epic journey, requiring landings at islands in the middle of the Pacific Ocean, and constant time zone changes. I flew over to the States to meet them at Harrisburg, in Pennsylvania. They had flown across from Los Angeles non-stop, and were all exhausted after weeks away. After taking part in the Harrisburg Air Day, at which Flt Lt Fred Grundy showed how the aircraft could be displayed in the right hands, I flew with the squadron to Goose Bay, in Newfoundland, and after a night's stay crossed the Atlantic back to Coningsby, where we were met by the Chief of the Air Staff and national media. Lloyd was rightly given a prestigious state award at the end of his tour; in all respects, he had been an outstanding squadron commander and supportive executive.

On reflection, Coningsby was an extremely challenging command tour, with a whole series of operational evaluations and a host of personnel issues. I didn't always get the leadership right, but I believe I always had the humility to accept when I was wrong and make corrections. In the debrief on my confidential report a few weeks before leaving, the new AOC, and an old friend, AVM Roger Palin, suggested that my performance fell short of 'the best'. I have to say, after a full career in the service, that his ideas and mine of who were 'the best' were severely at odds. But life is not always as you would wish it, and I had to make the best of whatever the RAF had in mind for my future.

CHAPTER 12

Shortly after leaving Coningsby, I was at a dinner at Bentley Priory in honour of the veterans of the American Eagle Squadrons, which readers may recall were those courageous young Americans who found a way to join the RAF before Pearl Harbor. Sitting alongside me was a lovely Texan, who mused that he often wondered what had become of his beloved Mk 5 Spitfire, AB910. Of course, I was able to tell him that the aircraft was still flying, and that I had flown it myself on many occasions. He looked at me incredulously: 'Chris, you gotta be shittin' me!' I assured him that I was not, and arranged for him to go to Coningsby the next day. Chuck very kindly sent me a photo of himself, after forty-three years, sitting again in the cockpit of AB910, tears streaming down his old face.

THE STELLAR YEARS

'You make all kinds of mistakes, but as long as you are generous and true and also fierce, you cannot hurt the world or even seriously distress her.'

'Keep buggering on.'

Sir Winston Churchill

Chapter 13

There was a time, as I saw my tour at Coningsby coming to an end, when I wondered if I wanted to stay in the RAF. I had an option point at age 44, which was only the following year; and I couldn't imagine anything better ahead. Worse, there was a good chance I might get stuck in a rut in the Ministry of Defence, or a staff job at Strike Command at High Wycombe, especially after my so-so report from the AOC. I had been at the top of the tree at Coningsby, with total authority, enormous responsibility and great flying. A few friends who had made the transition into the airlines tried to talk me into following down that path, but despite the cash incentive it didn't attract me. My very good friend Ali McKay had already made his decision, and subsequently joined the John Lewis Partnership on the fast-track executive stream. There were obvious options in the aerospace business as well. Before making my decision, I had asked for an interview with the Air Secretary, AVM Tony Mason. Shortly before my posting at Coningsby ended, I met up with him in the library of the RAF Club in London, where he read my fortune. The bad news was that all the faults identified by my headmaster at grammar school, Brother John, still seemed to be an indelible part of my character: took too much on, not interested in detail, more time for fun than work. The good news was that I had been selected for the Royal College of Defence Studies (RCDS), a sort of sabbatical for senior officers of many nations who had been earmarked to rise to very high rank. As this was known to be a fairly relaxed course, to accommodate the 'members' (not students, which might imply youth and diligence) from below the Olive Line, I decided to go for it.

During the latter stages of my time at Coningsby, I had become acquainted with John Wagstaff, who was a very successful entrepreneur, and ex-Lotus racing driver. In fact, he had won Le Mans twice in specialist classes, including the prestigious thermal efficiency one. After a day tramping round the airfield with our shotguns in pursuit of a few pheasant,

John kindly invited Irene and myself to his 'modest dwelling' in Derbyshire. As we were heading down to our new quarter in Stanmore towards late December, we thought this might be a convenient and convivial stop-off point for the night, which was 21 December 1988. We arrived in our VW Golf at the impressive gates of Langley Priory in the late afternoon, and as they swung open to reveal acres of lovely parkland ahead, Irene groaned 'Oh, my God, what's this? I've only got casual clothes!' The parkland gave way to an area of carefully manicured woods, with a magnificent lake in front of the Priory. We both felt just a little apprehensive. That is until John and his lovely wife, Jill, welcomed us into their beautiful home. We had a delightful supper with them both, and with another guest, Christopher Hackett, who was an amateur aerobatic display pilot, and who had introduced me to John at the Coningsby Air Day. We developed a strong and lasting relationship with John and Jill, and one which has survived the years, despite John's gradual decline into Alzheimer's Disease. But that evening with them both will remain in our memories forever, both for the warmth of their welcome, but also for the tragedy which Jill announced when she brought us tea the following morning. It was, of course, the tragedy of Pan Am Flight 103 at Lockerbie, over which I had streaked joyously in my Spitfire just a few weeks earlier.

I think we all realised then that this was the start of a prolonged period of terror and uncertainty that would in just a couple of years replace the troubled certainties of the Cold War.

The RCDS is situated in a delightful old residence in Belgrave Square, Central London. Surrounding it are several embassies and consulates, adding strength to its anonymity. But in this building have stepped some of the most important and influential people on the planet; some visiting speakers, others from the membership. Of the many nations represented, the Brits have nearly a half of the members; the USA normally have three or four, frequently one of them CIA, but a fact never acknowledged. The regime is unusual: coffee starts the day at 1030, followed by a visiting lecturer for an hour, including questions; aperitifs at noon and lunch at 1230. The afternoon is normally spent in private study, or other pastimes. Mrs Thatcher, when she was Prime Minister, came to address the College in the mid '80s. As she was leaving after lunch, she was rather brusquely overtaken by one of the hosting officers, a brigadier in the British Army, who then proceeded to pick up a set of golf clubs and make for the door. Mrs Thatcher exclaimed:

'Brigadier, isn't this a little early to be playing golf?' Clearly a man of independent means, he turned and retorted:

'Prime Minister, if I hadn't been having lunch with you, I'd have tee'd off an hour ago.'

Outraged, she went back to Number Ten and demanded that the College be closed down at once. 'RCDS, the Royal College of Deep Sleep,' she exclaimed. Of course, it never was closed down, as the Foreign Office, as well as the MOD, recognised its enormous role in building lasting relationships, and occasionally friendships, with officers who would often end up leading their nations. But her office had to conceal the fact for the next few years that her clear instructions had been disobeyed.

King Hussein of Jordan, Sir Laurens van der Post, the Supreme Allied Commander NATO Forces in Europe, the NATO Secretary General and so many other men and women of note came to speak to us. But the man who impressed me most was the Prince of Wales, who stood without notes and spoke with enormous vision for nearly forty-five minutes about the environment, architectural threats and Europe. At one stage he suggested that Europe had a functioning body, but no soul. In the question period afterwards, a German colonel said that he believed that Prince Charles could become that soul of the continent. He smiled, slightly embarrassed, and suggested that the compliment was no doubt an acknowledgement of his German ancestry.

Part of the course involved travelling to the regions of the UK, and I was fortunate enough to be in the group that went to Northern Ireland – still very much in troubled times. As part of our preparation, we had a series of lectures and talks from academics, diplomats and politicians, past and present. A memorable speaker was Enoch Powell, who late in his political life became a Unionist politician, firmly wedded to the preservation of Northern Ireland in the UK. Speaking with wonderful clarity and intellect, he expounded his firm belief that the British Government were scheming to divest themselves of Northern Ireland, as a troublesome, gangrenous limb which should be amputated. After he had delivered his powerful address, the Indian Navy Commodore sitting alongside me said: 'He's either mad, or he's right!' For some, the jury is still out on that one. At lunch later, I had the good fortune to be his principal host, and I asked whether he had ever regretted giving his infamous 'Rivers of Blood' speech in 1968, which was, and still is, seen

as racist, and resulted in his sacking by Conservative leader Ted Heath
from the shadow cabinet. He replied that he often wished he had kept the
quotation in its original Latin, which would have been incomprehensible
to his Birmingham Tory audience.

For many years, I had ensured that in any non-flying job, I associated
myself with an Air Experience Flight (AEF), which flew air cadets in
light aircraft. I had started when I was with the CTTO at RAF Abingdon,
in Oxfordshire, and moved progressively from Cambridge Airport to
Manston, in Kent, and in retirement flew at RAF Colerne near Bath.
Over half the instructors were RAF Volunteer Reserve, some of whom
were airline pilots and wanted to turn upside down from time to time,
others who had retired and wanted to impart their knowledge and
experience to young people. There were a few of us who, like me, just
loved to fly, and especially with enthusiastic air cadets. My weekend
trips to Cambridge to fly were a wonderful lifeline to my passion for
aviation, and there was nothing I liked more in those days in London
than donning my flying suit and setting off for a few hours enjoyable
flying. I shall return to this later.

But back to RCDS. Late in the course, the 'members' split into groups
and head off to various parts of the world to see at first-hand how other
nations dealt with internal and external threats, ran their economies (or
not) and maintained law and order. The commandant at the College was
a charismatic RAF 4-star, ACM Sir Michael Armitage. As well as being
extremely knowledgeable, he was also great fun, enjoyed a glass of wine
or ten and, being about to retire, saw the overseas phase as his swansong.
Accordingly, he declared that he would lead the Far East group, and for
some unaccountable reason selected me as his 'Personal Staff Officer',
aka Social Secretary. It was a fascinating few weeks, encompassing Hong
Kong, Brunei, Japan and South Korea. While in Japan, we were looked
after by the Air Attaché, no less than Wg Cdr Ted Edwards, who was my
predecessor on the OCU at Coningsby. On the last night in country, Ted and
his wife Veronica invited Michael Armitage and me to a drinks reception
to meet the Air Force officers and their wives from the Embassy. Michael
sternly warned me that we had to be up at 0300 the following morning to go
to the fascinating Tokyo fish market, and afterwards to the British Chamber
of Commerce for a working breakfast. As he was giving the keynote speech
there, we had to be away from Ted's no later than eight o'clock to get an
early night. Hmmm ... I eventually prised him away from his adoring
audience at nine o'clock.

On the way back to the hotel, a short walk of ten minutes or so, we passed a brightly lit bar – or to be precise, we didn't pass it. 'Fancy a glass of Sake?' Michael asked. How could I refuse. An hour later, and the worse for a bottle of the stuff, we found our way back to the hotel, to be greeted by sounds of revelry in the bar. 'Sounds interesting,' Michael remarked. 'Let's take a look.' Not a good idea, Sir. It turned out to be a group of young Australians, who appeared to be trying to drink the bar dry of Sake; so we felt obliged to join them. At or about midnight, I frog-marched the protesting commandant back to his suite, where he collapsed onto the vast bed. I went back to my room, set my two alarms for 0230, booked an early call with reception, and crashed out. After what seemed like only a couple of hours – probably because that's all it was – bells starting ringing everywhere. I dragged myself into a cold shower, phoned Michael's room to wake him up, and dashed downstairs to join the rest of the chaps on the bus. A few minutes later, the commandant arrived and we set off into the night. The trip around the bustling fish market was fascinating, but when they gave us what resembled a bowl of white worms to eat, my stomach started to protest. I noticed Michael was having similar problems.

At eight o'clock, we arrived at the Chamber of Commerce, and he was duly invited to stand and give his address, entitled 'Today's international landscape'. He was clearly having trouble both standing up and speaking, and after a minute of embarrassing silence, he pulled himself together and delivered an excellent 'tour d'horizon', producing spontaneous and rapturous applause, and deservedly so.

Back on the bus, he asked me how he had done. I replied, 'Bloody good, Sir,' to which he responded: 'Damned miracle, I forgot my specs and my notes!' A remarkable man.

After going back to the hotel to pack, we set off back to the airport for the flight to Hong Kong, where we were to stay for a couple of days before returning to the UK. On arrival, the Protocol Officer who met us passed me a slip of paper, which read, 'Please call Gp Capt John Preston as soon as possible.' John, who was a retired officer, was responsible for the postings of air officers. Interesting. I eventually got through to him, and he announced that I was to be promoted as Air Commodore Flying Training (ACFT) in Support Command, working for AVM Mike Pilkington, who was AOC Training Group, with AM Sir Michael Graydon as the Commander-in-Chief.

'The AOC has insisted on having an experienced QFI (Qualified Flying Instructor) to sort out flying training', John announced.

'But I'm not a QFI, I'm a QWI (Qualified Weapons Instructor)', I protested.

'Oh shit,' replied John helpfully. 'I think we'll keep that to ourselves.' And we did.

The headquarters of RAF Support Command was at RAF Brampton, near Huntingdon, a small town in Cambridgeshire. I arrived there in December 1989 with mixed feelings. I had been promoted to air rank, which had to be good; but I was moving into a non-operational training regime, which was new to me, other than during my cadet days, and which threatened to keep me away from the operational side of the RAF permanently. I knew I would be able to fly regularly, but gone were the days of air combat, air gunnery, radar interceptions and operational QRA missions. I recognised that such thoughts were unworthy, but they probably affected my first few months in the job adversely.

My immediate boss, AVM Mike Pilkington, was a charming man, and from my first interview with him I knew we would get on well. This was especially so when he told me that he didn't enjoy aerobatics, having been a Vulcan pilot, and that he wanted me to get current on the Jet Provost again, on the new Tucano turbo-prop and best of all, on the Hawk advanced jet trainer. I confess that I was having trouble keeping a grin off my face, but I gave up trying completely when he capped it all by instructing me to get up to the Red Arrows and fly with all of them as much as possible. Rather cheekily, I suggested that as helicopter and multi-engine training were my responsibilities as well, I needed to get checked out on the Gazelle and Jetstream respectively. 'Of course you should,' he replied, almost with a *why do you need to ask*? look on his face. All my fears were eradicated in those few minutes, and I decided then that whatever route the RAF had in mind for my career, this was going to be a tour I would enjoy immensely.

Many colleagues have teased me over the years about my determination to keep flying; very often, in my view, because they had long since lost their enthusiasm for aviation, or just couldn't be bothered with all the hard work associated with maintaining an acceptable capability. Such people would hide behind a range of excuses: 'I wouldn't want to drop down to pistons having flown jets', or, 'I think we should use flying hours for those who need them most', being the most common. For me, the role of a commander is first and foremost one of communication, and by far the best way to do so is in the workplace, not in a presentation theatre or, worse, via written edicts. That's not to say that flying for me was in any way a burden; it was, and remains, a joy. But after a sortie, where one is judged by fellow aviators on performance not rank, communication becomes much easier and more readily accepted. I was always keen to avoid any suggestion of cutting corners, especially in flight preparation or simulator requirements. Accordingly, when I pitched up at RAF Church Fenton, the first Tucano trainer base, I made it clear to my instructor, Wg Cdr Peter Stannard, that I was entirely in his hands for a week, and we would need to compress but not dilute the ground training, and that I intended to go solo before I left. Peter was understandably sceptical, but with a lot of hard work into the evening, that's exactly what I did, albeit not without some extra grey hairs appearing on his head.

Having completed the required preparation, we took to the air for a handling check on the Friday morning. The weather was atrocious, with driving rain and patches of low cloud. But we did all we needed to, and Peter climbed out, tied up the rear harness, and went to the air traffic tower to monitor my solo flight. I was planning to do about thirty minutes, including climbing to height for some aerobatics, but as I approached the take-off point, all the gaps in the cloud had disappeared and the visibility was rapidly decreasing. I called for take-off, fully expecting to be told to return to dispersal; but as luck would have it, Peter had nipped to the loo, and he got back to see me accelerating down a flooded runway, too late to stop me. It rapidly became obvious that I should have been more prudent, as I started to enter cloud at about 300ft. Without an instrument rating on the aircraft, a climb through the cloud would have resulted in an almost certain diversion to another airfield, with all the associated complications of recovery and engineering support. So I thought I'd better stay below the cloud, and do a couple of low-level visual circuits. I learned later that I had actually vanished from sight to those in the ATC tower, Peter included, who all thought I had climbed into cloud and was on my way to a faraway base. They were therefore somewhat surprised when I made my 'downwind low to roll' call. Fearing that to order me to land at once might have induced a panic attack, they let me get on with it. Despite the rain and gusty wind, I made a fair landing, put on the power and climbed up again to repeat the process. At this stage, Peter's nerve broke, and he advised me to land next time. I acknowledged. Unfortunately, the most appalling squall hit the airfield as I was heading downwind, and I lost sight of the runway completely. I turned to where I thought it should be, but by the time I picked it up it was too late to adjust my flight path to make a safe landing. I overshot, this time keeping as close as I dared to the runway. I completed what fast-jet pilots called a 'split-arse turn' round finals, and with a few frantic control inputs put the aircraft firmly down and commenced braking. Nothing. I was aquaplaning on an inch of water, gliding on the surface as though it were ice. Suddenly the brakes bit as I hit a dry patch, and I was back under control. As I taxied off the runway and called 'clear', I added 'You can tell the wing commander he can start breathing again!' Poor radio discipline, but much-needed humour at a time of high tension.

Following the firm direction of my new Boss, I quickly refreshed on the Hawk advanced jet trainer, anticipating some future flying with the Red Arrows. Over my two years as Air Cdre Flying Training, I managed to fly on many occasions with the team, enjoying the thrill of formation aerobatics, albeit as a spectator sitting in the back seat. Most readers will be aware of the effects of 'G-force' on the human body. As I mentioned earlier, but to recap, when direction is changed, laterally, vertically or longitudinally (as in acceleration/deceleration), the apparent weight of the human body increases or decreases. In normal civilised life, this effect is only barely noticeable. Put yourself in a jet travelling at up to twice the speed of sound, and the situation changes dramatically. Normally, with a G-suit, it is possible to endure up to 7-G without blacking out. Unfortunately, the expanding bladders around the legs can interfere with the rear cockpit control column, which – especially in the case of formation aerobatics – requires full freedom of movement for the front seat pilot. So, no G-suit protection for me as I prepared to enjoy flying with Adrian Thurley, the new leader of the Red Arrows. All was well until the 'break' to land at the end of the display. Perhaps I was relaxing too much, but as the 'G' came on, my vision went grey; then total oblivion. I gradually became aware of the radio chatter, but felt my arms and legs flailing, out of control. At first, I had no idea where I was, and thought I must have had a stroke or been in a traffic accident. Just as suddenly my vision returned, and I was wide awake as we touched down. But it shocked me; I had never gone into deep unconsciousness under 'G' before. In essence, I had gone into what is called 'G-Loc', or G-induced loss of consciousness. Little was known about this phenomenon for quite a while, but it goes a long way to explaining the loss of several high performance jets, when after some high-G manoeuvre, the aircraft appeared to be flying itself before crashing. I reckon I was 'under' for about fifteen seconds; easily enough to incapacitate a pilot and result in a fatal crash. Indeed, Red Arrow Flt Lt Jon Egging, who was killed in 2011 after completing a similar manoeuvre to the one that I experienced, almost certainly suffered G-Loc. And there are many more examples. Interestingly, when I came clean in the debrief, quite a few of the team pilots admitted they had fallen prey to this insidious killer when they were flying as rear seat passengers during the selection process. This led to a greater awareness of the potential hazard, but it was only after Jon Egging's death that real measures were taken to improve resistance to high G-forces. I arranged for an internal G-suit to be made, so constraining the bladder expansion inside my flying suit. No doubt this was non-standard, but I never had the problem again.

I loved my time as ACFT, although the First Gulf War in 1990 left me feeling isolated from the RAF's operational role. I put such feelings behind me and got on with my important function of providing aircrew for the front line units. I completed my conversion onto helicopters, going solo on the Gazelle and doing some operational flying in Wessex in the Stanford Training Area, which provided excellent and realistic training facilities for soldiers about to be deployed overseas. On one occasion, I heard the Loadmaster warning the troops to mind their language, as there was an RAF 'brigadier' flying them that day. They clearly didn't believe him, and were astonished when they climbed out and before donning kit and running for cover, took a look at the old guy in the cockpit!

Having refreshed on the Hawk, and done some flying with the Red Arrows, I felt very comfortable flying this superb little aeroplane. I had completed an Instrument Rating Test, and was qualified day and night. Typically overconfident, I decided after a year or so to do the Red Arrows flying test with the nine candidates offering themselves for selection. Sitting on Sqn Ldr Adrian Thurley's wing, with Gordon Howse in the back cockpit, we started with a normal pairs formation take-off, followed by some steep turns at 5,000ft. Then came the real stuff, starting with a loop and followed by the more demanding barrel roll. 'OK,' Adrian announced, 'now down to

1,000ft.' Gulp. We arrived over the airfield at Scampton and went straight into a loop, followed by a couple of barrel rolls and another loop. By then I was perspiring freely, my mouth as dry as a desert wind. 'Descending to 250ft', Adrian called on the radio. Further gulp, a very dry one. We raced back over Scampton at treetop level, with me hanging onto the leader's wing. Several steep turns later, we pulled up for a break, and we were on the ground a few moments later. We had been airborne for only twenty-five minutes and I was drenched and totally exhausted. In the debrief, Adrian was very complimentary, and said that I was second in the order of merit alongside the applicants. Hmmm. He went on to say that success in the flying test was only part of the selection process, and he had concerns about my other personal qualifications for the team, not least my age!

But the time spent in the air was never wasted. It was good for my credibility as a senior commander, but continued my pursuit of professional excellence, especially in a high-performance aircraft like the Hawk. This turned out to be just as well, as another bolt from the blue arrived in 1992. Mike Graydon had moved on with promotion to head up Strike Command, handing over at Support Command to AM Sir John Thomson, one of the RAF's shining stars. John called me into the office with Mike Pilkington, and announced that we needed to deploy two Hawks within a few weeks to the USA. The export version, the Goshawk, was on order for the US Navy and Marines, and was already being tested at Patuxent River naval air base. But there had been a lot of adverse press in the States about the aircraft, and Ministers had decided that the only way to scotch the rumours was to show as many influential Americans as we could what this splendid little aircraft could do. The big question was who should lead the detachment. I had no doubts: 'I should, Sir, and I suggest Bruce Latton comes as well.' Air Cdre Bruce Latton was the Commandant of the Central Flying School and a most respected aviator. John Thomson raised an eyebrow.

'Have you got time to get up to speed on the Hawk?' he asked, not unreasonably.

'Already current, with a full Instrument Rating', I replied. He smiled.

'Might have known. OK, get things moving, and work on a departure in early June.'

That was two weeks away. I gulped; had I bitten off more than I could chew again? Probably. Bruce was able to clear his diary, and we met to discuss logistics. We decided to take Gp Capt Tim Webb, CO at RAF Chivenor, who was a very experienced Hawk Pilot, and Flt Lt Andy Rands, a QFI from RAF Valley, who had done much of my conversion training earlier in my tour. Although we couldn't expect engineering support for the whole trip, we were able to take a few Red Arrows' engineers. They would fly in a Boscombe Down test aircraft, a lovely old Comet, called 'Canopus', that needed to do some research work in the USA anyway. Planning the route was interesting. The Hawk has a single engine, not a lot of navigation equipment, and a maximum safe range of about 650 nautical miles. The only sensible option was the 'northern route', via Iceland, Greenland, Northern Canada, Labrador and thence into the USA, planning to arrive in Washington DC on 8 June. We were booked in to see several key folk in the Pentagon on the 9th, and would then fly to Patuxent (Pax) River, in Maryland, to meet the US Naval test pilots. After that, the fun would really start!

On 6 June, we all met up at RAF Scampton, and Bruce and I briefed the entire team on the plans and the objectives. After the meetings in the Pentagon and the visit to Pax River, we were heading off to a selection of bases to demonstrate the aircraft, and hopefully to fly some interesting aeroplanes as well. It would be a very long and arduous detachment, with some very challenging flying. With that, we got changed into flying kit, briefed and set off on the first leg to Lossiemouth in Northern Scotland, where we refuelled, and set off for the long leg to Keflavik in Iceland. Arriving just before it became twilight (never dark there in the summer), we were met by an old friend, Sqn Ldr Phil Leadbetter, the Defence Attaché, who had been a Phantom navigator during my earlier days on the front line. He and Chris, his charming wife, had arranged a supper party for us in his residence, where we were able to meet several interesting local and USAF military friends of theirs. I was talking to a brigadier general, who commanded the US base Keflavik. He asked me when we were going back to UK, expressing his admiration that we had brought a couple of little jets so far. When I replied that we hoped to get back in about two weeks, depending upon how the trip to the States went, he looked incredulous.

'You're not taking those Hawks to the States?' I assured him that we were. 'But they've only got one engine,' he protested. 'How many times will you air refuel?' His incredulity increased when I told him that the Hawk didn't have an air-to-air refuelling capability, at least not the ones we were flying; he wandered away, shaking his head and muttering, 'Crazy Limeys.' It was a fun evening, with Phil and Chris the perfect hosts. But the morning's challenge was very much on our minds, and we made our excuses early, the sombre farewells of the local residents clearly implying that this was the last time we would ever be seen alive. I was in bed by midnight, thinking about the hazardous flight ahead, and marvelling at the light outside at such a late hour. I often wondered how the northern people coped with such extremes of day and night, from winter to summer. On a visit to Bodo in Northern Norway during my time commanding Treble One Squadron, I had asked this question of a local young lady, and she replied: 'Chris, in the summer, we fish and we make love.' When I asked her what they did in the winter, she replied: 'In the winter, we don't fish!' Eventually, after tossing and turning for a while, I dropped off and dreamt of icy waters and raging snowstorms; but there was a worse threat ahead, and one which we could never have predicted.

The Hawk is a lovely training aircraft. Virtually every control and instrument is replicated in both cockpits, and unlike many other tandem trainers the rear pilot sits high and has an excellent view ahead. Bruce and I agreed that we would fly together for the first few legs, alternating the front seat and with it the captaincy. With Tim Webb and Andy Rands in formation, we took off from Keflavik at 1000 hrs, Canopus just behind us, on the longest leg of our trip – over 600 nautical miles to Sondre Stromfjord on the south west corner of Greenland. It was right at the extreme of the Hawk's range, and we were going to have to be very careful about fuel management, treating the throttle like a wounded sparrow, gently coaxing every extra mile out of the aviation kerosene gushing through the thirsty engine.

One of the Comet's roles was to act as our guardian angel, but other than calling for more useful assistance on the radio, there was not much they could do if we had to ditch or eject. With the northern waters, even in summer, no more than five degrees centigrade, the chances of surviving for long enough to be rescued were slim. Best not to think about it. Before too long, the first icebergs started to appear, reminding us that we were closing in on arctic waters. After an hour we had to make a go/no-go decision, based on fuel used so far. The headwinds were fairly light, so we calculated that we could continue to Sondre Stromfjord, with an option to dive into a small airfield on the east coast of Greenland if we had an emergency or if fuel calculations changed.

A short time later we started to pick up the vast iciness of Greenland, white mountains and glaciers spreading out into the far horizon. The sea was washing up against the jagged coast as thick layers of snow, just the occasional small village breaking the solitude of the coastline.

After another thirty minutes, with the Tactical Air Navigation (TACAN) showing 100 miles to Sondre, we started a very gradual let down from over 40,000 ft. We were both down to minimum fuel, but in a slow descent, leaving the throttle at a low power setting, we were hardly using any fuel at all. I called Sondre on the radio to get the latest weather; it needed to be good. Oops … sea fog on the approach, but still accepting recoveries, using radar. Gulp, that would use more fuel than a visual approach. As we got closer, I could see the airfield, with the thick fog lurking out to the west.

'Bruce, why don't we let down visually and join downwind?' I asked. 'That way we save fuel and don't have to go into that dreadful fog bank.' He nodded, made a radio call to Tim, and we advised air traffic of our intentions.

'Negative,' came the heavily accented reply. 'We have two aircraft ahead of you; instrument approaches only.' Gulp times four.

We slotted into close formation on Tim and Andy, and started the slow descent to the west of the airfield, dropping down slowly to 5,000ft.

'Rafair Four One and Four Two,' (our callsigns) 'set the QNH 1012 and descend to 2,000ft. When level turn right onto three five zero and advise localiser established.' We were doing an Instrument Landing System (ILS) approach, which required us to do all the work from an instrument in the cockpit. The localiser would give centreline information, and eventually the glidepath bar would … well, you can work that one out for yourself. We were now in the thick fog, and Bruce was having to work hard to maintain visual contact with the lead aircraft. Suddenly we hit some turbulence, and Tim's aircraft just vanished from view. When this happens, it is vital to act quickly to avoid a mid-air collision; the pilot who breaks away has to switch from formation to instrument flying, and it can be a very dodgy time. But being a superb aviator, Bruce took it all in his stride and called:

'Rafair Four Two, lost contact; one orbit then will follow Four One down.' Air Traffic acknowledged, but I'm not sure that they really knew what we were doing. We rolled out slightly left of the centreline, as shown on the localiser bar. Bruce made a correction to the right. The glide path bar was coming down before we got settled, and suddenly everything was happening at once.

'Four One Glide Path descending, gear down,' I called out. We were down to 500ft, still in fog, and not yet back on the centreline. Suddenly we broke out into bright sunlight, and the runway was way off to our right. We were not going to make it.

'Shit,' Bruce exclaimed, in true fighter pilot fashion. And then to air traffic, 'Four Two, going round for visual low-level circuit, declaring fuel emergency.'

This time air traffic didn't argue. We did a very tight circuit at 300ft, watching that we didn't get sucked into the clutches of the fog as we came round the final turn. Bruce was breathing hard; so was I. We nudged the edge of the fog bank, then with great relief landed, and started to breathe easily again. The fuel was very low!

As we taxied in, I noticed that Tim and Andy were already out of the cockpit. Suddenly they started to jig around, waving their arms as though they were in some sort of devilish dance. 'What the hell are they up to?' I asked. A short time later, we had the answer. As soon as we opened the cockpit we were attacked by swarms of mosquitoes the size of rooks and as aggressive as hornets. It was no good trying to bat them away. The only course of action was to run like hell for the sanctuary of air traffic control. Apparently, had we read the brief carefully for the airport, we would have seen the dire warnings about the voracious insect life during the Greenland summer months; but even if we had, I doubt that anything could have prepared us for such a vicious and sustained attack. As we noticed once we were safely inside, everyone who ventured out was wearing a face and neck net protector, but from what I had already seen, the little blighters probably had wire cutters at the ready.

By the time Canopus arrived, we had organised Personal Protection Equipment (PPE) for them all, but it soon became apparent that we four were going to spend a few days looking like we had measles.

Two hours later, we had escaped the den of hornets and were climbing into a clear blue sky. Previous single-engine deployments had made a direct flight to Goose Bay, a NATO facility in Labrador, Canada, which had a permanent RAF element. But it was again on the limits of the Hawk's prudent range, and with changeable weather even in summer, we were disinclined to give ourselves another fright. With this in mind, we set off for Iqaluit, in Frobisher Bay, which is situated on the south east corner of Baffin Island in the north of Canada. After an uneventful flight, we arrived at the tiny airfield after a trip of less than two hours, and with comfortable fuel reserves. It was obvious that this civilian airport was sparely manned. It took five minutes to elicit a response on the radio, and even then I was not convinced we weren't talking to the duty cleaner. Our approach and finals calls were greeted with a rather bored and echoey, 'OK, Sir', and when we asked where we needed to park to refuel, the response was, 'at the fuel pumps, Sir'. He was right; there, over by air traffic control, was what looked like a motorway service station. We taxied up to the pumps, filled up, paid with a credit card to a native Canadian who had a voice very similar to the air traffic controller's, and after a coffee and a visit to a portaloo, set off again for Goose Bay.

The flight to Goose Bay took us down the glorious east coast of Newfoundland, hundreds of miles of bays and inlets, with a vast area of tundra out to the west as far as the eye could see. We let down slowly, fifty miles out from our destination, no concerns about the approach and landing as the weather was clear and the air traffic military, and well aware of our needs. There was a brief flurry of excitement, when a visiting Tornado fighter bomber declared an emergency with an engine problem, but after holding for ten minutes we were given clearance to land. An hour-and-a-half later, having sorted out the aeroplanes and made sure the groundcrew had decent accommodation, we were in the bar, alongside many other aircrew of diverse nations, doing what fighter pilots do best: shooting a line and drinking beer.

The next day was going to be arduous; yes, even more than the two days before. We had a long flight into the USA, were having to turn the aircraft round ourselves at a USAF base, and then we had the joy of going into American controlled airspace, followed by an approach and landing at one of the busiest airports in the world, Washington Dulles International.

After an early take-off from Goose Bay, we headed south into the United States, across the St Lawrence River, and into New York State. Immediately, we were into a descent towards Air Force Base (AFB) Plattsburgh, just twenty miles south of the Canadian border, on the western edge of Lake Champlain. The runway was massive, the base being home to Strategic Air Command bombers and refuelling aircraft. We taxied our tiny jets into the parking apron, surrounded by KC135 tankers and F111 fighter-bombers. Eventually the fuel bowser arrived, and we set about turning our aircraft round for the next flight to Washington. After a while, a massive 4x4 arrived, the flag on the front indicating someone of importance. It was the commander of the base.

'Hey, you guys,' he called out. I climbed off the wing, where I was monitoring the fuel flow. 'I'm looking for the two air commodore generals,' he announced.

CHAPTER 13

'Well,' I replied, 'I'm one and he's the other,' pointing to Bruce's legs sticking out from under the wheel bay, where he was checking for hydraulic leaks. He looked bewildered, and not a little suspicious.

'You two are the air commodore generals?'

'Not quite, err...' I looked at his shoulder insignia, 'Colonel. We are air commodores; same as your brigadier generals.' He came smartly to attention and saluted.

'I was hoping to take you gentlemen to the Officers' Club for lunch,' he announced. I held up my oily hands.

'Probably not a great idea, Colonel, but four sandwiches and cokes would be most welcome.'

'Coming up, Sir,' he replied, and disappeared in a cloud of blue smoke. Ten minutes later, he returned as promised and we sat down on the tarmac together and put the world right.

An hour later we set off for another interesting challenge. Landing a military single-engine jet at an international airport was a rare occurrence, and it was obvious from the reception we received as we made contact with Dulles that we were to be treated the same as a Boeing 747. I have never understood why some air traffic controllers believe that a fighter pilot is sitting in an airborne office, surrounded by assistants and executive secretaries. Thus,

'Rafair 401 and 402, you are cleared to Point Echo at Flight Level 210, Squawk 3624; when level turn onto 240 degrees, set the Dulles QNH of 1012 and call Dulles Centre on 256.40; readback please!'

If you get a word wrong, you are in big trouble, and your ignorance is trumpeted across the ether for all on frequency to hear. One such jet pilot, who got a couple of things wrong, was given a tongue lashing so public and severe, that he timidly retorted: 'Excuse me, Ma'am, wasn't I married to you once?'

But somehow we overcame the tribulations of civilian air traffic, not to mention language, and landed safely at Dulles, our small jets a source of amusement and curiosity in the cockpits of the queue of wide-body jets trundling their way towards ten hours of total boredom. The head-scratching must have reached frantic proportions as Canopus landed, aircraft recognition not being a subject taught to commercial pilots, and certainly not of vintage aeroplanes.

We were met by one of the British Defence Staff (BDS), Gp Capt Hilton Moses, an ex-Jaguar pilot, who most of us knew from the past. We serviced the jets, had a word with the engineers about some minor problems, collected our suitcases from Canopus and headed for our hotel, looking forward to a large Manhattan cocktail, a long shower and a change of clothes, a steak the size of a doormat – and not in any particular order.

Following a day briefing in the Pentagon, a place which never ceased to amaze me for its size, air of frantic activity and more stars drifting around than you can see on a clear night, we flew the short leg to Pax River, the US Navy Flight Test Centre. They had a couple of the T45 Goshawks flying, and we did a memorable sortie in formation with two of their test pilots. The main issues of concern, and we had picked this up also in Washington, was the progressive 'requirement creep', which had led to increased cost and weight, with consequences to handling and carrier operations. They were reassured at our praise for the aircraft, both its handling and its serviceability. We were left in no doubt that no number of defence company reps could replace the honest appraisals of fellow aviators; manufacturers take note!

Having sung the praises of the Hawk, we then hit a problem on start-up for the return to Dulles. The generator, which provided electrical power and topped up the battery, stubbornly refused to come on line, a red 'Gen' light illuminating the Warning Panel. After a quick discussion, we flew it back to Dulles, where the groundcrew could take a closer look at the problem. The usual head-scratching produced no solution, so we looked back through the aircraft's engineering record. Sure enough, just before we had departed UK, a Line Replacement Unit (LRU) had been changed following generator problems. All we had to do was find the right LRU. That done, we realised to our dismay that we didn't have a spare, and it would take a couple of days minimum to fly one out from the UK. 'Let's try this, Sir', the warrant officer engineer suggested. He clambered under the aircraft, asked us to start up, and then gave the LRU a mighty bash with a large rubber mallet. Immediately, the generator came on line. There was, however, a slight problem. Canopus, with our engineers and the big mallet, were setting off for a pre-arranged trip that afternoon, and we were not setting off until the next morning. A suitable briefing was given to Hilton Moses, who accepted the responsibility for the essential engineering work.

Accordingly, the next morning, as we started up at Dulles en route Corpus Christi, Hilton waited for us to start up, then lying on his back under the aircraft, gave the troublesome LRU a mighty kick with a size ten boot;

immediately the generator came on line. After a refuelling stop, during which we had to persuade an American mechanic to repeat the process, we arrived at the massive Naval Air Station of Corpus Christi, on the Texas Coast, south of San Antonio. We were met by a Rear-Admiral, who made it clear that we were his special guests, and handed us over to a smart young Ensign who was to act as our guide. We had a great time with the US Navy and Marines, all of whom appreciated the efforts we had made to get there to see them, and to take as many of them as possible for flights in our Hawks.

On the second day, the young Ensign sought reassurance that all was going well. When we told him that we were delighted with the arrangements and his assistance, he breathed a sigh of relief and confessed that: 'The Admiral said that if there were any problems, he'd cut my balls off.' Good old fashioned Naval discipline!

After flying with the great guys at Corpus, we made the short flight to Randolph AFB, near San Antonio. Randolph was, and remains, the home of the Euro NATO Jet Training Programme (ENJTP), a valiant if patchy effort to coordinate NATO initial training, in the good weather of southern Texas. The aeroplanes used were relatively old, but the big problem was the concentration on procedural flying, very much under control of Air Traffic and rarely below 1,000ft. The consequence was that when European students returned home, they had to be given additional advanced flying to get them up to speed on the weather conditions, greater freedom to operate and especially flying at low level. Typically, the UK would have six students going through the course, which for obvious reasons was extremely popular. Our visit coincided with a graduation, so we planned to stay there for a few days. We were especially pleased to be able to thank a few local people, who had taken the Brit students under their wings, by offering them a Hawk flight. Only one refused, a rather proper lady, who reported to us that some of our students had been drinking beer in the evenings. Heaven forbid!

On the second day, Bruce called me into his room in the Officers' Mess for a chat. 'Sorry, Chris', he reported, 'I have a problem at home and I need to get back to the UK asap.' In fact, he had already booked his flights, his bags were packed and he was leaving within the hour. This presented a bit of a problem. Although we were still left with three competent pilots, operating solo in American airspace was going to be a major challenge; and we had a long way home, including going via Dulles to debrief the British Defence Staff on our discussions with US Navy and Marine pilots and senior officers. Bruce's Aide-de-Camp (ADC), Gordon Bruce, had been travelling with the Canopus team, but he was an RAF Regiment Officer, and although he had flown in the back seat of the Hawk a few times, his ability to stand in as a useful crewman was questionable. But we had no other choice, and Bruce left us to sort it out ourselves.

There was another problem. I had had a bit of a personality issue with Tim Webb. I liked him very much, and he was a very sound pilot. But for one reason or another, he seemed to resent my authority, possibly because he saw me as a staff officer rather than a fellow pilot. Things went well until the return through Goose Bay, when I was concerned that Iqualuit was showing scattered cloud at 200ft, and light snow showers. Without a strong diversion, I thought it was too risky, and Tim was clearly incensed as he favoured a quick departure. In the end, we got airborne an hour later, and I thought Tim was trying to make a point when he declared, some fifty nautical miles out from Iqualuit, that he was visual with the airfield, which was clearly bullshit. On the ground, over a coffee, I asked him for a quick word. I decided to use a light touch rather than risk confrontation, and asked whether he had a problem with me and could we sort it out before we set off on the long trip home. He appeared surprised, we shook hands and set off for an uneventful recovery back to the UK. I was glad I had raised the issue; there is no place in high-risk, edge-of-the-envelope flying for additional tensions caused by misunderstandings or personality clashes.

I flew the last leg back to RAF Scampton with Gordon Bruce in the back seat, and it was a great joy to see my driver and car waiting to take me home to Brampton. I could have a bit of a rest after such a hectic two-and-a-half weeks, during which we had flown over 12,000 miles, including crossing the North Atlantic and braving complex transits through American airspace. I could then catch up on my in-tray, and have a couple of weeks summer leave. But my Commander-in-Chief, John Thomson, had other ideas; and a new adventure was waiting for me, and boy was it different!

★ ★ ★ ★ ★

The RAF's Aerobatic Team, the Red Arrows, are not just a showcase for the excellence of the air force, they are also very much a national asset, contributing to diplomacy and trade overseas. In 1990, as part of a good will gesture, they performed at the Moscow Air Show, delighting the Russian crowds and impressing the many great and good present. Perhaps it was a coincidence, but the following April the Soviet Union formed its own team, the Russian Knights, flying six SU-27 'Flanker' fighters.

A few weeks after I had returned from the epic journey around the USA, John Thomson called me in to his office, and cheerily announced that the Russian team would be visiting the UK in September. The plan was for them to arrive at Scampton, where they would be hosted by the Red Arrows. Thereafter, they would perform at the Finningley and Leuchars Air Shows before returning home. Then the rub.

'They will have a Soviet 3-Star as top cover, and I'd like you to be his host for the entire duration of their visit.'

'Yes, Sir.' I gulped.

'The general will have an interpreter, as he doesn't speak any English; oh, and there will be a 2-star KGB man with them the whole time as well.' Further gulp. 'I have had a call from CAS, and he wanted me to be clear that this is a very high-profile visit, and everything has to go smoothly. Understood?' Only too well, I was tempted to say, but didn't. 'I will be there to welcome the general and the team when they arrive at Scampton; after that, it's down to you. The general's name, by the way, is Nicolay Antoshkin; he's quite a man, apparently – fighters mainly. But see what you can find out yourself.' I saluted and left, making for the library to do some research – pre-Google days!

Quite a man indeed. Certainly fighters in his younger days, but in 1986 he directed the clean-up operation of the Chernobyl nuclear plant, flying with the helicopter crews right into the reactor area; and for this he was awarded the honour of Hero of the Soviet Union. Reading between the lines, it seemed that like many of those involved in the recovery process, he had contracted leukaemia. I could find nothing on the KGB 2-star!

In late August, John Thomson and I stood on the aircraft pan at RAF Scampton, the home of the Red Arrows, watching in wonderment as aircraft with a red star on their tails flew across the airfield. For my whole service career, these had been the bad guys, the ones we were trained to hunt down and kill without mercy. And now we were welcoming them as friends; funny thing war. We often spoke to old fighter pilots from the Second World War, who could be intensely aggressive in the air, put lead into a man's skull, but be the first to rush to help him if he bailed out and was injured. The beautiful SU-27 fighters landed and as they parked up, the Red Arrows' pilots, John Thomson and I walked out to greet the Soviet aircrew, including Antoshkin, who was in the back seat of a two-sticker, with the team leader. His interpreter and the KGB officer, along with their groundcrew, had landed an hour before in their IL-76 transport aircraft. The three turned out to be inseparable, in the case of the interpreter to facilitate conversation, the

KGB man's role being less clear. But as they had obviously been friends in the past, it didn't seem to matter much.

That evening, we took them to a nearby pub for a few beers and a basket meal. After a while, two of the Russian pilots came up and asked me who were the civilians drinking by the bar. When I explained that they were local people and this was their pub, they looked at me in surprise: 'Are they allowed to drink with you, General?' one asked. I smiled and took them across to meet the 'suspicious characters', who were typically friendly Lincolnshire folk, and in no time at all they were gassing away like old chums. It gradually dawned on me, and sadly on them too, that all the propaganda about divided societies was just that – fake news. Their whole upbringing and education had been based on a lie about the moral superiority of the communist model, and when they realised they had been duped by their political masters, it must have been a turning point in their lives. Indeed, we were alerted to the possibility of a defection, but it was made clear to us that any hint or suggestion from any of their people should be ignored or discouraged, as it would present Her Majesty's Government with an embarrassing situation, during what was after all a goodwill visit.

The following day, the Knights were flown with the Red Arrows on a practice display sortie. A special flight was arranged in a Hawk for General Antoshkin; the KGB minder declined. Then, to his surprise, John Thomson was bundled into the back of the 2-stick SU-27, given an in-cockpit brief, and launched off with the solo display pilot. I was full of envy as he climbed out afterwards, his face alight, if just a little green. Suddenly, I found myself being pushed up the ladder, strapped in and a helmet firmly pushed down on my head. The radio crackled:

'What your name?'

'Chris,' I replied.

'OK, me Anatole. No English, so I say Anatole fly or Chris fly. OK?'

What could I say? We lined up on the runway, the massive engines spooled up to full power, into reheat, a terrific kick in the back.

'OK, Chris fly.' By that time we were racing down the runway, with me frantically trying to find the air speed indicator. Anyway, it was clear the aeroplane wanted to fly, so I lifted off, Anatole raised the gear and flaps, and then called out exuberantly: 'OK, Anatole fly!'

At that stage, with a cloud base no more than 800ft, he pulled up into the vertical and then, oh my gosh, kept the pull going into a loop. I just had time to reflect on the irony of being killed by a Soviet fighter pilot, when we broke cloud, the nose still firmly down, and then pulled about 6-G to level at 100ft, accelerating rapidly. 'OK, Chris fly,' he suggested, indicating with his hand that I should repeat the manoeuvre. I elected not to, probably diminishing irrevocably the deterrent credibility of the RAF. But it was an amazing experience. The aircraft was a delight to fly, very similar to the American F15 Eagle in handling, but a generation behind in avionics. It was built like the F4 Phantom – basic engineering but obviously effective. We landed after thirty minutes, I was bundled out of the cockpit by two Russian airmen smoking cigarettes, and was then given an SU-27 pilot's badge. Phew!

The following day, we made the short trip to RAF Finningley, near Doncaster, by road. General Antoshkin insisted on strolling round the large crowd at the Air Show, looking resplendent in his uniform and large hat. Michael, the poor interpreter, struggled to understand and then translate from scores of Yorkshiremen, most with thick north-country accents which I barely understood myself. I suspect that he was making most of the questions up, because even a highly aggressive man received a warm handshake from Antoshkin in response to his wish that we would one day nuke the Russians into the Stone Age. But he was very much the exception; the majority ranging from kind to just curious.

The following morning, we all flew up to Leuchars, Antoshkin in the back of a SU-27, myself with the Red Arrows, sitting behind the leader, Adrian Thurley. After the two teams had flown practice display sorties, we went back to our respective hotels; I was staying in St Andrews at the delightful Old Course Hotel, along with Antoshkin, the KGB general and Michael, the interpreter.

That evening, the station commander of Leuchars, and an exec from 11 Group, joined me in hosting the senior Russians at a local restaurant, famous for its Aberdeen Angus steaks. When asked how they liked it cooked, they all replied, 'Very well done', no doubt used to poor quality meat alive with bacteria and maggots. The Maître d'Hôtel whispered in my ear that the chef was Spanish, inclined to be temperamental, and might appear with a meat cleaver if he were asked to burn his signature steaks. I suggested as well cooked as the chef would tolerate, but definitely no blood. That seemed to work, both for the chef who didn't appear with homicidal intent, and also with the Russians who, after checking that the meat wasn't moving around the plate, seemed to enjoy it.

When we got back to the hotel, I asked Michael to check if the two generals would care to join me for a malt whisky in the bar. Not surprisingly, they agreed enthusiastically. Three doubles of Talisker later, I noticed a group of attractive ladies chatting amicably and sipping cognac. It turned out that they were the wives of Scottish Widows executives, who were attending a conference at the hotel. They leapt at the opportunity when invited to join us, and before long Antoshkin, through the interpreter, was telling them everything about himself, about the Soviet Union and just about everything else. I left him to it, and sat watching the light from Bell Rock lighthouse illuminating the sea outside. I must have dropped off, because I suddenly became aware of a vacuum cleaner buzzing around, with Antoshkin still in full flow to an adoring group of ladies. I encouraged him to leave, before he was swept up and discarded in the bins outside.

The next morning I came down to the dining room to find him, together with Michael, tucking into a massive Scottish breakfast of smoked salmon, scrambled eggs and a loaf of buttered toast. I wished them good morning, and ordered something lighter myself. The general muttered something over his breakfast in Russian. Michael translated: 'The general says he enjoyed speaking to the Scottish ladies last night.' I acknowledged. He muttered again: 'They were saying they want their independence from the English,' Michael explained. I nodded again. Antoshkin raised his eyes and looked around the sumptuous, marble-clad dining room. Another mutter, face expressionless: 'The general says he can see how very suppressed and impoverished the Scottish people are!' I burst out laughing; he just gave me a wink.

The following day, at Her Majesty's request, the Red Arrows and the Russian Knights overflew the Queen Mother's Castle in the north of Scotland. As the Red Arrows' Royal Patron, this was not unexpected. But General Antoshkin had been adamant that he wanted the Knights to be involved, and he and I flew with our respective teams, watching this dear lady waving at us as we flew past in salute. She very graciously sent a telegram, which was read out in the Officers' Mess at Leuchars that evening, thanking all the pilots, but especially mentioning General Antoshkin. He was glowing. Strange, but the affection for our Royal Family reaches way beyond expected geographical, religious and cultural boundaries.

The following morning, we returned to Scampton, ahead of going with both teams to a Reception in the Soviet Embassy that evening. As I had my car at Scampton, I invited Antoshkin and Michael to accompany me to meet Irene in our home near Peterborough; a convenient watering hole on the way to London. A quick call to Irene to get some champagne ready, and we headed south, arranging for the bus with the rest on board to collect us at 1600. As I had witnessed with the Scottish Widows ladies, the general charmed Irene, giving her a beautiful piece of porcelain and complimenting her on our beautiful house. Despite being a 3-star, he was not among the 'Nomenklatura', and lived in a modest apartment in the Moscow suburbs, so our average four-bedroomed detached house probably seemed luxurious.

On time, the bus collected us, and after two hours we were in the Embassy quaffing half-pint glasses of a vodka, Campari and orange mix; there appeared to be a shortage of orange. The journey back to Scampton was slightly hazy.

In the morning the Russian Knights gave us one last flypast and disappeared East, Antoshkin in the leader's 2-seater; back to an uncertain future in an empire which was already crumbling. I never saw him again, but I heard that he had been promoted to 4-star, and in retirement became a politician, with special interest in environmental issues. Michael wrote me a nice letter of thanks, but I was advised not to respond. The KGB general left with the ground party on the IL-76; I couldn't help but notice that he had tears in his eyes as I bade him farewell. For him especially, he knew the game was up.

In the spring of 1992, AVM Mike Pilkington called me into his office. I was expecting a posting to another 1-star job, probably in the Ministry of Defence. To my surprise and delight, he announced that I was to be promoted and succeed him as AOC Training Group. To be honest, I had mixed feelings. I welcomed the promotion, but it would dash any lingering hopes of returning to an operational AOC job. But I soon put such ignoble thoughts behind me, went home that evening, cracked a bottle of bubbly and passed the news on to Irene. Little did I know that within weeks of assuming command of the Group, I would be involved in a tragedy which affects me to this day.

One of the trickiest manoeuvres practised by Hawk pilots was the 'turnback'. At an airfield with a single runway, under certain circumstances it is possible, with an engine failure after take-off, to execute a turn back and land on the reciprocal of the runway in use. This necessitates very careful handling and judgement, as the parameters for success are extremely fine, and the risk of it going wrong quickly are quite high.

On 30 September 1992, two pilots on the Qualified Weapons Instructor (QWI) course from RAF Chivenor taxied out to practise a turnback. Both were qualified instructors on the aircraft; the front seater was the captain, and was planning to do a demonstration for the QWI student, Flt Lt Philip Martin, known as P-Mar. As briefed, shortly after take-off, the captain closed the throttle, simulating engine failure. After taking the immediate actions needed, including climbing straight ahead, he judged that he could safely execute a turnback, which he commenced from about 1,200ft. It was only very late in the manoeuvre that he realised he could not make the runway, so put on full power – but too late to spool up the engine in time to avoid a severe impact. Just before hitting the ground, the captain ejected; the QWI student did not. The aircraft hit the ground with sufficient force to render P-Mar unconscious. By the time the emergency services arrived, the aircraft was burning fiercely. The brave firemen at the scene risked their own lives and pulled P-Mar out of the cockpit to the ground, where they gave first aid until the on-site Search and Rescue helicopter arrived and rushed him to Derriford hospital in Plymouth, Devon.

I was told of the accident within minutes, and managed to get a helicopter down to Chivenor in short order. After a brief on the circumstances of the accident, and setting in train the necessary Inquiry procedures, I set off in the chopper to Derriford. P-Mar's parents, his fiancée and his brother were already at his bedside in the Intensive Care Unit. The poor boy was badly burned, had already lost an arm and was in a deep coma. Only his exceptional physical fitness kept him alive. I spent a lot of time with his parents, John and Nora, over the next few days. Very sadly, P-Mar died ten days after the accident, from complications following smoke and flame inhalation. At the funeral, at Chivenor, I was able to introduce John and Nora to the fire crews who had at least given their son a chance. It was a very moving moment.

I have never had any problems dealing with injuries, or even death itself; but grief is an awful emotion to witness, and it is John and Nora's grief for their beloved son that haunts me still.

It was no surprise to anyone when John Thomson announced that he was to be promoted to 4-star and take over Strike Command. He was an outstanding man and clearly destined to be the Chief of the Air Staff (CAS). But fate and destiny have a funny way of confounding man's best laid plans.

The new CinC was an old friend, John Willis, with whom I had worked closely when he was the Director General of Training policy in the MOD. Like Mike Pilkington, he had been a Vulcan pilot, and was more than happy to see me continue flying as much as possible, especially with the Red Arrows. Bruce Latton had been appointed as ACFT, in quick succession to another old friend, Bob Lightfoot, who had been a Lightning man like myself. Both were bitterly disappointed that they were confined to the office while I did all the flying; but I always believed that there was no point in having power and not using it. I also continued my flying with the Air Cadets, at Cambridge Airport, with the Air Experience Flight on the base, commanded by a lovely man, Sqn Ldr Ced Hughes. Ced was a perfect gentleman, and forgave me for last minute changes in plan, and the occasional call from my ADC to see if I could get some last-minute flying. It was an idyllic time in my service career, but the storm clouds were gathering and I was to be under them when the storm broke.

In the wake of the fall of Communism, politicians leapt at the opportunity to drive down defence expenditure. The catchphrase 'the peace dividend' increasingly gained momentum in Whitehall, ignoring two realities: first, the dividend was actually peace itself, and you don't stop your insurance just because you have made a big claim; and second, history is very cruel to those who ignore it, and discounting any other existential threat because one had gone was naïve in the extreme. But politicians tend to have short horizons, so we got on with implementing their policy, knowing only too well that it would prove flawed.

The policy, or should I say 'wheeze', which emerged in the early 1990s was the Defence Cost Study, aka 'Front Line First', to give it an operational flavour it didn't deserve. The marketing spin was attractive: cut out the unnecessary 'tail' and focus on improved front-line capabilities; oh, and by the way, slash the defence budget while you're at it. Anyone who has run a business (stand fast the vast majority of Ministers) knows that hollowing out support functions has a real impact on operational capabilities, but we had a whole range of politicians, advisers and even some military men, intent on mass outsourcing, 'rationalisation' (cut) of operational elements, and reorganisation (cut) of command arrangements. We were not Luddites, and recognised political and global realities driving change, but the irresponsible behaviour of government to defence needs was outrageous, and of course came home to roost later.

The RAF took a particularly devastating hit, with more than forty tactical squadrons being progressively whittled down to just six; less than many allied nations which had in the past earned our contempt. As the guardian of flying training standards, which were admired and indeed replicated across the planet, I found myself defending our record for excellence against some who just wanted to contract out the whole package, and to others who would have had us replicate the Israelis, both in training and equipment. Of course, the Israeli Air Force enjoyed enormous respect, but their geopolitical situation was very different to ours, and they concentrated almost entirely on an enemy of limited capabilities, especially in bad weather and at night. We, on the other hand, even post-Cold War, had to prepare and train for a much more complex set of scenarios. It was during this period of transformation that it was decided to form an RAF Personnel and Training Command (PTC) at a new HQ at RAF Innsworth in Gloucestershire, merging the MOD policy functions of the Air Member for Personnel (AMP) with those of Support Command, under a 3/4-star CinC. The first incumbent was nominated as ACM Sir Andrew (Sandy) Wilson, who enjoyed a mixed reputation around the RAF, not least as he was perceived as being ambitious and ruthless. In reality, he was at heart focused on delivery, and drove himself as hard as his subordinates. I came to like him and his talented wife, Mary. The inauguration of the new Command was scheduled for 1 April 1994. During the month before, the first crack of thunder of the gathering storm pealed loudly, shaking the RAF to the core.

I was lying in bed on a Sunday morning, when the background news pervaded my senses. I sat bolt upright; surely not? But it soon became clear. The much-respected, admired and charismatic Peter Harding, who was by then the Chief of the Defence Staff (CDS), had resigned after a devastating revelation in the *News of the World*. He had admitted having had an affair with a certain Lady Bienvenida Buck, the wife of a Tory MP, Sir Antony Buck, and just at a time when policy letters had gone out in all Government circles, reminding people of the importance of integrity, especially in leadership roles. It turned out to be a dreadful business, with the most sordid details being revealed, some as a result of Sir Peter having foolishly written intimate letters to the woman. He was set up by the publicist Max Clifford, but in the end the fault was his, and he and his family, and the RAF, paid a heavy price for his folly. It was little consolation that the woman chosen for his affair was blessed with a name extremely helpful to limerick writers such as me – Buck...!

While this particular gust of wind was hitting the headlines, there was a rumbling in the background that was slowly, but unstoppably, picking up greater volume. The press had picked up that Sandy Wilson had secured agreement for an investment of circa £387k for the refurbishment of his new residence, Haymes Garth, a delightful property on the edge of the Cotswolds, overlooking Cheltenham Racecourse. That he would not be the long-term benefactor of this so-called 'appalling misuse of public funds' mattered not a jot to the voracious media; they had him in their sights. On a weekly basis, there would be some journalist or other, who had picked up the scent and believed they were acting in the public interest and piled increasing grief on Sandy and Mary, not to mention political pressure on the Government.

One morning, after we had moved to Innsworth, my office door burst open, and Sandy's Personal Staff Officer (PSO) appeared, looking extremely agitated.

'Sir,' he exploded in a rush of breathlessness. 'Please don't argue or ask questions; there's no time. You have to be in the helicopter (he pointed towards a Gazelle on the sports field) in five minutes. Your steward is bringing your number one uniform. I'll give you the brief on the way across.'

The brief was simple in explanation, but startling in its execution. I was heading off to join the Second Sea Lord and the Army Adjutant General, who were waiting to greet The Queen at the formal opening of a new Skills Learning centre for injured servicemen and women. We were then going to have lunch with Her Majesty. The CinC had become indisposed, the Queen would be informed. Gawd!

I clambered into the back of the tiny Gazelle, and after lift-off tried to get out of my working blue into my best one. It was a nightmare, rather like trying to do a dance routine in a phone box, and one that was bouncing round. Eventually, having strained my back and shoulders, I succeeded; just in time to see the red helicopter of the Royal Flight appearing a few hundred yards ahead. We flew across in front of it, and I leapt out to join the reception party.

I knew 'Second', Sir Mike Layard, who looked surprised, but I suspect soon got the message. I positioned myself alongside Adjutant General (AG) Sir Michael Wilkes, as the door opened and the Queen was escorted across to meet us.

'Who are you?' AG asked.

'Chris Coville,' I replied. He either decided out of courtesy not to repeat 'Who?' or didn't have time, as he was by then bowing to the Queen. I looked across at her Equerry, who nodded towards me; the word had obviously got to them in time to avoid embarrassment. I introduced myself, offering an apology that Sir Andrew was indisposed. She smiled graciously:

'I hope he recovers soon,' she replied, more out of kindness, I suspect, than expectation.

I spent the next hour following the group around the remarkable facility, seeing severely disabled servicemen learning new skills to equip them better for life outside. We then retired to a quiet area, where with the two eminent gentlemen and the Queen, we were served a light lunch and enjoyed wonderful conversation with this quite remarkable lady. At breakfast that morning, if you'd told me I would be breaking bread with the Queen a few hours later, I'd have declared you insane.

I never got to the bottom of the full story, but tying the strands together, it would appear that Sandy arrived in his office that morning to be shown headlines in the *Times* newspaper, vehemently denouncing him and arguing that it was his poor example which had earmarked the RAF for special surgery in the Defence Costs Study. Understandably, he had thrown a complete wobbly, to the extent that his personal staff became concerned and called the nearest doctor. As it happened, proximity was a bad idea, as the medical staff officer summoned had not practised medicine for many years, and the sedative he gave the apoplectic Air Marshal was enough to knock out a horse for a week.

While he slumbered, I was racing for the helicopter. But it all worked out, at least on that day. Unfortunately, the Defence Secretary of the time, Malcolm Rifkind, bowed to pressure from the baying media and the self-righteous senior civil servants, and demanded Sandy's resignation, which he honourably tendered in August 1995. It was a shabby end to a brilliant career, and while he could have been accused of imprudence, the implications of feathering his own nest were both outrageous and, at least from his political masters, totally hypocritical.

But there was another bolt out of the blue just before Sandy departed. In June of that year, I had attended a senior officers' conference in London. I sat alongside John Thomson, who had recently been pulled from his job heading up Strike Command, to fill a new and prestigious NATO appointment. I thought he looked tired and unwell, and asked if he was OK. He muttered something about having had to work hard recently. The next month he was dead, cut down so cruelly by a cerebral haemorrhage. He was a man of immense quality, and losing him, Sandy and Peter Harding within months of each other was a terrible blow for the RAF. In his eulogy for John Thomson, Sir Mike Graydon, by then CAS, made it clear that John was his preferred successor. In the end, Sir Richard (Dick) Johns who was at the time the CinC Strike Command, was eventually to carry the torch onwards; and this was to have implications for my future in ways which I could never have foreseen at the time.

Chapter 14

Just before his part of the imperfect storm broke, Sandy Wilson called me in to his office.

'You're going to be posted soon, and there are three jobs coming up: Senior Air Staff Officer (SASO) at Strike Command; Commandant Cranwell and Assistant Chief of Defence Requirements Air Systems,' (ACDS OR (Air) in MOD). What do you think?'

It was unusual for Sandy to ask for someone else's opinion, so I suppose it threw me a bit.

'I don't think Cranwell would be a good idea,' I ventured; he nodded. 'And I've never served in MOD, so I guess that's out?' He didn't respond. I knew that the MOD job was going to be the most challenging by far, especially as the RAF was lining up its biggest re-equipment programme since the Second World War, and the ADCS OR (Air) would be right in the thick of it. 'So I guess that it has to be Strike Command,' I concluded.

'No', he answered sharply. 'If you go to Strike you'll never pick up a third star. I'm going to get you into MOD, where you can make a name for yourself.' I thought I'd already done that, albeit not in the manner he probably meant. I had learned from experience not to argue with Sandy once he had made his mind up, but I did wonder why he'd asked my opinion in the first place. 'There's a Board meeting tomorrow to discuss these postings', he explained. 'I'll see what I can do.' I was tempted to say don't try too hard, but wisely decided against it.

The following day, I had just arrived home when the phone rang. It was Sandy.

'It was bloody hard work, but I got you into MOD', he announced.

'Thanks, Sir', I replied, but not I suspect with any obvious conviction.

Irene had also learned that there was little point in challenging the wishes of the RAF, and as we had been allocated a delightful senior officer's residence at the old Biggin Hill camp, she was quite relaxed about the move. I had switched my AEF flying to Manston, which was about an hour's drive from Biggin Hill, so that should do to keep me sane(ish). I was taking over from an old friend, Ian Macfadyen, who had agreed to accept the Director General Saudi Arabia Project (DG SAP), which gave him a third star but meant he and his wife, Sally, would have to live in Kingdom, with all its limitations, especially for her. It did mean I had to get to MOD quicker than was ideal, but everything slotted into place, and I pitched up, feeling somewhat apprehensive, to the famous portals in Whitehall in September 1994. Oh well, I thought, it won't be for long. Wrong again.

CAS, Sir Mike Graydon, made it clear in my arrival interview that I was probably in for a long haul, and that I had to deliver the equipment programme which had been awaiting funding approval for years. I gulped. Finding my way back to my office, my Military Assistant, Sqn Ldr Clive Bairsto, had all the briefings ready to fill my next three days. I groaned as I saw the pile of folders on the desk, and the queue of staff officers waiting to impress me with their knowledge of their particular programmes. I was blessed with an excellent deputy, Air Cdre Bill Tyack, who made my first weeks much easier, guiding me through the main issues and discarding those which could wait for later.

Alongside him, heading up my team of research scientists, was Dr Lionel East, and together we forged a future for military air systems which has made today's RAF and air arms of the Army and Navy, second to none.

It soon became apparent that I was leading a really top-notch team, many of whom had been front-line executives, and were very sharp and full of ideas and the stamina to follow them through. It was just as well, because the workload was at times overwhelming. But there were wonderful distractions. For a start, I was enjoying my flying at Manston, in the delightful Chipmunk aircraft. I recall that it was after a flight there that I received my last aviator's bollocking, at least so far. The flight commander, Pete Stonham, had asked me to fly a weather check, as I still had a valid instrument rating. It made sense to take one of the cadets, who no sooner than we were airborne asked if we could do a loop. A quick look around the murky weather revealed no other air traffic, so I obliged; only when inverted did I see an S-76 civilian helicopter right below me. Rolling out well clear of him, I kept fingers crossed he hadn't seen me. Wrong again. There was an angry bellow over the radio, the chopper pilot suggesting he had been 'attacked' by an RAF aircraft. In the subsequent Air Miss Inquiry, I was rightly held responsible, and the flight commander was charged with interviewing me to make sure I understood the serious nature of my misdemeanour. Poor Pete, a flight lieutenant, had to invite a serving air vice-marshal into his office for a sound telling-off. I brought him a cup of tea, we closed the door, and reflected on how twitchy commercial pilots had become these days.

I was also able to get a bit of fast-jet flying, although it tended to be in the back seat, with all the problems of limited visibility forward. A good friend and colleague was French General Jean-Georges Brevot, who was doing a similar job as myself in the French MOD. Later, when he moved back into a command appointment, we flew together in a Mirage 2000; no less than seven stars in the same aeroplane – possibly a record.

I also made many good friends in the defence and aerospace companies. The Controller Aircraft at the time, Sir Roger Austin, explained to me on arrival that I would be sought after by the many defence contractors vying for the numerous lucrative contracts in the pipeline. He advised me strongly to accept no invitations, as to show favouritism could be seized upon by a losing bidder in a competition. I heeded his advice, never showed favour, and accepted every invitation to lunch or dinner over the four-and-a-half years I was in the MOD.

But my closest colleague in Whitehall was a most unlikely companion for an old fighter pilot. I recognised right from the start that the senior civil servants were the ones who had the ear of Ministers. The 2-star equivalent Mandarin in the equipment area was David Fisher, who held the title of Assistant Under Secretary (AUS) Systems. He had a double first from Oxford, wrote books and articles on Philosophy, and was perceived by many military people as devious and duplicitous. Indeed, he was known as 'the Prince of Darkness'. Sounded like the sort of chap I needed on my side to drive through the immense number of programmes on my slop chit. So I went to meet him after a few days in the job, told him I saw his contribution as crucial to delivering the much-needed air systems programmes, and invited him out to lunch. Somewhat surprised, he accepted, and despite our totally different personalities, we got on famously and became good friends as well as staunch allies against the Treasury and other evil forces. Indeed, when I look back on what was seen as a very successful tour, I can think of no better partner through good times and bad, and the RAF, as well as the Fleet Air Arm and the Army Air Corps, owe him much gratitude.

At about the three-year point in my MOD tour, with a host of equipment programmes already in the bag, and several more maturing nicely, the Air

Secretary, AVM Bob O'Brien, came to see me. To my surprise, bearing in mind that I thought I was doing a good job, he asked me whether I had thought of applying for the redundancy programme. I think I concealed my annoyance, and asked if there was any chance from his discussions with CAS that I might get a third star. After sucking his teeth, he confessed that there were a few others ahead of me, but that Ian Macfadyen might be leaving the Saudi job soon, and I could throw my hat in the ring for that if I wanted. I nearly threw him, not my hat, out through the door, but chose to ride with the punch. After he left, I decided to raise the subject at my next meeting with Mike Graydon, but I came away with the distinct feeling that he didn't see me as a front-runner for promotion, a feeling that was reinforced shortly after with an appointment that nearly resulted in me and a few other two-stars throwing ourselves out of the top floor of the MOD. I thought I would look outside. Most of my programmes were approaching completion, and there was a good financial package attached to the redundancy programme. One particular job caught my eye: CEO of the National Society for Epilepsy (NSE), based in the Chilterns. Why not? I boned up on this terrible affliction, and made sure I was well-briefed on the available treatments being administered by the Society. I attended an initial interview in London, was shortlisted to the last four, and spent a day at the centre, before the formal interviews in the late afternoon. I was extremely impressed with the care and dedication shown by all the staff, and rather hoped I would get the job. In the end, I got a rather nice letter advising me that I was runner-up, and that if the winner declined the appointment, I would be offered the job. He didn't and I wasn't, and just as well, as my future would have been totally different had my direction in life taken me to the Chilterns. And there was something else just round the corner, something which had profound implications for the Navy and the RAF.

My RN colleague, Rear Admiral John Trewby, with whom I had developed a strong professional relationship, had been posted, and replaced by Richard Phillips, an ex-carrier captain, who was well up to speed on the RN/RAF issues surrounding the future carriers and the aircraft that were needed to fly from them. The Harrier vertical/short take off and landing aircraft would need to be replaced, and there was the prospect of another bloody and fruitless cutlass fight between the two services, similar to that in the 1970s, when the RN didn't get their carriers and the RAF didn't get the TSR-2 tactical bomber. The Treasury had nicely put the two services in opposite corners of the ring, let them beat each other to death, and had walked away the winners, with no major programmes to fund. I came up with a wheeze, which I decided to try out on Richard over lunch.

It was looking increasingly likely that, of the available options to replace the Tornado GR4 bomber and provide a carrier capability, the American Joint Strike Fighter (JSF) would emerge as the best option. I suggested to Richard that we should write a systems-focused paper, proposing that the two services should support each other's aspirations, with the RAF standing behind the carrier programme and the RN agreeing that the aircraft chosen should be broadly the same for both services, that there should be an equitable mix of dark and light blue manning, but that ownership of the aircraft would remain with the RAF, to simplify acquisition, training and support. The actual command and control arrangements would depend upon the scenario, the platform used and could be addressed at the time. Initially, Richard was sceptical that the Navy would accept such an arrangement, but in the end I convinced him that the support of the RAF would be crucial for the carrier programme; and wasn't that the Navy's priority? He agreed to talk it over with the Assistant Chief of Naval Staff (ACNS), Jonathan Band, and I did the same with Tim Jenner, the Assistant Chief of the Air Force (ACAS). The outcome was a paper signed off by Richard and me, presented in such a way to argue the logic from an equipment/systems perspective. This was eventually turned by the Assistant Chiefs into a policy paper. In due course, the new CAS, Dick Johns and the First Sea Lord, Jock Slater, marched arm in arm down to the Defence Secretary's office to announce a 'Historic Agreement between the Royal Navy and the Royal Air Force'. Richard Phillips dropped me a very kind note as the fanfares and spotlights were focused on the two top men: 'I don't suppose anyone will chose to remember your initial paper!'

Success has many fathers....

One of the interesting challenges facing anyone working in Whitehall is the range of politicians, many with different backgrounds and all with different agendas. My first experience was with the charismatic and very likeable Nicholas Soames, who was Minister Armed Forces, and asked for a brief on the RAF's air-launched anti-armour weapon. I suspect he had been set up by his army chums, who wanted their own system rather than hoping the RAF would be there on the day; and there was only enough funding for one option. I was led into his office by his well-groomed private secretary (PS), to find the Minister with feet on his desk, jacket off, revealing red braces, a striped shirt and a massive paunch. I introduced myself. 'Ah, yes,' he said, 'I want a brief on this anti-armour thing, and nothing technical; I'm just a simple soldier.' This was a well-known line of his, but I resisted the temptation to say that I was aware of this, even if he did only serve in the Army for three years.

I went over and sat at his table, refusing to demean myself and my rank by briefing anyone with his feet on the desk. He got the message and came across, groaning when he saw I had a set of printed slides to show him, all of which had been simplified to an appropriate level. After five minutes, I suspect he pressed a hidden button as his PS returned advising the Minister that he was needed by the Defence Secretary urgently. Reopening his drooping eyes, he thanked me for an excellent briefing, excused himself and left. Ah, well, democracy! There were many Ministers who were very impressive, and most were courteous and respectful of rank. I especially admired the (then) young James Arbuthnot, who replaced Roger Freeman as Minister for Defence Procurement. James, despite his relative youth, was a perceptive man who kept us on our toes, demanding explanations for changing requirements or expensive upgrades. I count him among my friends today.

But the man who stood out during my long tour in the MOD was Michael Portillo. Despite having come from the Treasury, where evil officials and politicians were spawned, he was a delightful man, warm and highly intelligent. Shortly after he arrived in post, he held a lunch in his office for the 2-star community, and with only a few months as Defence Secretary gave a quite outstanding tour d'horizon of the major issues facing his department. He was also a skilled and robust negotiator, driving through in one package three of my programmes which were vital to the operational effectiveness of the RAF, and against fierce Treasury opposition. In 1996, he lost his seat as an MP and, of course, his Cabinet job. It must have been the worst night of his life, as Tony Blair's Labour Party swept the Tories aside in a landslide victory. But he found time to come into the MOD that morning, and gave a heartfelt speech of thanks to us all for supporting him during his period in office. I wrote to thank him for what he had done for my programmes, and he kindly replied. A wonderful man, and a great loss to the British political scene. That said, I love his railway travel programmes!

In looking back at my experience of politicians, both in the Service and later in business, I conclude that the majority are good people, but that massive gaps remain, especially in crisis management, judgement and leadership qualities. Many, indeed the majority of, politicians believe that they are natural leaders, can manage any crisis and do not need further training let alone advice; thus, they depend almost entirely on intuition. The reality is that very few match these perceptions, but that constant deference from officials encourages their exaggerated self-belief. As complexity, uncertainty and change become the norm in modern societies, politicians and those who appoint them would do well to take a look at their real, as opposed to imagined, capabilities, and make appropriate adjustments to their attitudes and preparedness. Virtually all other decision makers are turning to artificial intelligence, algorithms based on mathematics alongside wisdom and experience, to deliver systematised solutions. Sadly, and with profound implications for national security and prosperity, politicians do not. I return to some implications of all this shortly.

I had been in the MOD for four years, and was considering setting up an escape committee to dig a tunnel to freedom, when Bob O'Brien came to see me again. He announced that I was to take over a NATO appointment from Tony Bagnall, who was Deputy Commander-in-Chief Allied Forces Central Europe (DCINCENT), a 4-star job in the past, but like so many others had been downgraded by the Brits. There is an adage that there is only one good Deputy job – the Pope – on the basis that his Boss never gives him any trouble.

The HQ was in Brunssum, at the southern end of the Netherlands, and the residence was known to be delightful. Irene and I were very happy, and started to prepare for another house move.

When I look back on my time in Whitehall, I have to agree that Sandy Wilson was right. I was certainly in the thick of things, working at the top level of politics and defence, as well as defence companies. Moreover, I had been given the weighty task of providing my Service with a range of new capabilities that were vital for its future. In every respect, it was a fulfilling time, but I was ready for new challenges and locations and becoming increasingly frustrated at the bureaucracy of decision-making, especially in the Government acquisition process. Too many people were involved in scrutiny, hiding behind 'the need for strong governance of public finances', resulting in delays, shifting funding profiles and consequent increase in costs to the taxpayer. 'Sir Humphrey' was alive and flourishing, and nothing I have seen then or since has persuaded me otherwise. Perhaps more in my second career, I have become increasingly aware of the myopic approach of decision-making in Whitehall, with scant regard for the medium and long-term consequences across departments. There are, at the time of writing, some glimmers of hope, with the impact on supply chains and national prosperity at long last featuring in acquisition decisions. That it has taken so long for us to get to this utterly obvious position, with all the devastating consequences in the past to our manufacturing and supply bases, to jobs and to national cohesion, speaks volumes about the paucity of foresight and wisdom displayed by our erstwhile political leadership.

Chapter 15

Ahead of taking up my new appointment, Tony and Pam Bagnall kindly invited us to visit them during the summer of 1998 to look at the domestic arrangements and meet a few personalities. I was also scheduled, ahead of my takeover, to join the Allied Forces Central Europe (AFCENT) team in Nova Scotia, Canada, at the Pearson Peacekeeping Centre (PPC), where they were preparing a Combined Joint Task Force (CJTF) HQ staff for possible peacekeeping and peace enforcement operations in the uncertain post-Cold War years ahead. After a couple of very pleasant days with the Bagnalls at the residence, known as V33 (address 33 Vroenhof), we set off back to UK for some leave before heading off to the PPC. At least that was the plan. But I had picked up some important information in Brunssum: I had at my disposal, along with several other UK NATO 3- and 4-stars, a precious asset, a Gazelle Helicopter flight at RAF Bruggen. And, of course, I was qualified on the Gazelle. There was a little snag: the flight was run by the Army Air Corps, not the RAF. Somehow, I had to get myself an army tick in my logbook to fly their helicopters.

One of my good friends at the RCDS had been Brigadier Simon Lytle, who was by then a major-general and the Director of Army Aviation. After a quick call ('Thought I'd phone to see how you and Pam are, and by the way...'), he kindly agreed to run me through a short course at the army's aviation centre at Middle Wallop, near Salisbury. Feeling somewhat self-conscious, as a 3-star and light blue officer alongside army junior officers and SNCOs, I duly pitched up for my two-week course instead of a holiday in the South of France. My instructor was a somewhat bemused Warrant Officer Second Class (WO2) Dave Monk, who steered me through five sorties before sending me off solo again, and rounding the course off with a couple of challenging test trips. I got the necessary certificate from the Chief Flying Instructor, who praised my efforts but announced that I was probably a little too old for an Attack Helicopter recommendation. Appalling ageism again in the army!

The visit to the Pearson Peacekeeping Centre was just the right way to start my new tour, giving me an opportunity to meet a lot of the AFCENT staff, and most importantly my new boss. General Joaquim (Jochen) Spiering was a Panzer man, a true commander and a perfect gentleman. We hit it off right away, and have remained lifelong friends. Jochen was in Nova Scotia for just a couple of days, but he made it clear to me that all this 'fluffy' peacekeeping stuff was not for him, and he was perfectly content for me to take the lead in developing the new CJTF concept, while he focused on high-end conflict. It meant that for the most part, he left me to do my job and he got on with his, mutually supporting each other when necessary. He left me also to look after the aspirant NATO nations, initially the Czech Republic, who enjoyed a good reputation as potential allies, but recognised that they needed to mature and prove their capabilities before they could be admitted into the integrated military structure of the Alliance. It was a great joy to develop professional and social relationships with these marvellous people, who had risen out of the communist years ready to move forward into a new democratic future. I made a very special friend in Lt Gen Jiri Martinek, who worked alongside me for over a year to prepare his HQ and front-line forces for the scrutiny needed before accession. I had only one beef with my Czech colleagues: every time we met we exchanged gifts; I would pass over a bottle of malt whisky, and in return would receive a litre of Slivovitz, a potent damson brandy that sounds better than it tastes. Irene found a few uses for it when redecorating, but also as a host for garlic in producing a most effective cold cure. It was certainly useful in guaranteeing social isolation.

The Czech Republic was formally admitted into NATO in March 1999, shortly after I had run an evaluation of their command and control capabilities in the south of the country. There was still much work to be done, especially in modernising their equipment and training enough people in the English language. But I felt, as did others, that their enthusiasm and westward-looking policies would carry them through the progressive integration process. The Chief of their Defence Staff, General Sedhivy, kindly awarded me the nation's Gold Commemorative Medal as a sign of their gratitude; he also gave me another bottle of Slivovitz!

In the summer of 1999, my ADC, Ian Butler, brought me a copy of the Whitehall magazine, *Focus*. It was a useful way of keeping up to speed with civil service and ministerial appointments. Right on the front was a photograph of a rather portly man, the new Minister for the Armed Forces, a certain Peter Kilfoyle. Interested at the coincidence of a name from my past, I took a closer look, and was astonished to see that this was the very Peter Kilfoyle, the son of Mrs Kilfoyle our housekeeper in 1962, who I had last seen all those years ago, planning to go to Australia. I asked Ian to contact his front office in London, and we arranged to meet for lunch at Shepherd's, a well-known restaurant close to Westminster. It was an amazing experience: two boys from Liverpool, both at grammar schools, brought together by the loss of my mother, and reunited in the most extraordinary way. Peter explained that he had gone to Durham University, then entered local politics in Liverpool, before finding his way into Parliament. Unfortunately, we became aware that a national newspaper had got wind of the story, and had positioned a cameraman and a journalist at an adjacent table. Rather than have them thrown out, we agreed to give them a photo-shot session later. They took full advantage of the opportunity, and the story hit the headlines in several newspapers the next day. 'Blood Brothers Reunited' was a common theme, as was the suggestion that Mrs Kilfoyle had become our surrogate mother. But it was a delightful reunion, and Peter and I have stayed in touch ever since.

During this fascinating tour, working alongside several different nations, each with their own capabilities and limitations, I trained HQ staffs for operations in the Balkans, visiting the theatre of operations on several occasions. The level of hatred was shocking, and on all sides, but in retrospect the NATO interventions were perhaps the only truly successful ones of the post-Cold War decade, leaving at least an element of peace behind in the region, albeit a very fragile one.

Readers will not be surprised that I was able to fulfil my wish to fly as first pilot in the Gazelle helicopter on many occasions, frequently landing back on the lawn behind our delightful residence. But as always, lurking around the corner in aviation, is the opportunity at best to frighten yourself, at worst to pay the ultimate price. One day in the winter of 1999, I was flying down to the USAF and NATO base at Ramstein, in southern Germany. The weather forecast was reasonable, with just a chance of snow showers. The Gazelle arrived at the HQ to collect me, and with my overnight bag and working papers on the back seat, I took the captain's place in the front right.

Initially, everything was as routine as it had been on many similar visits in the past. But as we approached fifty miles from Ramstein, the cloud below filled in, and we flew between two layers with heavy overcast above. Suddenly, and without any warning, we were in heavy precipitation, and it was every aviator's worst nightmare – freezing rain. This most unpleasant phenomenon is caused by super-cooled raindrops falling into a cold surface, and immediately turning into clear, hard ice. It can sometimes be seen on roads as 'black ice'. On an aircraft, especially one travelling slowly, it can rapidly add weight and reduce the aerodynamics, with potentially lethal consequences. In a few minutes it was obvious that we had a problem. The rotor blade was resonating, no doubt gathering ice on its turning surfaces, and the canopy was becoming opaque, despite our best efforts to clear it. We declared an emergency to Ramstein, but it was clear that several other aircraft were experiencing similar problems, and air traffic control had become saturated. We had to look after ourselves. I continued flying the helicopter, while my warrant officer co-pilot concentrated on navigation. Ramstein is in a valley, surrounded by high ground. We needed to line ourselves up in the valley, and make a direct approach to the main runway; and all we had was the Tactical Air Navigation System (TACAN) to get us safely through the cloud into the lower ground. Fortunately, the TACAN remained locked-on as we slowly descended into the murk, the controls feeling decidedly lumpy. After a few anxious moments, we broke out of the cloud, ice slowly breaking off the blades and canopy, and ten minutes later were safely on the ground. Phew!

On one of my frequent visits to London to share thoughts with senior colleagues, CAS Sir Richard (Dick) Johns asked to see me. After a few pleasantries, he grimly advised me that it had been decided that a British Army general would replace Jochen Spiering, and that I would need to leave my post when he arrived, not least as he would need my residence. Then came the real shock. Dick announced that he didn't have another job for me, so I would need to leave the service in early 2001. I had been honoured with a knighthood the year before, which softened the blow, but I wasn't ready to leave my beloved RAF and felt devastated.

I had arranged to meet up with an old friend, Sir Mike Knight, for supper that evening. Mike, after a distinguished RAF career, was at the time Chairman of Cobham PLC, and a great character with just the right personality to help me through a difficult patch. In fact, when I left him that evening, perhaps partially as a result of a lot of fine Italian wine, I was feeling quite optimistic about the future. Mike had pointed out that I still enjoyed a strong reputation in the defence and aerospace world, and he was sure that it wouldn't be long before the word was on the streets. He was right. By the time I returned to my office at Brunssum, there were two calls to follow up. Within a month I had agreed to become the Senior Defence Advisor to Matra Bae Dynamics, with a lucrative package of options and salary, and some great people to work alongside. Life was looking quite good, and I got back to finishing off my work in NATO.

Early in January 2001 on a Friday afternoon, I had a call from my old friend Tim Jenner, who was the deputy commander at Strike Command. He advised me that he had just received a call from the new CAS, Sir Peter Squire, who had offered him the job of CinC Personnel and Training Command, dual-hatted with the Air Force Board post of Air Member for Personnel. For personal reasons, he had declined and decided to retire. The bottom line was that Tim had worked out that I would be getting a similar call on Monday, so I'd better think through the pros and cons. On the face of it, with a knighthood and a third star, and a bit of redundancy cash, as well as having an excellent job in the bag, there didn't seem any reason why I should change my plans. But it was everything I had wanted to do: to have an Air Force Board position and my own top-level command. I would be back in the RAF, and there was always a chance of another star, unlikely though that seemed at the time. I discussed it with Irene over the weekend, and as always she supported my wishes.

As predicted, Peter Squire called me on the Monday morning, and asked if I had signed a contract with Matra Bae Dynamics. He was relieved that I hadn't, although I did have it for signature in my briefcase. Five minutes later we had agreed the deal, and with great joy I prepared for my next assignment.

Chapter 16

So it was back to Innsworth, but this time at the top of the team, and with MOD responsibilities as Air Member for Personnel. Being dual-hatted meant I would have to spend a fair amount of time on the road, or in a train, commuting to London. Losing one's presence in London was a recipe for obscurity in the intricate web that is Whitehall, but I had no intention of giving up on flying, especially as this was almost certain to be my last tour. Most exciting was the prospect of again flying with the Red Arrows, for whom I was now responsible on behalf of the Air Force Board for giving Public Display Authority (PDA).

My predecessor, John Day, in a major reshuffle at the top, was taking over from Tony Bagnall at Strike Command. Tony, in turn, was going to be the next Vice Chief of the Defence Staff (VCDS), a prestigious and challenging job, for which Tony was admirably suited. A most effective and hard-working man, he was the perfect fit for a job which required energy, balance and intellect. It was, alongside the very personable Peter Squire as CAS, a good deal for the RAF.

Before he left, John Day and I spent some time going over the major issues confronting the Command. As always, money was tight, and there were several initiatives in the pipeline to reduce costs by contracting out several services and functions, including an element of flying training in the so-called UK Military Flying Training System (MFTS). There was as expected a list of people issues, not least the following Monday morning when I was required to kick a young trainee pilot out of the RAF. I took a pile of work home with me, and dug down deep to find more about the planned dismissal. That evening, Irene and I were kindly hosted to supper by my new PSO, Wg Cdr Mark Ashwell and his charming wife. I mentioned the issue, but it was clear that it was considered just a rubber stamp on a decision already made.

Normally, only the full Air Force Board, endorsed by the Defence Secretary on behalf of the Government, may terminate an officer's commission. Even then, the individual has the right to appeal to The Queen if he or she feels unfairly treated. But in the case of a trainee, only an acting officer's rank is held, allowing dismissals to be conducted summarily by the Air Member for Personnel, following informal agreement by the Air Force Board. Williamson (not his real name) was in this position. After a graduation ball at Cranwell, he had found himself alone in the bar; enter a pretty young airwoman steward to tidy up. Exit Williamson and pretty girl, with a bottle of champagne, to his room in the Mess. Very naughty in the RAF, though less so in the Navy. Unfortunately for Williamson, he failed to check that the coast was clear before kissing the girl goodbye in the morning, and they were both nicked by an elderly and obviously strait-laced Station Duty Officer, who at once reported their misdemeanour. The airwoman would be reprimanded and posted; Williamson was to be dismissed from the service, as already determined by the Air Force Board. All I had to do, was inform him of the decision. Hmmm.

On Monday morning, I was clear what I needed to do. With the Senior Personnel Staff Officer (SPSO) standing behind me, my hat on and seated behind my desk, I summoned in Williamson. The poor lad was marched in, turned towards me, and looked totally miserable. I waited a few minutes, looking him straight in the eye. He was shaking.

'Williamson, you have let down your parents, your instructors and yourself.' Pause for effect. 'You have betrayed the trust that was placed in you when you were selected for a commission in the RAF.' Further shaking, quivering lower lip, perhaps the trace of a tear. 'Worse, Williamson, you have let down a young, vulnerable woman, who as a result of your poor officer qualities now has a black mark on an otherwise unblemished service record. I hope you are ashamed of yourself.' Not a question; a statement. He nodded, his lower lip now definitely quivering. SPSO grunting with approval so far.

'Williamson,' I went on, 'I am sending you to RAF Linton-on-Ouse to complete your flying training, with a formal reproof, and a clear warning that any repetition of this behaviour will certainly result in your immediate dismissal. Do you understand?' He looked astonished; SPSO coughed to catch my attention. I silenced her with a wave of my hand. Williamson found his voice:

'Do you mean...?'

'Get out, Williamson,' I replied to his stuttering. 'I never want to see you again.' He saluted, even though he wasn't wearing a hat, spun round and left.

I turned to Michele Codd, the SPSO: 'I know what you're thinking, Michele, but I'm not kicking a young man out of the RAF for one mistake.'

'There is the issue of the Air Force Board', she reminded me.

'I know. I'll speak to CAS.'

Michele left, probably wondering if her next big personnel issue was going to be my court martial.

For my first phone call to the Chief since taking over my new job, I can't say it was the easiest of discussions. But Peter was a pragmatist, and reminded me of the importance of collective decision-making. I concurred, and assured him that he should consider this an exceptional case. I think he agreed, not least as I was still in the job after lunch.

Despite having told Williamson that I never wanted to see him again, I did, many years later after I had left the service. I was in the bar of a fighter station, in my capacity as President of the Aircrew Association, when there was a beer thrust into my hand. 'I think I owe you this, Sir.' It was Williamson.

On 19 February 2001, an abattoir in Essex reported confirmed cases of Foot and Mouth disease. By the time the disease had been eradicated in September that year, over six million animals had been slaughtered, businesses had been ruined and individual lives blighted. The initial response by the Ministry of Agriculture, Fisheries and Food (MAFF) was calamitous, with poor organisation and communication, compounded by a lack of resources and, crucially, the expertise and processes to deal with a national disaster. During the early spring, the military were brought in and, in the words of the official report on the outbreak, 'made an impressive contribution, providing leadership, management and logistical skills'. Most importantly, with farmers openly rebellious at MAFF's incompetence, the military brought order and communication, and a fair amount of compassion.

Several RAF units were involved in the unpleasant, heart-breaking job of removing and destroying thousands of carcasses, as well as dealing with the distress of the farmers and their families. I visited many of our people engaged in this most challenging task, and one for which few had been trained. But the astonishing resilience and flexibility of our soldiers, sailors and airmen allowed them in short order to adapt to the task, and deal with the human aspects in a way that seemed beyond the capability of MAFF officials. On several occasions, I saw grief-stricken farmers and their families, weeping openly as their stock were slaughtered, but being comforted by our wonderful servicemen and women in a show of empathy and compassion that brought a lump to my throat. It is, to me, a source of great sadness that at a time of falling standards and values in society, the military continue to be reduced in numbers, denying many disadvantaged groups the role models and leaders that in the past ran their youth and sports organisations. There is also surely a lesson to be learned in crisis management, including pandemics such as we are suffering in 2020, for the unique command and control capabilities of the military to be deployed early, rather than as a last resort, when the incompetence of civilian authorities to manage crises has become all too evident.

Every year, the RAF Aerobatic Team, the Red Arrows, go through a transformation. Of the nine pilots, three leave in the autumn and are replaced by three FNGs (see Glossary of Terms!). The whole team revert to green flying suits, formation positions change, and an extensive six-month training programme starts in preparation for the following season. In the 1990s and just after the turn of the century, the 'Reds' would deploy for the final few weeks of their work-up to RAF Akrotiri in Cyprus, to get away from the dreadful British winter, but also to help bond the group into a real team before the rigours of a very busy season. It was my job, on behalf of the Air Force Board, to award Public Display Authority, based on my satisfaction of their safety and overall performance. In principle, this could be limited to my attendance for just a few days, but for reasons which by now will have become obvious to readers, I felt my presence needed to be at least a week, enabling me to get a real feel for the team, as well as getting a period of concentrated flying myself. The daily routine was exhausting, but exhilarating. The first take off was 0730, followed by two more practices at 0930 and 1130. My plan was to fly in the back-seat for the first two, attending briefs and debriefs, and watch the third display from the ground. I would then have a quick sandwich, and fly from the front seat on a general handling sortie, including aerobatics over the airfield. Landing by 1330, it still gave me time to deal with the usual monstrous amount of staff work, which my outstanding new PSO, Wg Cdr Christine (Chris) Elliott, would have ensured was faxed out to me when the fun stopped. On the last day, when the team were flying for my clearance, I would position myself as a crowd would be, and watch critically for safety breaches, including overflying the crowd line or busting other display criteria. Many will remember the tragedy of Ramstein in 1988, when a mid-air collision by the Italian aerobatic team resulted in seventy deaths, and many more terrible injuries, including to children in a families' enclosure. Since then, the rules governing airshows have been tightened, and teams or individual aerobatic aircraft can be ordered to land if they bust any of the stringent safety criteria.

Only when the CinC was happy with safety and performance would PDA be awarded; and then the team were allowed to don their red flying suits, formally be designated as the RAF's Aerobatic Team and start cracking open the champagne. Indeed, the 'Red Suit Party' was quite an event, normally starting at 1700 hrs with a large strawberry laced with vodka, a few glasses of champagne and then descending into brandy sours and the like. I need hardly say that the following day was one of recovery, meditation and commitment to temperance thereafter. In the early hours following the formal part of one particular Red Suit Party, I happened to find myself back in the block used by the team. For some unaccountable reason, they had been given a one-wheel bike, which all had to master before being acceptable to their team mates. As I always believed in leading from the front, I decided to have a go myself. I was coming round a corner back into the main throng, when I became aware of a very angry-looking man in a dressing gown, who was remonstrating with the team leader, Spike Jepson, about the appalling noise. Spike was just about to suggest that the wing commander admin, as he turned out to be, should direct his complaint to the senior officer present, when I crashed into the poor man, destroying his slippers and my authority. A glass of bubbly and an apology later, he departed believing he had achieved enough to go back home and report limited success to his wife.

I suppose I should say at this stage, that my job as a CinC and AMP was massively complex, dealing with all the Human Resource issues of an organisation of 95,000 people, as well as the flying and ground training, legal, chaplaincy, medical elements of the RAF, and such emerging topics as diversity and equal rights. I also had the good fortune to be the president of RAF Football, and eventually of Combined Services Football. In acknowledgment of this, I was made a vice-president of the Football Association, a position I held for about ten years. During this time, I made lots of wonderful friends, including Pat Jennings, the Tottenham Hotspur goalkeeper, and his lovely wife, Eleanor. I also met a series of fascinating celebrities, who I would host to lunch before international matches. Perhaps my biggest blunder in this role was inviting a very attractive lady to my table, as she was sitting alone, and after introducing myself had to admit that I had missed her name, largely as she had omitted to mention it. There was a groan around the table; it was Victoria Beckham, but then Miss Adams, Posh Spice. I had a great time with Frank Bruno as a guest; he insisted as an ex-Army man in calling me brigadier, the highest rank he had ever known. More recently, my focus has been on veteran's football, and it has been a delight to renew friendships with footballers from the past who are either still playing, or involved in coaching. Wonderful people.

But this book has focused principally on aviation and human stories; perhaps another is needed for everything else.

In early 2003, it was obvious that I would be retiring that summer; so I arranged a holiday to Australia, principally as a thank-you to Irene for her steadfast support, much of it without thanks or even recognition. She had endured many periods of long separation, as well as thirty house moves, during my service career, although I know she would agree that it was a lot of fun, albeit tinged with some heartache and tragedy.

But then an event which I had thought unimaginable occurred: a coalition, led by the USA and UK, using Weapons of Mass Destruction as a pretext, launched an attack on Iraq with regime change as its objective. This is not the place to argue for or against the conflict, but perhaps the current state of the Middle East, and especially Iraq, speaks volumes about the wisdom of the decision. I was appointed as the UK Commander of all sensitive sites, especially American air bases, and was given a Company of Gurkhas and a couple of helicopters to safeguard their security. Working alongside the local police forces, we prevented attacks and demonstrations by diverse groups, many of whom had already caused havoc on military bases and defence establishments. But the dream holiday had to be cancelled, and I lost all my three months terminal leave, finally handing over command to Sir Joe French at the end of May 2003. There was a wonderful farewell dinner in our honour the day before the change of command; many old friends attended, and all of our adult family were there to celebrate and commiserate, in equal measure.

The next day, as I left my HQ, and handed in my ID card, I realised that my life would now fundamentally change, that after thirty-nine years of service I was now history. I determined to forge a new and exciting second career, with aviation at its core. Maybe that would make for an interesting sequel to these memories.

As I saw the main gate of my HQ disappearing in the rear-view mirror, I could swear that I heard the sound of a Lightning's mighty Avon engines roaring in the distance, followed by the sweet melody of a Merlin, taking a Spitfire up into the clear blue sky.